Murdering Indians

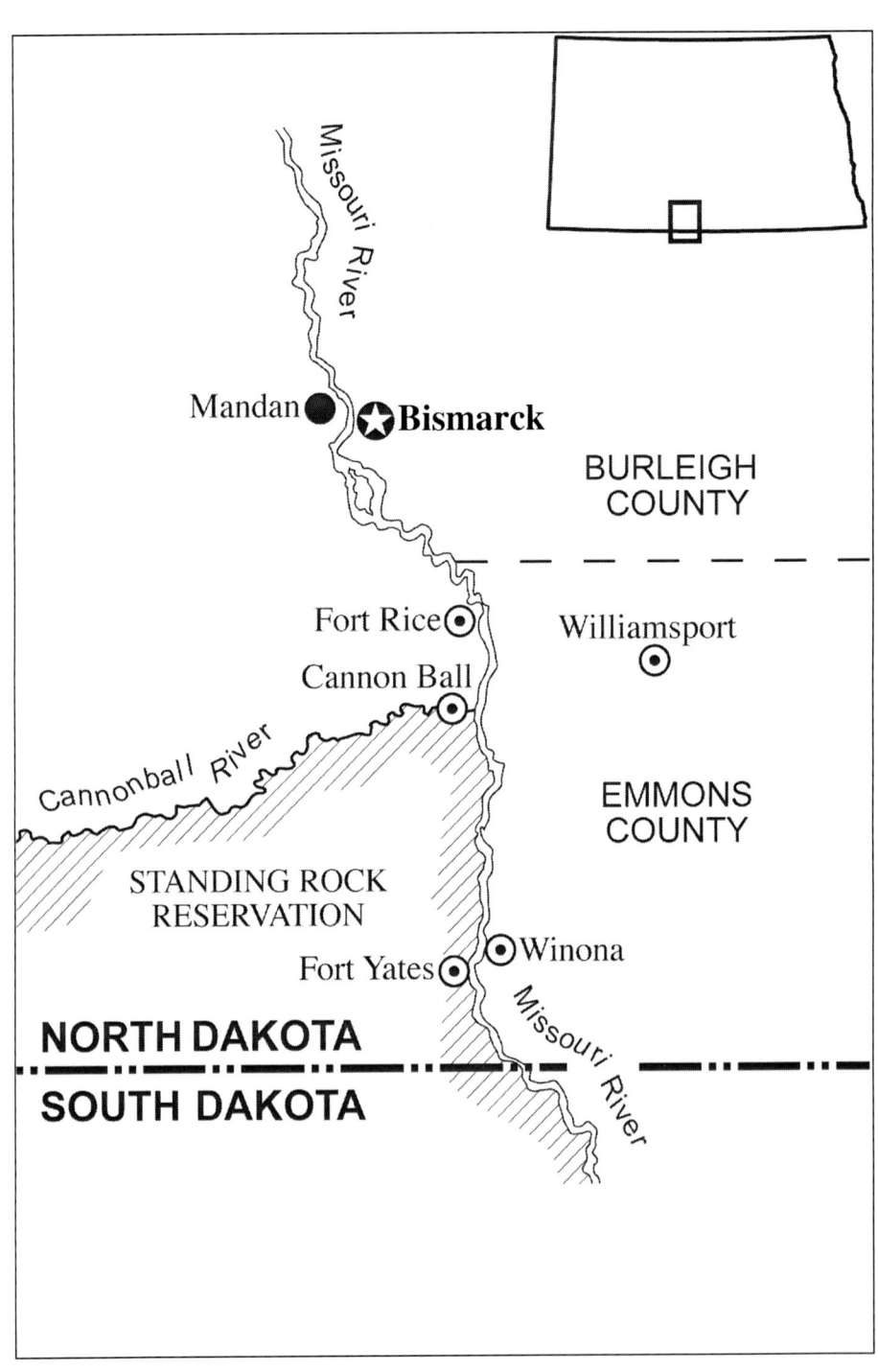

Murdering Indians

A Documentary History of
the 1897 Killings That Inspired
Louise Erdrich's *The Plague of Doves*

PETER G. BEIDLER

McFarland & Company, Inc., Publishers
Jefferson, North Carolina, and London

Frontispiece: Map showing parts of Emmons County, Burleigh County, and the Standing Rock reservation in south-central North Dakota, adapted from a map of 1895. Both Winona and Williamsport later were abandoned and no longer appear on maps of the region. The small inset map of North Dakota at the upper right locates the area enlarged.

LIBRARY OF CONGRESS CATALOGUING-IN-PUBLICATION DATA

Beidler, Peter G.
 Murdering indians : a documentary history of the 1897 killings that inspired Louise Erdrich's The plague of doves / Peter G. Beidler.
  p. cm.
 Includes bibliographical references and index.

 ISBN 978-0-7864-7564-3
 softcover : acid free paper ∞

 1. Dakota Indians—Standing Rock Indian Reservation (N.D. and S.D.)—History—19th century. 2. Dakota Indians—Standing Rock Indian Reservation (N.D. and S.D.)—Social conditions. 3. Dakota Indians—Legal status, laws, etc.—Standing Rock Indian Reservation (N.D. and S.D.)
 4. Homicide—North Dakota—History—19th century.
 5. Frontier and pioneer life—North Dakota—History—19th century. 6. Standing Rock Sioux Tribe of North & South Dakota—Trials, litigation, etc. 7. Standing Rock Indian Reservation (N.D. and S.D.)—History—19th century.
 8. Standing Rock Indian Reservation (N.D. and S.D.)—Trials, litigation, etc. I. Title.
 E99.D1B43 2014
 978.4'88—dc23   2013036368

BRITISH LIBRARY CATALOGUING DATA ARE AVAILABLE

© 2014 Peter G. Beidler. All rights reserved

No part of this book may be reproduced or transmitted in any form or by any means, electronic or mechanical, including photocopying or recording, or by any information storage and retrieval system, without permission in writing from the publisher.

Front cover: (*From left to right*) Alec Coudotte, Philip Ireland, and Paul Holy Track the morning after the lynching. In the background is the Emmons County Courthouse in Williamsport, where they had been imprisoned (State Historical Society of North Dakota 0281–0038). *Background:* map of North Dakota (iStock/Thinkstock)

Manufactured in the United States of America

McFarland & Company, Inc., Publishers
 Box 611, Jefferson, North Carolina 28640
  www.mcfarlandpub.com

For good people everywhere
who sometimes do bad things

Contents

Acknowledgments — ix
Preface: Six Murders, Then Three More — 1
Author's Notes — 7

1. Despair — 9
2. Murder — 33
3. Whiskey — 45
4. Confessions — 55
5. Trial — 89
6. Reversal — 154
7. Lynching — 162
8. Recollections — 197
9. Healing — 217
10. Epilogue — 232

Key Dates and People — 235
Questions for Discussion — 239
Index — 243

Acknowledgments

James A. Davis, head of reference services in the State Archives of the State Historical Society of North Dakota, and his assistant Sarah M. Walker kindly helped me gain access to the transcribed proceedings of the Alec Coudotte trial and patiently helped me to locate photographs (listed by number in the caption under each photograph). Ellen Fitzgerald and other librarians in the Seattle Public Library helped me track down many documents and facts. Tracy Foster and other librarians at the University of Washington libraries helped me locate various other materials.

Glenn McCrory, the great-grandson of Thomas and Mary Spicer, grandson of Ella Spicer (a sister of Lillian Spicer Rouse, one of the murder victims), gave encouraging and helpful answers about his compilation of documents relating to his family, *Tragedy on the Prairie* (Linton, North Dakota: Emmons County Record, 1999).

Allan Burke, publisher of the *Emmons County Record*, gave me permission to quote Henry A. Armstrong's 1934 article. Jean Tracy Hanson gave me permission to quote from her grandfather's "The Win Tracy Story." Karen Curr helped me prepare the map of the region.

I am grateful to LaDonna Brave Bull Allard, Mary Louise Defender Wilson, and Archie D. Fool Bear, relatives of the Indians who were lynched, for kindly agreeing to talk with me about what they knew or guessed or felt about what happened in 1897, and for their willingness to let me publish some of what they said. LaDonna has been particularly generous in agreeing to read a draft of this book.

Louise Erdrich's 2008 novel *The Plague of Doves* first aroused my interest in the real Paul Holy Track and the factual history of the killings in Emmons County in 1897.

Marion Egge typed from faded and smudged copies many of the documents that I present here, and her sharp editing eye has guided me in many ways.

Finally, I am grateful to Anne, my wife of five decades, for her help with typing and for her sensitive reactions to the materials. "I think Paul Holy Track is a tragic hero," she proclaimed at one point. "Will others see that," she went on, "or will they just condemn him as the drunken, butchering fiend he is said to be in all those old newspapers? Will they see that he was striving to be an old-time warrior in an environment that called for a new-time farmer? Will they see that all those contradictory confessions were evidence that he was cleverly playing with the white men who surrounded him?"

Preface: Six Murders, Then Three More

In 1863 a U.S. Army post was established on what came to be known as the Standing Rock Sioux reservation in south-central North Dakota. The purpose of the post was to control the actions of the Hunkpapa, Blackfeet, and other bands of Sioux Indians located or relocated there. In 1878 it was named Fort Yates in honor of Captain George Yates (1843–1876), a cavalryman who had died with Custer two years earlier at the Battle of the Little Bighorn.

In Emmons County, just across the Missouri River from Fort Yates, a small town known as Winona came into being. Winona existed to serve the pleasure needs of the soldiers stationed at Fort Yates, though it catered also to the baser needs of some of the Indians.

A mile and a half north of Winona on a small homestead lived a farmer named Thomas Spicer. Thomas and his wife, Mary, had both been born in the northern British Isles, he in Scotland, she in Ireland. They had emigrated several years earlier to Canada. Then, having learned about the availability of cheap land across the U.S. border, they moved with their three daughters to North Dakota in about 1892. They were welcomed by Thomas's brother Jack Spicer, who was by then well established in Emmons County. He owned a store in Winona and a prosperous ranch just south of town. Thomas and Mary Spicer moved onto a farm just to the north of, but within sight of, Winona.

Thomas Spicer sometimes preached lay sermons in the local church where his wife Mary was superintendent of the Sunday school. An unlikely and unfortunate series of events led to the deaths of Thomas and Mary Spicer and four other members of their family. We will never know all of the details, but it appears that an Indian African American named Frank Black Hawk and an Indian Frenchman named Alec Coudotte needed some cash, mostly to pay for whiskey they bought from Winona saloon keepers. Although it was against the law to sell liquor to Indians, money talks louder than laws, so some saloon-keepers sold readily enough to Indians, especially to mixed-bloods. Indians who wanted a drink knew which dealers to approach. To get the cash to pay for the whiskey, Frank Black Hawk and Alec Coudotte would from time to time butcher stray or stolen cattle and sell the meat or trade it for whiskey.

The story becomes less certain after that, but one scenario has it that when stealing cattle as a source of income dried up because of the harsh winter conditions of 1897, the two mixed-bloods decided to try outright robbery. They enlisted the help of two younger full-blood Standing Rock Dakota Indians, Paul Holy Track and Philip Ireland. A fifth Indian, George Defender, was apparently later brought into the group. They selected Thomas Spicer's farm to rob because they knew that only one man lived there, and he was too old to offer effective resistance. They were not worried about Mary Spicer and her elderly mother, Ellen Waldron.

Frank Black Hawk, apparently the leader, planned the raid. The other Indians knew from previous experience, however, that he might not give them their fair share of the take. These others decided to kill and rob the Spicers themselves, bypassing Frank Black Hawk. On Wednesday, February 17, 1897, Alec Coudotte, Paul Holy Track, Philip Ireland, and George Defender all went to the Spicer farm. One of them carried a muzzle-loading shotgun. Two of them, Paul Holy Track and Philip Ireland, had visited Spicer a day or two earlier under the pretense of buying a horse from him. Spicer was expecting them that Wednesday with the money.

The two younger men got to the Spicer farm just after lunch. Alec Coudotte and George Defender soon joined them. The Indians followed Thomas Spicer to his stable, saying they would help him muck out the stalls. As Spicer was wheeling out the last wheelbarrow load of manure, Paul Holy Track shot him in the back with the old Winchester shotgun they had brought. The others then finished the killing with farm tools that lay at hand: a spade, a pitchfork, and an axe.

One of the Indians went to the house and told Mary Spicer that her husband wanted to see her in the barn. When she arrived she was shot and then repeatedly stabbed with a pitchfork. The Indians then moved to the house, where they clubbed Mary Spicer's elderly mother, Ellen Waldron, to death. Visiting the Spicers at that time were the Spicers' married daughter, Lillie Spicer Rouse, and her twin sons, Alvin and Alfred Rouse, about eighteen months old. Lillie Rouse put up a fight with an empty rifle and a garden hoe, giving small wounds to both Alec Coudotte and Paul Holy Track before she was overpowered. She and her two young sons were then murdered with clubs and an axe.

That is one scenario. There are others. One states that Frank Black Hawk and Alec Coudotte had tried to buy whiskey from one of the Winona saloon-keepers. Fearing a raid by state officials, however, the saloonkeeper had hidden his stock elsewhere. As a kind of joke, he told the two Indians that they could go up to the Spicer place, where they would find it stashed in the basement. Another scenario claims that only the two youngest Indians, Paul Holy Track and Philip Ireland, visited the Spicers and committed the murders themselves. According to that scenario, the three older Indians had nothing to do with the murders. Still another scenario maintains that all five of the accused Indians were innocent.

The following Saturday, February 20, State's Attorney Henry A. Armstrong rode from the county seat of Williamsport to the scene of the murders and began his investigations. Meanwhile, Alec Coudotte and Frank Black Hawk had been arrested for butchering other men's cattle. They were encouraged to provide evidence against a saloonkeeper named Frederick "Red" Caldwell, who was being investigated for selling whiskey to Indians. They soon, however, became suspects in the Spicer murders.

Before long the two younger Indians also became suspects. Paul Holy Track and Philip Ireland had been seen returning to Winona after the murders, and were later found to be in possession of certain items that had belonged to members of the Spicer family. Confronted with the evidence against them, Paul Holy Track and Philip Ireland ultimately confessed to their part in the crime and agreed to be state's witnesses against Alec Coudotte and George Defender. In June, on the basis of their testimony, Alec Coudotte was tried, found guilty of murder, and sentenced to death by hanging. George Defender's trial, however, ended in a hung jury. Both Alec Coudotte and George Defender denied taking part in the murders.

Not long after the trial of Alec Coudotte, the North Dakota supreme court ruled that the testimonies of Paul Holy Track and Philip Ireland, self-confessed accomplices in the Spicer murders, were an insufficient basis for Alec Coudotte's conviction. In a lengthy statement issued on November 8, 1897, the justices reversed the verdict of the lower court. They ordered a new trial and demanded more corroborating evidence.

A week later, early in the morning of Sunday, November 14, 1897, almost nine months after the Spicer murders, some thirty or forty local citizens, convinced that a new trial would result in acquittal, rode to the Williamsport Courthouse where Alec Coudotte, Philip Ireland, and Paul Holy Track were incarcerated. They overpowered deputy sheriff Thomas Kelly, placed ropes around the necks of the three Indians, dragged them from their cells, and hanged them from a butcher's beef windlass not far from the courthouse.

Because of space limitations in the Williamsport jail, the other two suspects, George Defender and Frank Black Hawk, had been placed in the Bismarck jail forty miles to the north. Now, because the only witnesses to the murders were dead, there was no way to bring the surviving two to trial.

George Defender and Frank Black Hawk were eventually released. None of the men who took part in the lynch mob were ever arrested, tried, or punished.

The story of the Spicer family murders and the lynching of the three accused Indians came to the attention of Ojibwe novelist Louise Erdrich in the first decade of the twenty-first century. In a short story called "The Plague of Doves" that she published in the *New Yorker* in 2004, later revised and expanded in her 2008 novel *The Plague of Doves*, she gave a highly fictionalized account of the Spicer murders. It is certain that Erdrich knew the basic facts of the Spicer murders and the resulting lynching. On her acknowledgments page in *The Plague of Doves*, she says that "the reservation, towns, and people depicted are imagined places and characters," with the notable exception of "the name Holy Track. In 1897, at the age of thirteen, Paul Holy Track was hanged by a mob in Emmons County, North Dakota" (*The Plague of Doves* [New York: HarperCollins, 2008], p. 313).

Erdrich so alters the facts of the Spicer murders and the resulting lynching that it is almost impossible to see them as the same events. In her account the murdered family is named Lochren, not Spicer. The Lochrens live in Pluto, a town just outside an Ojibwe reservation in northern North Dakota, not in Winona, a town just outside a Sioux reservation in southern North Dakota. One of the Lochren children is spared and eventually becomes the town doctor, whereas none of the Spicer children were spared. In *The Plague of Doves*, none of the accused Indians ever confesses to the murder, none are arrested, and none are put in jail or put on trial. Holy Track and his two fellow lynch victims are taken from the sanctuary of a church on the reservation, not from the off-reservation county jail. They are hanged from a tree branch, not from a beef windlass. And whereas there is little question that the 19-year-old real Paul Holy Track was guilty of at least some of the Spicer murders, the fictional 13-year-old Holy Track is unequivocally innocent of any of the Lochren murders. The real murderer of the Lochren family turns out (discovered many years later) to have been an insane white man.

Vastly different though it is, the novel version of *The Plague of Doves* still originates in the factual murder of the Spicer family and in the ensuing lynching of three Indians by a mob of white men. Part of my motive in bringing together here the documents relating to the Spicer murders is to provide literary scholars with the fundamental historical facts out of which Erdrich "imagined" her novel. For my own analysis of some of the changes Erdrich made, see "'Imagined places and characters': Louise Erdrich's Recasting of *The Plague of Doves*" on my website, PeterGBeidler.com.

My central motive, however, is historical. I gather together here many documents relating to the Spicer murders and the lynching of the three Indians because they tell a true story of racism and revenge, a true story of the misery, mistrust, frustration, and impatience that are the unfortunate origins of modern America. Among those documents are newspaper accounts of the discovery of the six Spicer bodies on the farm, the funeral, the arrests of the five Indians, the various — and sometimes contradictory — confessions of some of them, transcripts of Alec Coudotte's trial, the North Dakota supreme court's decision reversing the verdict, newspaper accounts of the lynching, the recollections of some of the principles in these events, and the thoughts of some of the living relatives of the lynched Indians.

These documents will be of interest to anyone wanting to know more about the history of the westward settlement by white families, about the desperation of displaced Sioux Indians on their reservations, about Indian-white relations at the end of the nineteenth century when the so-called "Indian wars" were over, about the power of Indian agents, and about the administration of the law in a time, just eight years after North Dakota became a state, when white settlers were still inclined to take matters of justice and revenge into their own hands. It is a truism that the victors get to write the history, and that is true about the history of these murders. What we get from the documents is mostly the white American view of what happened in 1897 in Emmons County, North Dakota. The limitations and the biases of that view will be evident to anyone who reads the documents. By placing the events of 1897 within a broader historical context and by consulting several of the current residents of Standing Rock, I have attempted to present what I could of the Native American view.

Author's Notes

The Dakota-Lakota-Nakota People

Some of the Indians known collectively as the "Sioux" resist that name because it is not from their own language and was originally another culture's insulting name for them. Most, however, have come to use it from time to time to refer collectively to a series of loosely related native bands of the Great Plains with somewhat similar languages and customs. It is more accurate to refer to three branches of the people: **the Lakota or Teton or Western Sioux** (Oglala, Sicangu [Brule], Hunkpapa, Miniconjou, Oohenonpa [Two Kettle], Itazipco [Sans Arcs], and Sihasapa [Blackfeet]); **the Dakota, Santee, or Eastern Sioux** (Sisseton, Wahpeton, Wahpekute, and Mdewakanton); and **the Nakota or Yankton or Middle Sioux** (Yanktonai [middle Sioux bands], Yanktonai-Ihunktonwana [upper Yanktonais], Hunkpatina [lower Yanktonais], Pabaska [Cut Head], and Assiniboine). That third group is sometimes divided into two smaller groups. Paul Holy Track, Philip Ireland, George Defender, and Frank Black Hawk are mostly associated with the Dakota, though they all have mixtures from other bands. Alec Coudotte was mostly associated with the Lakota.

The Texts

In presenting the various published documents, I have silently corrected obvious typographical errors. I have let stand the multiple spellings of the names of the principal personages, including the half-dozen variations on the spelling of "Coudotte." His first name, variously "Alec" and "Alex" is sometimes spelled with a period after it: "Alec." and "Alex." I have removed the period. I have somewhat regularized punctuation, spacing, and spelling (e.g., spelling "whiskey" with an "e" even though it is sometimes spelled "whisky," and "axe" with an "e" even though it is sometimes spelled "ax"). I have occasionally divided extra-long paragraphs into shorter ones, particularly in the transcript of the trial of Alec Coudotte. I have occasionally expanded abbreviations and have slightly edited a sentence here and there to make the intended meaning more obvious to modern readers. I have somewhat regularized the format of the headlines, provided in the articles. Where no headline was given, I have devised one, typically a quotation from early in the article, and placed it in square brackets. I have silently dropped the subheads that immediately followed the headlines, because they merely repeated what was said in the article itself. I have occasionally added a comma for clarity, changed a semicolon to a period, and otherwise avoided distracting inconsistencies and confusions. The transcripts of the court proceedings in the trial of Alec Coudotte were typed hastily in 1897 and without a view to publication. I have been more boldly intrusive in editing that document. See early pages of Chapter 5, "Trial," for more about that editing.

1

Despair

The Spicer murders were both illegal and immoral. Surely no one can condone the bloody shotgun-, pitchfork-, spade-, club-, and axe-murders of innocent white men, women, and children, allegedly by Indians whom they had never harmed — indeed, by Indians whom they had befriended. The torture and murder of three accused Indians by a vigilante mob was also illegal and immoral. Surely no one can condone the pre-dawn murder of young men, one of them a man whose conviction the state supreme court had just reversed, two of them little more than children.

How can such bad things happen among civilized people? It is the purpose of this book to approach a deeper understanding of the Spicer murders and the resulting lynchings. To do so we need in this chapter to examine some of what happened in the years that preceded those terrible events. Doing so permits us to see that the North Dakota murders on the Missouri took place within a context of oppression, corruption, racism, fear, and anger.

It is difficult to know where to begin to provide a context for the tragic events of 1897. It may make some sense to start with the arrival of Columbus's three little ships laden with greedy Europeans and their diseases, but I will begin much later and closer to the Standing Rock reservation.

Inkpaduta and the Spirit Lake Massacre of 1857

In 1851 many of the leaders of the Dakota Sioux who lived in Minnesota signed the treaties that turned over to the United States government most of their land. The land was to be used for white settlement, except for specified areas "reserved" for the native people. Among those who refused to sign the papers or to stay on one of the designated reservations was a minor Santee Dakota Indian chieftain named Inkpaduta (1815–1879). His name can be translated as either "Red End" or "Scarlet Point," but unlike more famous

Sioux leaders (Sitting Bull, Crazy Horse, Little Crow, etc.), he is usually referred to by his Indian name.

Inkpaduta had a cousin (a "brother" in the Indian way) named Sintominiduta. In 1852, near Fort Dodge, Iowa, a white whiskey trader and horse thief named Henry Lott axe-murdered Sintominiduta and most of his family — his mother, two wives, and two children. Inkpaduta reported the murders to army personnel at Fort Dodge, thinking that the white man's military and legal officers would arrest and punish Henry Lott. Lott, meanwhile, had run off. The authorities made some effort to find him but failed. Instead, they indicted him in absentia. The prosecuting attorney, in full view of the Dakotas, then nailed Sintominiduta's head to a pole in front of his house. Henry Lott never came back to Iowa and was never punished.

Four years later, during an especially hard winter in which his band of Dakotas nearly starved to death, Inkpaduta asked for rations and an annuity from the United States government. Most of his tribesmen were confined to reservations, where they received — in theory if not always in practice — an annuity and rations from the government. Unfortunately, many of the agents were dishonest in dispersing the money, food, and clothing they were entrusted to give out, making available to the Indians, for example, only spoiled and often inedible food. Dishonest traders arranged things in such a way that the Indians' annuities, when they did come, were always owed to them, the traders. Inkpaduta knew that, but he was desperate and asked for food and money for his band. Because he had refused to sign the 1851 treaty or live on a reservation, however, the government would give him nothing.

Inkpaduta decided that he had had enough of what he saw as the white man's injustice, greed, and stinginess. Enraged at the heartless ways of the whites who refused to share their food with Indians, Inkpaduta led his people to Spirit Lake, Iowa. (This Spirit Lake, just south of the Minnesota border, is not to be confused with Spirit Lake in central North Dakota.) On March 8, 1857, Inkpaduta asked for breakfast at the home of a white settler named Rowland Gardner. Gardner lived in a cabin with his wife, two daughters, and two grandchildren. Gardner apparently did give the Indians some food to eat, and Inkpaduta then led his people away. There seemed to be some trouble with other families in this recently settled part of Iowa, and at nightfall Inkpaduta returned to the Gardner cabin with others in his band, asking for more food.

Gardner apparently turned to fetch the food, though it is possible that he turned to fetch a weapon of some sort. In any case, Inkpaduta and his followers shot Rowland in the back, then beat to death Rowland's wife, one of his daughters, and his two grandchildren. The second daughter, a girl of thirteen named Abbie, was spared, but she was carried off by the Indians. Abbie was eventually released in exchange for a ransom payment, and years later

1. Despair

This drawing appeared on the cover of *Frank Leslie's Illustrated Newspaper* for January 22, 1887, just a decade before the Spicer murders. It depicts a ceremony honoring the sacred "Standing Rock" that gives the reservation its name. Indian agent James McLaughlin stands to the left. Sitting Bull stands to the right. The Indian in the center with the paint brush is Fire Cloud. The brief article accompanying the drawing reports that Fire Cloud is dedicating the rock to a future full of peace, forgiveness, harmony, and healing.

wrote a small book about her captivity. In it she describes Inkpaduta as tall and strong, but with a face marred by smallpox scars. She calls him and his band "inhuman, fiendish monsters" (Abbie Gardner-Sparks, *The History of the Spirit Lake Massacre and Captivity of Miss Abbie Gardner* [Lakes Okojobi, Iowa: Arnold Press, 1885, 1912], p. 87). The most balanced treatment of Inkpaduta's life is Paul N. Beck's *Inkpaduta: Dakota Leader* (Norman: University of Oklahoma, 2008).

Inkpaduta then led his small band of renegade Dakotas in an attack on several other settlers. The final death toll was thirty-two white men, women, and children. The soldiers chased Inkpaduta, but he disappeared.

Inkpaduta was never caught or punished. He played prominent roles in several more important events, including the Sioux uprising of 1862 in Minnesota, the massacre of Dakota Indians at Whitestone Hill in 1863 in North Dakota, and the defeat of Custer at the Little Bighorn in 1876 in Montana. He fled with Sitting Bull to Canada and never returned. He died in Canada.

To the white settlers, of course, Inkpaduta was a diabolical murderer, but to the Indians, particularly those related to him by blood or by tribal affiliation, he was a visionary hero. Not only had he refused to sign treaties that opened Indian land to white settlement, but he had fought back by attacking the white settlers and by helping to defeat the hated Custer. Furthermore, he cleverly evaded the police and the soldiers who tried for decades to kill or capture him. Is it any wonder that the Dakotas looked up to him?

The Minnesota Massacre of 1862

Henry H. Sibley (1811–1891) was a U.S. congressman from Minnesota. Before taking that office he had lived among the Sioux, learned their language, and married an Indian woman. As one of the traders, he made a lot of money in his dealings with the Sioux Indians. Later, as a congressman, he introduced in 1850 a bill that would give to Indians certain rights then enjoyed only by white citizens. In his speech defending the bill he condemned the government's current policy toward Indians as one of

> injustice, cruelty, treachery, violation of treaties the most sacred, stipulations and promises being regarded as a convenient means of public robbery and private fraud. [...] [T]he red man [was] forced to surrender his possessory rights in immemorial tenures of country endeared by the traditions and graves of his tribe, or bayoneted, rifled, shot, or driven from one so-called "reservation" to another, until, at last, turning enraged on his foe, he sought vengeance in massacre, crime, and deeds of brutality for which the government itself, and its horde of vagabond "Indian agents," worse than the Indians themselves, were alone responsible [quoted in Duane Schultz,

Over the Earth I Come: The Great Sioux Uprising of 1862 (New York: St. Martin's Griffin, 1992), p. 91].

The bill did not pass, of course, but that last sentence, about Indians seeking violent vengeance, proved to be prophetic, not only in Minnesota on a large scale but also but also at Standing Rock on a smaller scale.

Indian lands in Minnesota, just to the east of the Dakota territory, had been parceled out to white settlers after the treaty of 1851. For a while the Indians on their reservations got along well enough with the white settlers, but in August of 1862, frustrated at the broken promises of the U.S. government officials and by the greed of the Indian agents and the traders, the Santee Dakota Sioux, aided by some of their relatives, embarked on an orgy of killing. It started when several young Santee men of the Whapeton band called each other cowards and accused each other of being afraid to take a white farmer's eggs and chickens. To prove their courage they entered a settler's home near Acton in Meeker County. Not long after, three white men and two white women were dead. Ready or not, a war had begun. A Dakota man named Little Crow became its reluctant leader.

Before long other Indians attacked and burned the Redwood agency and killed several of the white men who worked there. Then the Dakota headed toward Fort Ridgely, calling in at white men's homes along the way. They sometimes entered pretending to be good friends of the family, then turned on them in murderous violence. They bashed in heads, whacked off the breasts of women, sliced off the genitals of men, and helped themselves to whatever they wanted. Then they went on to the next cabin. As one modern historian put it:

> At one cabin a dozen braves killed the homesteader and his two sons in a hayfield and murdered the settler's wife and his two youngest children in the house. Only a thirteen-year-old daughter remained alive. Her clothing was torn off and she was raped in turn by the twelve.
> At another homestead on Sacred Heart Creek the raiders found John Schwandt repairing the roof of his cabin. He toppled to the ground, shot through the heart. Then the invaders killed Schwandt's wife, Cristina, his pregnant daughter, Caroline, his sons, Christian and Frederick, Caroline's husband, John Waltz, and a hired man.
> August, a twelve-year-old son, was tomahawked and thought dead. He regained consciousness, watched the murders of other members of the household, saw the Indian rip Caroline open with a knife, remove her unborn baby, and nail it to a tree [C. M. Oehler, *The Great Sioux Uprising* (New York: Oxford University Press, 1959), pp. 49, 57].

Another modern historian argued that the killing of white women and children was criticized by most of the Santee leaders:

> As the braves congregated in camp that evening, intoxicated by their tales of pillage and murder, they did not receive the accolades they expected

from the chiefs and tribal elders. They were awarded no eagle feathers for bravery, no praise or congratulations, only scorn and contempt from Wabasha, Wacouta, and the other peace chiefs, as well as from Little Crow. The chiefs berated their warriors when they proudly displayed fresh scalps, reminding them that killing helpless settlers was cowardly and undeserving of eagle feathers. It was not honorable; it was not like the killing of Chippewas in battle.

"You ought not to kill women and children," Little Crow said, repeating the admonition he had voiced many times over the past two days. "Your consciences will reproach you for it and make you weak in battle. You were too hasty in going into the country. You should have killed only those who have been robbing us so long" [Duane Schultz, *Over the Earth I Come: The Great Sioux Uprising of 1862* (New York: St. Martin's Griffin, 1992), p. 101].

The reference to "those who have been robbing us" was to the Indian agents and traders, too many of whom had exploited the illiteracy, inexperience, and trust of the Indians to line their own pockets with money and goods meant for the Indians.

In 1862, of course, the U.S. military was busy with the American Civil War, but the generals diverted enough soldiers to Minnesota to put down the uprising. Lincoln sent General John Pope (1822–1892), recently relieved of his command of the Army of Virginia after a humiliating defeat at the second battle at Bull Run, to deal with the situation in Minnesota. Meanwhile, the governor of Minnesota asked Henry Sibley to head up the state's military effort to put down the rebellion. Pope sent a letter to Sibley:

> It is my purpose utterly to exterminate the Sioux if I have the power to do so. [...] Destroy everything belonging to them and force them out to the plains. [...] They are to be treated as maniacs or wild beasts [quoted in Duane Schultz's *Over the Earth I Come: The Great Sioux Uprising of 1862* (New York: St. Martin's Griffin, 1992), p. 245].

The soldiers soon enough quelled the rebellion and arrested hundreds of the Santee Indians. Many others — including Inkpaduta — escaped capture and fled north, south, and west. Hasty military tribunals resulted in the conviction and condemnation to hanging of more than three hundred of the captured Indian men. President Lincoln reviewed the cases and authorized the execution of only thirty-eight of the three hundred Indian men. The Indians' names, however, were often confusing to the white men. Sometimes the wrong man was hanged because his name sounded or looked similar to another name.

On the day after Christmas, 1862, the U.S. Army hanged those thirty-eight in the largest mass execution America has ever known. The Indians whose death sentences Lincoln had commuted were imprisoned. Many died in prison. Those who survived their prison sentences were eventually relocated in the Dakota territory. Some of the Santees had managed to evade capture and escape to the Dakota territory to the west and south. In retaliation for the rebellion, Congress closed the Sioux reservations in Minnesota, and most of the remaining Indians were forcibly relocated to the west.

The Minnesota rebellion would have served as a reminder to the white settlers in Emmons County, North Dakota, that their own Indian neighbors might go on a similar rampage and attack them. In 1897 the white settlers who lived in Emmons County might not have known much about Inkpaduta or the Spirit Lake massacre down in Iowa, but they would surely have heard or read the lurid stories of what the Sioux had done just across the eastern state border in Minnesota — the carnage, the burnings, the vicious raping and killing. The white settlers of Emmons County would have heard that next door in Minnesota perhaps as many as a thousand white settlers, many of them friends of the Indians who attacked them, had been tortured and mutilated. When the Spicers were murdered in February of 1897, then, it no doubt occurred to the settlers of Emmons County that the murders of one family might be the brutal precursor to a second great Sioux uprising by the unpredictable Indians just across the Missouri River. Not surprisingly, the settlers were fearful, assumed that Indians were responsible for the Spicer murders, and demanded that the guilty ones be arrested and punished with all deliberate haste.

The Whitestone Hill Massacre of 1863

Although the white settlers might not have known about Inkpaduta's Spirit Lake massacre in 1857, the Indians of Standing Rock would have known about it, if only because some of Inkpaduta's relatives now lived on the reservation. They would have known about Little Crow's Dakota massacre in Minnesota in 1862 because some of the refugees were now enrolled tribal members at Standing Rock. These Indians were soon to find themselves, in 1863, on the receiving end of a different kind of massacre.

Colonel Alfred Sully (1821–1879) was sent to chase down some of the Santees who had escaped capture in Minnesota. In early September of 1863, Sully led 1200 soldiers to Whitestone Hill, about a hundred miles east of the Missouri River and just a few miles north of what would become the South Dakota border. Sully discovered at Whitestone Hill a large Indian camp of around a thousand men, women, and children. He wrongly assumed that they were runaway Santees who had participated in the uprising in Minnesota a year earlier. These Indians, however, were mostly Yanktonai and Hunkpatina Sioux who had nothing to do with the Minnesota uprising. They were at Whitestone Hill hunting buffalo and drying the meat for use during the winter months.

When the Indians learned of Sully's approach, they rushed to pack up their lodges and their meat so they could avoid a confrontation. Sully ordered his soldiers to block the Indians' retreat route. Then he ordered his soldiers to open fire, killing several hundred Indians, more women and children than men. There were only around twenty soldiers killed, some of them caught in their own crossfire. Then the soldiers destroyed the abandoned lodges that were still standing and burned the dried buffalo meat that was to have sustained the Indians in the coming winter.

The bodies of the many Indian dead apparently were not buried. Many years later the site was discovered by a man named Frank Drew who made a business of collecting wagon loads of buffalo bones for sale in nearby Ellendale, North Dakota, where they were ground up for use in fertilizer or shipped east. Someone noticed that some of the bones Frank Drew was selling were human, and that eventually led to the discovery of the location of the massacre at Whitestone Hill.

In a taped interview on August 20, 2012, at the Standing Rock agency in Fort Yates, Archie D. Fool Bear, a relative of Philip Ireland, gave his account of the historical backgrounds of the 1862 Minnesota uprising and the 1863 massacre at Whitestone Hill. Especially interesting is his account of the journey that he and some others made to Whitestone Hill to feed the hungry spirits of the men, women, and children who had perished there in 1863:

> Interview with Archie D. Fool Bear
> Fort Yates, North Dakota
> August 20, 2012

It Was a Massacre

My name is Archie D. Fool Bear. My parents are Agatha Ireland and Charles Fool Bear, Jr. My mother's mother's name was Martha Ashley. Her father's name was Francis Ireland. Francis Ireland's mother's name was Mary Moccasin. Mary Moccasin had three children, Philip being the youngest.

The great Sioux uprising in Minnesota in the summer of 1862 was caused by a greedy government official, putting into his own pockets and the pockets of his friends food and money meant for the Indians. As a result of his greed, a couple of young boys were out hunting. They were almost starved to death and got into an argument about killing a white farmer's chicken. The two young boys were going to steal a chicken from this farmer. As one of the young boys turned around, the story goes, he accidentally shot the farmer with his gun.

The boys came back to their camp and said, "This accident happened when we were hunting." The chiefs all said, "Well, we'll get hold of Little Crow because Little Crow is the war chief. He'll know what to do."

Little Crow came to the meeting. He was sitting there. When asked for advice, he told them, "Well, the best thing to do is to take these two young boys and go to the Indian agent and explain what happened, and resolve it." But at the back of the room in this big council meeting, you've got young men hollering, "You're a coward, Little Crow, you're a coward!" When you said that back in those days, said that someone was a coward, you challenged that man's whole being, his whole existence. So Little Crow stood up and said, "I'm not a coward! I'll fight to the death with all of you." And that's how the 1862 Minnesota uprising started, over a chicken.

Anyway, the Minnesota uprising happened. I don't need to go into the whole story, but the Indians were defeated. Some were captured and given some sort of trial, and of those around 300 were sentenced to die. President Lincoln said they could only hang thirty-eight. They were supposed to be hung on the 19th of December, but they didn't have enough rope, so they put the execution off until they could get enough rope. So the execution didn't occur until the day after Christmas, December 26, 1862. That morning, at 9:00 in the morning, they brought them all out and hanged them. All the relatives were outside of the fence there listening to their war cries and their death songs. One of those men who was hanged was a man named His Nation. He was my great-grandfather. When her husband was dead, my great-grandmother and her parents fled this way.

General Sibley was sent out to round up the escaping Indians, determined to destroy as many as he could. But he had a hard time finding the Indians. I think he found one Indian, but he said one Indian wasn't worth killing. Meanwhile, another army officer named Sully came upon an Indian encampment. The ones he found were friendly Indians hunting buffalo and drying out the meat for use in the winter. The people in the camp were Indians that the white government used to go to and ask them to help talk to these other tribes about not fighting anymore. So when Sully's scouting party of about 150 rode into their camp, the Indians were not afraid. The Indians weren't afraid to talk to them because they had been doing this all along. Sully's men started asking for certain hostile leaders, like Little Crow and other Indians who had been involved in the Minnesota uprising, but none were there. Meanwhile, Sully sent for Sibley's troops.

Sibley's larger force — some 1700 soldiers — attacked the camp at Whitestone Hill, in September of 1863. They call it a battle, but it was a massacre. The Indians who could escape did. Among them was my great-grandmother, Mary Moccasin. That family is from northern Minnesota. In 1862 she and her family fled west in hopes of staying alive. Meanwhile, Sibley's and Sully's soldiers, armed with good rifles and cannons, devastated the Indians, who fought back with whatever obsolete firearms and bows and arrows they could lay their hands on. They did fight back, but were able to kill only twenty of the white soldiers. But in the melee, some 300 natives were killed.

Doing my research on this massacre, I could not find any references to the grave of those 300 native people who were killed at Whitestone Hill. The story comes back from my great-grandmother that the survivors of the massacre scattered in all directions, but that my mother and her uncles snuck back to see if there were any survivors. They could still hear gunshots in the morning. So the uncles crawled to a point where they could watch and hear. They saw soldiers going around where somebody was wounded or whatever and shooting them. The one story that stuck to my mind to this day is of a soldier walking up to a baby and bayoneting it and throwing it into a pile. So when they say they threw them into a pile, well where's the grave? Where did they put all these bodies?

At Wounded Knee, later in 1890, they dug a grave for all the bodies. But Sully and Sibley apparently never bothered at Whitestone Hill. They did burn lots of stuff, the dried buffalo meat, the tepees, and so on, but what did they do with the bodies? Burn them, too, or just let them rot out in the open?

Then I heard that a man showed up one day in Ellendale with a huge wagonload of bones. He collected them on the prairie and shipped them back East for sale, for fertilizer or for buttons or whatever. Anyhow someone noticed that some of the bones were not of buffalo and asked him, "Where did you get these?" He mentioned a location, and there's an older gentleman standing there, and he says, "That's where that battle was." So these bones were not only buffalo and horse, but there were also humans. When they made the statement that they could see that fire burning for miles and miles and miles, the black smoke coming off of the animal meat, to me, that means they probably burned the human bodies, too.

My mother was a strong believer in our cultural ways. In 2003 she told us to organize what's called a Wiping of the Tears ceremony and go over to Whitestone Hill and hold a ceremony there. And so we did. We contacted one of our local spiritual leaders, contacted our veterans group, contacted relatives of people that come from there, and we went over there. I think we had about thirty-five people who went over there to hold a Wiping of the Tears ceremony.

And my mother brought along what are called "wesna balls." Wesna balls are a mixture of deer meat and berries, and it's really something to eat. But anyways, she says that a long time ago, they would use wesna balls to feed the spirits at different times for different functions. So when we got done with the Wiping of the Tears ceremony, she brought out those wesna balls. She had a big old tub-looking thing, all full. She said, "You take these, and you walk out there because nobody wants to say where those bones are and the bodies are. You take this and walk out there, and when you get to a certain spot, you'll feel it. I'm telling you boys this."

And so there was us five boys, or four boys, and then there was three other guys that came to help. So we spread out and started going all around that battlefield, I mean massacre-field. I was a skeptic. I'm a trained cop, believer in science, and facts, and what is in writing in front of me. And there I was walking along with six, seven balls of this stuff. I got to a certain spot, and it's just like a cool air came up. I mean this was a nice, warm day. This cool air came up.

My mother says, "You'll know when there's a body or someone there or remnants of them. Take part of that and put it down for their spirits and tell them that we prayed for them. Put some tobacco down so they will have what they need." We went all over that whole area, and we put stuff down all over. Because some places, there's either remnants of bones, part of a person, or maybe they were buried there. Who knows? After I got back to the car, my youngest brother at the time, Charles, walks up. He says, "I didn't believe what mom said, but when I started walking, I felt that cool air just like it came up from the ground."

After 1900 the state of North Dakota set the Whitestone Hill site aside as the place where the "battle" took place. The monument was officially dedicated in October of 1910. The "Whitestone Hill Battlefield State Historic Site" can be found on detailed maps of North Dakota about midway between Kulm and Ellendale. The Standing Rock reservation, about a hundred miles to the west, is now home to many families who are descendants of the Indians killed or captured at Whitestone Hill. Among those families are those of four of the five men arrested in connection with the Spicer murders.

The Indians of Standing Rock have tried to get the state historical society to refer to Whitestone Hill not as the site of a battle but as the site of a massacre. They have not succeeded. Few people today have heard anything about the massacre at Whitestone Hill. It has unfortunately been overshadowed by other massacres, like the one at Sand Creek a year later, in 1864, and the one at Wounded Knee a quarter-century later in 1890.

Life at Standing Rock

Before the coming of the white man, the Dakota-Lakota-Nakota Indians, usually referred to collectively as the Sioux, had roamed the vast great plains. That vastness included not only the areas now known as North and South Dakota, but areas of Minnesota, Iowa, Montana, Wyoming, Nebraska, and Colorado. In that wide open territory the Sioux moved about almost at will, following the great herds of buffalo that were their main sustenance. North Dakota and South Dakota, carved from part of that vast territory, were officially granted statehood and admitted to the Union on November 2, 1889. By the time of the Spicer murders eight years later, the various tribes had been confined to a series of small reservations: Rosebud, Pine Ridge, Brule, Crow, Yankton, and Cheyenne River in South Dakota; Fort Berthold, Spirit Lake, and Turtle Mountain in North Dakota; and Standing Rock, mostly in South Dakota but extending across the border into North Dakota.

The five men accused of murdering the Spicer family lived on the northern extension of the Standing Rock Sioux reservation in North Dakota. Like other Indians there, they lived as defeated wards of the United States government. There was little work for them to do. They were supposed to become farmers, but they, the land, and the climate were not well suited to agriculture. Most Standing Rock enrollees showed up periodically at the agency at Fort Yates or one of its substations to get their issues of food and clothing from the people who had robbed them of their land and their way of life. The men of Standing Rock, particularly, were at a loss. They were reluctant to accept what they were told — that their warrior way of life was dead. With the buffalo gone and most of their weapons confiscated, they had no way to demonstrate their manhood. Farming was foreign to them and was not well suited to the land. Idleness, bitterness, whiskey, tuberculosis, hunger, and grief consumed many of them. They were now almost totally in the power of the crass and confident newcomers who had defeated them. They had lost family members, independence, land, freedom, health, and dignity. The closest they could come to the old way of life was the occasional chance to poach a stray cow from a white settler's herd, sell the meat, and spend their meager earnings on the whiskey that helped them forget how much they had lost.

The Indians on the Standing Rock reservation at the end of the nineteenth century had every reason to despair. They had been forced to relinquish more and more of their land to make way for white settlers, most of whom were granted land through Abraham Lincoln's Homestead Act of 1862. To "earn" their 160-acre piece of the earth, the white settlers had to do little more than live on it for five years and "improve" it.

The white settlers came flooding to the Dakota Territory during two large waves. Some 100,000 came between 1879 and 1886. Then, between 1895 and 1914, another 250,000 arrived. Not only was the land the Indians had previously ranged over made available to white settlers (many of them immigrants from northern Europe), but the Indians discovered that the U.S. government too often failed to keep its promises to protect the remaining reservation lands from further encroachment by settlers and gold miners.

Boarding Schools

The whites took away their lands. Then the whites took away their children. A federal law in 1893 forced Indian children to go away from their homes, usually far away, to school.

If you lived on the Standing Rock reservation in the 1890s, and for a long time afterward, your child, instead of going off to a local kindergarten as many American children do today, would be forcibly taken from you and sent to live in a boarding school. You would not see each other for months. The idea, as freely expressed by our federal government, was to take the Indian out of the Indian children and make them act and talk and live like white people.

Try to imagine it. At age six you would say goodbye to your family and neighbors and climb aboard a train all by yourself. The train alone would be scary, but to ride on it for hours or days to Pennsylvania or Virginia would be even more frightening. You would have to sit beside another child who was from another tribe, perhaps even an enemy tribe, who spoke a language you could not begin to understand. You would be told when you got to the boarding school that you would be punished if you spoke the only language you knew, the one you learned at home. You would be told that you would have your hair cut and would wear white man's clothes and never, ever, think about or mention your religion. You would be told that your name was no longer your name, but that you must use a new one that sounded really weird to you. You would hear stories from the older children, once you learned some of the strange new English, about the people in charge and how they would abuse and punish children who did not comply with all the rules. You would be taught by your teachers that Indian ways were wrong and that you needed to be civilized. You were taught that the Indian ways of dancing were bad and that you had to dance new steps to new music.

In August 2012, Mary Louise Defender Wilson, the grand-daughter of George Defender, one of the five Indians accused of complicity in the Spicer murders, kindly consented to an interview. In part of that interview she gave a brief account of her grandmother's experience in a boarding school. Her grandmother was a Hidatsa Indian who eventually married George Defender:

> Interview with Mary Louise Defender Wilson
> Fort Yates, North Dakota
> August 21, 2012

Every Day, I Cried

My grandmother was named Mary Packineau. Her father was a Frenchman who had a boat on the Missouri River, a freighter actually. He married a Hidatsa woman named Plenty Sweet Grass. They had Mary and her two brothers. I remember her telling her story about school in St. Louis. Mary refused to speak English, although she must have known how because her father sent her to a Catholic school way back in those early times down in St. Louis. He took her down there on the freighter. She would talk about that trip. She would talk about that terrible time in St. Louis. She did not like the nuns. She didn't like anything about it in that school. She said the food was bad. Of course, it wasn't what she was used to. She said, "Every day, I cried. Every day, I cried." So finally, I guess the nuns sent word to her father that he better come and get his daughter or she might become ill. By that time, the Missouri froze over, so he wrote back and said, "As soon as the Missouri thaws out, I'll come down and get her." And he did.

Like virtually all of the other surviving Sioux of their generation at Standing Rock, the five men accused of the Spicer murders had all been to boarding schools. Obviously, most of the Sioux children survived boarding schools, despite the great pain of leaving home for so long and being taught that the way they were was the wrong way to be. But many were scared and confused and traumatized. Trauma is no excuse for murder, of course, but it begins to explain the despair and fear and grief that must have filled every home on Standing Rock.

The white settlers on the other side of the river probably knew little about the boarding schools that became the new homes of virtually all of the Indian children on the reservation. They would have been too busy trying to make something of their newly-acquired land, trying to feed their families, trying to stay warm in the winter, trying to have a little fun along with all the hard work. Busy with their own struggles, they would have had little idea of the suffering on the other side of the river.

Sitting Bull

In the late nineteenth century the taking of lands from the Indians and giving it to white settlers was almost universally viewed — except, of course, by most of the Indians — as the practical thing to do. Among the advocates of Indian sovereignty was the famous Hunkpapa holy man Sitting Bull (1831–1890). More than any other man, Sitting Bull had orchestrated the defeat of Custer's Seventh Cavalry at the Little Bighorn in 1876. To evade capture, Sitting Bull had then moved to Canada. He lived there for five years and would have liked to have stayed, but the Canadian government, not comfortable with having Sitting Bull and his band of followers living there, encouraged them to go "home." In 1881 Sitting Bull came back to the United States and turned himself in to the authorities, who eventually allowed him to settle, with some of his followers, on the Standing Rock reservation. After working for a short time in 1884 in Buffalo Bill's Wild West Show, Sitting Bull returned to Standing Rock. He reported to the agency at Fort Yates, ironically named for one of the soldiers his warriors had killed at the Little Bighorn.

When the government agents enticed the various tribal leaders to sign a new treaty in 1889, opening still more of the Standing Rock reservation to white settlement, Sitting Bull resisted. By then, however, his power over other Indians had waned, and enough of them signed the treaty to make it legal, more or less. Shortly after the new treaty was signed, this poem appeared in a North Dakota newspaper:

Daily Argus
Fargo, North Dakota
August 17, 1889

Sitting Bull Is Matched

And so at last the treaty's signed;
Though Sitting Bull has done his best
To thwart us in our grand design,
He could not quite control the rest,
For names enough are now attached,
And Sitting Bull for once is matched.

It won't be very long before
Industrious white men till the ground
Where ages upon ages gone
The Indians have loafed around;
Nor bettered self nor bettered land,
Now let the pale face try his hand.

Our many people need the lands
And these few Indians worked them not,
They'll never use what they have left;
But are at best a shiftless lot,
And blessed, indeed, will be the day,
When every one shall pass away.

The Indians, of course, soon enough got it: the white man's "grand design" referred to in line 3 of that poem was that all the Indians would "pass away." There was plenty of evidence of that design, famously expressed in General Philip Henry Sheridan's statement in 1869 that "the only good Indian is a dead Indian." Just a year later an editorial in a Wyoming newspaper proclaimed that grand design less tersely.

White Attitudes Toward Indians

To understand said editorial we need to know that the Big Horn Association was a group of ambitious men in Cheyenne who had banded together to explore the Big Horn mountains in search of gold. There was a problem, however. The Fort Laramie Treaty of 1868 contained specific provisions keeping the white man out of designated Indian territories. The Big Horn mountains were in one of those designated territories. Only two years after that treaty was signed, however, the white citizens of Cheyenne showed their disdain for all such treaties and for the treaty rights of Indians. After all, since they believed that God had ordained the "doom of extinction upon the red men of America," for white men to ignore the treaties was simply speeding along the work of the Lord. The members of the Big Horn Association planned an exploratory expedition to "our" Big Horn mountains, ignoring or circumventing objections of the Indians and of the federal government:

Cheyenne Daily Leader
Cheyenne, Wyoming Territory
May 3, 1870

[The Indians Must Stand Aside]

The Big Horn Association is rapidly perfecting its plans and making the preliminary arrangements for the forthcoming expedition. [...]

The rich and beautiful valleys of Wyoming are destined for the occupancy and sustenance of the anglo-saxon race. The wealth that for untold ages has lain hidden beneath the snow-capped summits of our mountains has been placed there by Providence to reward the brave spirits whose lot it is to compose the advance-guard of civilization.

The Indians must stand aside or be overwhelmed by the ever-advancing and ever-increasing tide of emigration. The destiny of the aborigines is written in characters not to be mistaken. The same Inscrutable Arbiter that decreed the downfall of Rome has pronounced the doom of extinction upon the red men of America. The attempt to defer this result by mawkish sentimentalism in favor of the savages is unworthy of the spirit of the age. To clog the chariot wheels of progress by effeminate scruples and ill-grounded sympathies for a cruel and incorrigible race is unworthy of a great people.

The Big Horn Association did send forth a 150-man, well-armed and well-supplied, expedition, but they found little gold in the lands they were permitted to explore. They were deeply disappointed that they had not been permitted to prospect in the Big Horn mountains after all. The editor of the *Cheyenne Daily Leader* issued a report three months later. Even though the prospectors had not been permitted to enter the Big Horn mountains, he was still optimistic. Once the Indians were extinct, the white gold-seekers would have their day in the Big Horns. These three sentences are from the closing paragraph:

Cheyenne Daily Leader
Cheyenne, Wyoming Territory
August 23, 1870

[The Tedious Process of Indian Extinction]

[...] The key to the richest gold mines in Wyoming, or perhaps in the world, is not yet within the grasp of white men. The tedious process of

Indian extinction must go on, perhaps for years, before this realization. The process, though slow, is sure.

No one ever did find much gold in the Big Horn mountains, but within a couple of years, gold worth mining was found in the Black Hills, another place protected by treaty from white encroachment. That treaty was soon abrogated, and the miners and farmers swarmed in. The whites were pretty well convinced that "Indian extinction" was not only inevitable but right. The Indians knew that the whites, by and large, considered them to be intellectually and morally inferior. How could they not know it when they read or were told about what Theodore Roosevelt (1858–1919) said about Indians in a speech he gave in 1886:

> I suppose I should be ashamed to say that I take the Western view of the Indian. I don't go so far as to think that the only good Indians are the dead Indians, but I believe that nine out of every ten are, and I shouldn't inquire too closely into the case of the tenth. The most vicious cowboy has more moral principle than the average Indian. [...] Reckless, revengeful, fiendishly cruel, they rob and murder, not the cowboys who can take care of themselves, but the defenseless, lone settlers of the plains [recorded in Hermann Hagedorn, *Roosevelt in the Bad Lands* (1921), p. 355].

In that last sentence Roosevelt was presumably alluding to the 1862 uprising in Minnesota. He made that statement just fifteen years before he became president of the United States in 1901. As a politician he knew that he could not win Western votes by showing sympathy for Indians, who were still a quarter-century away from being "given" citizenship in the United States. In any case, for Indians who understood what the future president was saying, the road ahead must have looked grim indeed, no matter what the local Indian agent told them.

Indian Agents

James McLaughlin (1842–1923) was the Indian agent at Standing Rock from 1881 to 1895. After that he took up supervisory duties as an inspector in the Indian Department in Washington, D.C. In 1910 he published a book about his lifetime of working with Indians. Entitled *My Friend the Indian*, the book is largely about his experiences as agent at Standing Rock and his dealings with Sitting Bull. In a chapter entitled "On the Making and Breaking of Treaties," he set forth his views of the inevitability of the "dominating influence" of the "white man" in North America:

> I do not hold with those people who contend, and generally without much knowledge of the subject, that the red man has been pillaged,

debauched, impoverished, and driven to desperation by the acts of the white man. In the nature of things, it must have come about that the Indian should go to the wall before the dominating influence of the white man. When the first white placed his foot upon the shores of this continent, it was predestined that he should come into the inheritance of the Indian. And there is no use quarreling with the processes of natural law [*My Friend the Indian* (Boston: Houghton Mifflin, 1926), p. 260)].

A blacksmith by trade, and married to a Santee woman, James McLaughlin had gained early experience as an Indian agent at the Spirit Lake reservation to the north and east of Standing Rock (not to be confused with Spirit Lake in Iowa). He thought he knew what the Indian people of North Dakota needed: they needed to become farmers. Shortly after he took up his duties at Standing Rock in 1881, McLaughlin summoned the Indians under his jurisdiction to a meeting to hear his proclamations. An Eastern reporter who attended that December 1881 meeting at Fort Yates filed a long report with his New York newspaper. The early paragraphs set the tone for the final paragraph in which McLaughlin explains his view of his relationship, both powerful and paternalistic, with the Indians at Standing Rock:

New York Daily Telegram
New York, New York
December 9, 1881

The Wily Sioux

Whatever the failures the government may have met with in its endeavors to settle that paradoxical and, withal, costly problem, the Indian question, there can be no doubt that the complete domestication of the Sioux will be accomplished within a very short period, and thus the last vestige of hostility be removed from the historical shores of the Missouri River. [...]

The manner in which the hostile tribes have been dealt with upon their return from the warpath is open to the most serious criticism. For instance, when Sitting Bull returned to Standing Rock he was lionized and petted by the officers of the remaining two companies of "the fighting Seventh" regiment, whose comrades and heroic commander were so barbarously butchered by direction of the very man they wined and dined. I was surprised to see the greatest kindness lavished on men who were never known to do any useful work, but here spent their lives in waging war upon our settlers and soldiery. As the red man reasons only from his own standpoint and there is no motive attributed to the action of a white man in doing them a generous turn other than fear, the misdirected and often questionable philanthropy of government officials and others must have their logical result. [...]

The prairie surrounding the camp was littered with the bones of animals killed by the bucks, and on lines in front of some of the tepees was hung jerked beef and otter skins. The whole plain was covered with Indians, all strolling toward the fort to attend a great peace council which Major McLaughlin, the new Indian agent, had called; and even the blue rim at the hills was dotted with the chiefs and braves on their way to talk with the new "father" whom the "Great Father " had sent. [...]

The agent's remarks

"My friends, chiefs and braves of Standing Rock: I am pleased to shake hands with you and tell you what the Great Father has sent me to do. He has sent me to take care of you and to labor for your interests. I intend to do my duty as a man and I shall expect the hearty co-operation of every man and chief here. I occupy the same relation toward you that a father does toward his children. And as the first thing that is necessary on the part of the children is obedience, I look to you to willingly obey me and listen to the commands of the government without demur. Such a course will enable me to represent your wants to our friends in the East. The eyes of many noble men and women are turned toward you, for the white people believe that you have at last abandoned savagery and will follow peaceful pursuits for the rest of your days. I have great confidence in you and hope that your conduct will be such as to be commended by all. I appeal to you, great chiefs, to bury the hatchet forever and learn what happiness you may have with your children by tilling the soil. May yon hills be covered with corn and vines, and may the smoke of your cabins rise in the midst of peace and plenty. Each individual must do his part. If the whole Sioux nation joins hands it can be as comfortable and as wealthy as the whites." [...]

Though Sitting Bull was not present at McLaughlin's great council at Fort Yates, he heard about it. Naturally, after his triumph at the Little Bighorn, he was not much interested in playing the role of Indian child who must obey the commands of a white "father" on a small reservation or even the "Great Father" in Washington. Sitting Bull, however, had few options. He was growing older. He had few warriors and weapons at his command. He had been made to feel unwelcome in Canada. And now he found himself the powerless "child" of a white father to whom he was expected to give unquestioning obedience.

Ghost Dance

It was at the end of a decade of discouragement, displacement, degradation, and despair that in 1890 word of a Paiute prophet named Wovoka reached the Indians at Standing Rock. Founder of what came to be called the Ghost Dance religion, Wovoka described his vision that Christ had returned to earth as an Indian. This messiah, he said, would cause the white man to leave Indian lands and would bring back the abundant buffalo herds. Some of the Plains Indians were convinced — or wanted to be — that if they wore special shirts and performed the Ghost Dance described by Wovoka their old way of life would return.

Fearing that the Ghost Dance might unify and mobilize the various Plains tribes and lead to armed attacks against settlers and military installations, white military and political leaders wanted to do all they could to suppress it. One of those who was most worried was agent James McLaughlin. He assumed that Sitting Bull would support this self-proclaimed Paiute prophet who said that if Indians across the West would take part in the Ghost Dance, the white man would disappear, the buffalo would return, and Indians would once more occupy their own country.

Sitting Bull never supported the Ghost Dance, but he was curious about it. When Sitting Bull asked McLaughlin for permission to visit the Cheyenne agency to find out more about the new phenomenon, McLaughlin turned him down. When McLaughlin learned that Sitting Bull had invited to his home several Indians who could tell him more about the new "religion," he was concerned. Later, when McLaughlin learned that a Ghost Dance was in session near Sitting Bull's residence on the Standing Rock reservation, he became even more concerned. When he learned that Sitting Bull, despite his orders, intended to visit Pine Ridge to learn more about the Ghost Dance, McLaughlin decided to act. On December 15, 1890, he sent forty Indian policemen to arrest Sitting Bull at his home. Crowds sympathetic to Sitting Bull gathered to protest the arrest. When Sitting Bull tried to pull away from the policemen, an Indian named Catch the Bear fired a shot. Soon Sitting Bull, eight of his supporters, and six of McLaughlin's Indian policemen from the agency lay dead.

Sitting Bull was dead, but his presence is still felt on the Sanding Rock reservation. Visitors still leave gifts at his two grave sites, and the tribal college in Fort Yates is named Sitting Bull College.

On December 19, just a few days after the murder of Sitting Bull, General Nelson A. Miles sent this telegram from Rapid City to Washington, D.C. It was addressed to John McAllister Schofield (1831–1906), the commanding general of the United States Army:

> The difficult Indian problem cannot be solved permanently at this end of the line. It requires the fulfillment of Congress of the treaty obligations that the Indians were entreated and coerced into signing. They signed away a valuable portion of their reservation, and it is now occupied by white people, for which they have received nothing. They understood that ample provision would be made for their support; instead, their supplies have been reduced, and much of the time they have been living on half and two-thirds rations. Their crops, as well as the crops of the white people, for two years have been almost total failures. The dissatisfaction is wide-spread, especially among the Sioux, while the Cheyennes have been on the verge of starvation, and were forced to commit depredations to sustain life. These facts are beyond question, and the evidence is positive and sustained by thousands of witnesses.

It is the same story over and over again. The Indians are starving; the whites are impatient and greedy.

Wounded Knee

After Sitting Bull's murder, around 200 of his Hunkpapa band, no longer feeling welcome at Standing Rock, rushed south to join Big Foot's Miniconjou band at the Cheyenne River reservation in South Dakota. Not long after, nearly a fourth of these Hunkpapas left the Cheyenne River reservation with Big Foot (also known as Spotted Elk) and his band. With him they made their way further south to seek shelter with Red Cloud on the Pine Ridge reservation.

A few days later, when they got to Pine Ridge but before they met up with Red Cloud, a detachment of the Seventh Cavalry, under the command of Major Samuel M. Whitside (1839–1904), intercepted Spotted Elk's band of Miniconjou and Hunkpapa Sioux near Porcupine Butte and escorted them to Wounded Knee Creek, where they made camp. While there Whitside's detachment was joined by other cavalry units. The cavalry quickly surrounded the encampment and set up four rapid-fire Hotchkiss guns — portable repeating cannons with a range of more than 2,000 yards. On the morning of Monday, December 29, 1890, Whitside sent his men into the camp to confiscate the weapons of the Indians. Some of them resisted, a scuffle ensued, and a rifle went off, probably by accident. The cavalry then opened fire and cut down Big Foot's band. By the time the shooting was over, more than 150 Indian men, women, and children lay dead. A third as many lay wounded. To Indians, of course, the killing at Wounded Knee was further proof, as if any were needed, that the grand design of the whites involved the extinction of Indians, and that it was working.

The massacre at Wounded Knee was of particular interest to the Indians at Standing Rock, if only because it included so many of the former Hunkpapa residents of the reservation. It was written up in the *Bismarck Daily Tribune*.

Bismarck Daily Tribune
Bismarck, North Dakota
December 30, 1890

Conflict at Last

Official dispatches from General Miles, dated [December 29], Rapid City, South Dakota, were received tonight by General Schofield [in Washington, D.C.], telling of a fight in the Bad Lands today between Indian hostiles and white troops. [...] "At 8:30 this morning, while disarming the

Indians, a fight commenced. I think very few Indians escaped." [...] General Schofield, though deeply regretting the occurrence, was not greatly surprised when he learned of the treachery displayed by the Indians in the fight referred to above. He had been on the lookout for treachery all the time; it was almost inevitable. That the trouble would end without a conflict of this kind was almost too much to be hoped for.

The "trouble" he referred to was the Ghost Dance movement. Reports the next day were more detailed:

Bismarck Daily Tribune
Bismarck, North Dakota
December 31, 1890

Worse and Worse

In the morning [of December 29, 1890], as soon as the ordinary military work of early day was done, Major Whitside determined upon disarming the Indians at once, and at 6 o'clock the camp of Big Foot was surrounded by the Seventh cavalry and Taylor's scouts. The Indians were sitting in a half circle. Four Hotchkiss guns were placed upon the hill about 200 yards distant.

Every preparation was made, not especially to fight, but to show the Indians the futility of resistance. They seemed to recognize this fact, and when Major Whitside ordered them to come up, twenty at a time, and give up their arms, they came, but not with their arms in sight. Of the first twenty, but two or three displayed arms. These they gave up sullenly, and observing the futility of that method of procedure, Major Whitside ordered a detachment of the K and A troops, on foot, to enter the tepees and search them. This work had hardly been entered upon when 120 desperate Indians turned upon the soldiers, who were gathered closely about the tepees, and immediately a storm of firing was poured upon the military. It was as though the order to search had been a signal. The latter, not anticipating any such action, had been gathered in very closely, and the first firing was terribly disastrous to them. The reply was immediate, however, and in an instant it seemed as if the draw in which the Indian camp was set was a sunken Vesuvius.

The soldiers, maddened at the sight of their falling comrades, hardly awaited the command, and in a moment the whole front was a sheet of fire, above which the smoke rolled, obscuring the central scene from view. Through this horrible curtain, single Indians could be seen at times flying before the fire, but after the first discharge from the carbines of the troopers there were few of them left. They fell on all sides like grain in the course of a scythe. Indians and soldiers lay together, and the wounded fought on the ground. Off through the draw toward the bluffs the few remaining warriors fled, turning occasionally to fire, but now evidently caring more for escape than battle. [...]

> The remnant fled and the battle became a hunt. It was now that the artillery was called into requisition. Before the fighting was so close that guns could not be trained without danger of death to the soldiers. Now, with Indians dying where they might, it was easier to reach them. Gattling and Hotchkiss guns were trained and they began heavy firing, which lasted a half hour, with frequent heavy volleys of musketry and cannon. It was a war of extermination now with the troopers. It was difficult to restrain the troops. Tactics were almost abandoned. About the only tactic was to kill while it could be done. Wherever an Indian could be seen down into the creek and up over bare hills, they were followed by artillery and musketry fire and for several minutes the engagement went on until not a live Indian was in sight.

The author of that piece claimed that the Indians were still in ownership of their weapons and that it was they who opened fire on the soldiers. Later investigation called both of those claims into question. The author rightly called the battle "a war of extermination," but neglected to point out that many of those exterminated were women and children. That particular error was corrected in the next issue:

Bismarck Daily Tribune
Bismarck, North Dakota
January 1, 1891

Death Toll Still Increasing

> The Episcopal church has been turned into a hospital, and this morning it contained thirty-eight of the hostile Indians wounded or captured at Wounded Knee. Most of them are squaws, and a majority will die. [...] A journal correspondent at Pine Ridge sends full particulars of Monday's battle at Wounded Knee creek. One hundred and sixteen Indian bucks were found dead upon the field and surrounding hills. In the confusion squaws and children mingled with the men, and forty of them were killed on the field. [...] Among the troops thirty-three were wounded, three dying last night. More Indians were killed than in any one Indian fight for the past twenty-five years.

The loss of their land to white settlers, the slaughter of their buffalo by white hunters, the disappearance of their children into white boarding schools, the killing of Sitting Bull by the white agent's Indian policemen, the snuffing of the Ghost Dance dream by the U.S. white cavalry, the massacre of men, women, and children by white Hotchkiss guns and Gatling guns at Wounded Knee — these would all have been recent history, living memories, for most of the Indians at the Standing Rock reservation. Is it any wonder that the Indian men who survived were ready to retaliate in strange and violent ways against whites? Is it any wonder that some of them seemed not to care much if they got caught, seemed almost to want to get caught? Did they see getting caught as a way of calling attention to the fact that they were warriors seeking revenge against a powerful enemy?

At the age of fourteen Sitting Bull proved himself a man by taking part in a fight in which a half-dozen enemy Crow warriors met their deaths. Did Paul Holy Track and his friend Philip Ireland think it was high time they proved themselves men? Did they think that they could prove it by following the example of Sitting Bull, a Lakota Indian, and Inkpaduta, a Dakota like themselves?

2

Murder

On the third Wednesday in the cold month of February 1897, readers in and around Bismarck, the state capitol of North Dakota, could have read in the local *Bismarck Daily Tribune* a short article about a murder on a Sioux Indian reservation further down the Missouri River in South Dakota:

Bismarck Daily Tribune
Bismarck, North Dakota
February 17, 1897

Two Killed

The bodies of Anton Sharp and his wife were found this morning at their house on the Yankton reservation, fifteen minutes west of Tyndall. The wife had her throat cut and she was shot in the breast. The man was shot in the head. The couple had been married two months. They had $300 in the house and this is supposed to have been the cause of the murder. There is no clue.

Readers could not have guessed that, even as they read that article about the killing of the Sharps, another "no-clue" family murder was taking place just across the Missouri River from the Standing Rock reservation. On that same day, on a small farm a short distance north of Winona, North Dakota, just sixty miles south of Bismarck, a man named Thomas Spicer was murdered. So was his wife. So was his mother-in-law. So was his daughter. So were his infant twin grandsons. The bodies were not discovered until the next morning. The day after that an account of the discovery was given in the Friday issue of the *Bismarck Daily Tribune*, the newspaper published in the state capitol. The writer, emphasizing the "inhuman butchery" of the "hellish" murders, assumed that Indians — by implication, Indians from the nearby Standing Rock Sioux reservation — must have committed the crime:

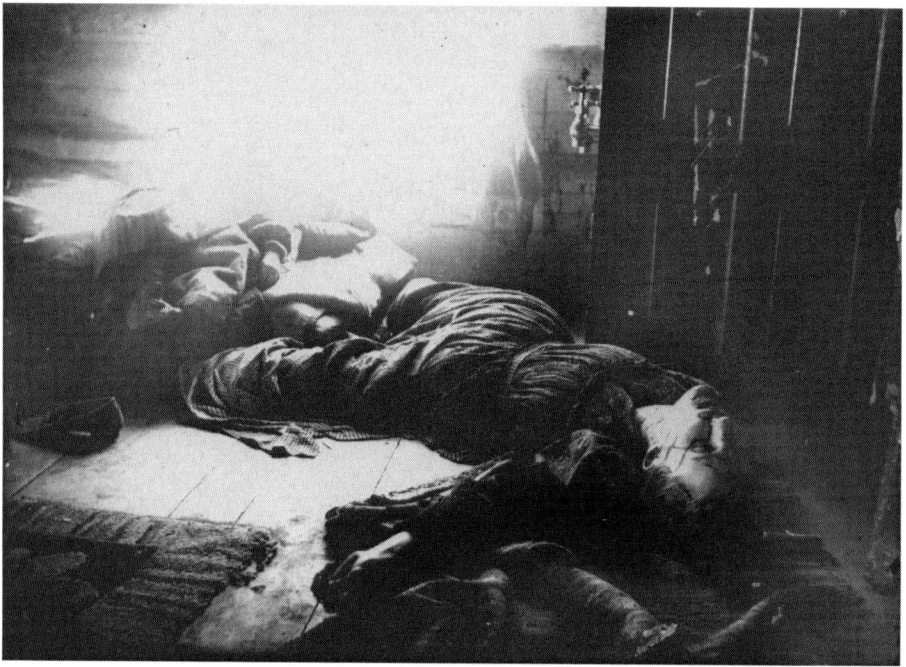

Lillie Spicer Rouse's body in the living room of the house owned by her parents. The bodies of her twin infant sons are concealed in the bedding on the couch at her feet (State Historical Society of North Dakota 1952–3337).

Bismarck Daily Tribune
Bismarck, North Dakota
February 19, 1897

Foully Murdered

About 10 A.M. this morning [Thursday, February 18] as Jack Spicer was going after a load of wood, he drove past his brother Thomas's house, which is situated about a mile and a half north of [Winona]. Upon receiving no response to his knock on the door, he pushed it open and found Mrs. Waldron, the mother of Mrs. Thomas Spicer and of Jack Waldron, lying on the floor dead and a hole crushed in her skull; he then passed on to the next room where he found Mrs. William Rouse, the daughter of Mrs. Spicer, and Mrs. Rouse's twin sons about a year and a half old lying dead on the lounge. Mrs. Rouse had been struck twice on the back of the head with the leg of a table and the children were struck over the eye and right side of the head, evidently with the same instrument that killed their mother. Mr. Spicer then went to the barn and found Mrs. Thomas Spicer lying in the stable with a hole in her skull and a deep cut on her chin, evidently produced by an axe.

He immediately came to town and notified the deputy coroner and a number of citizens who went out to the scene of the awful tragedy. After a careful search the body of Thomas Spicer was found in the cow shed, his head and throat were mutilated in a horrible manner and a knife wound over the heart.

The work is thought to be that of one or more Indians, as an Indian was seen there by a passer-by yesterday evening. [...]

The entire family were killed, except two daughters, Miss Ella and Maggie, who were away from home at the time. William Rouse, the husband of Mrs. Rouse, and the father of the two little ones, was on the Cannonball River at the time, having left here only last Monday to fix up things on a new ranch which he purchased recently, leaving his wife with her parents. A courier was sent for Mr. Rouse, who was fortunately met about fifteen miles from Fort Yates, coming home. He arrived here this afternoon, but was not allowed to witness the scene until after the dead bodies were cared for. The excitement is running high. [...]

Mail carrier LeBrock, who came up from Winona yesterday morning, saw two Indians at Winona, two of whom had painted faces, and there seems to be no reasonable doubt that the Indians are at the bottom of the devilish deed. Mr. Spicer was a M. E. minister, working under the direction of presiding Elder Ryan. He was about 52 years of age and his wife about the same. Mrs. Waldron was about 80 and Mrs. Rouse about 22. The family was one of the most respected in the whole county, and there could exist no valid reason for any one to have any enmity against the family. [...]

It is impossible to believe that such cruel and inhuman butchery of women and children could have been perpetrated by other than Indians.

That same day a somewhat similar report appeared in the weekly county newspaper, the *Emmons County Record*, which came out every Friday. Its opening headline proclaimed the view that the murders were the work of a devil doing what is described in the article as the hellish work of a fiend:

Emmons County Record
Williamsport, North Dakota
February 19, 1897

Devilish!

One of the most horrifying sights that ever met the gaze of human eyes was that which presented itself to the startled vision of those who were first on the scene at the residence of Thomas Spicer, one mile north of this village, on Thursday morning, February 18, about 10 o'clock.

Six human bodies lay cold in death, as a result of the vengeance of some fiend or fiends in human form. [...] The particulars of the horrible affair, as near as can be ascertained, are as follows:

Mr. John Spicer, a brother of the murdered man, had occasion to call at the latter's place Thursday morning about 9 o'clock, to get a set of bobsleighs. As he occupied some time in hitching to the sled and no one came out of the house and as he also noticed the cattle at the stack, and that no smoke was coming from the chimney, he went to the door and rapped. There was no response. He opened the door and was horror stricken to find the old lady, Mrs. Waldon, lying on the floor, dead, with deep gashes in her head. In the next room lay Mrs. Rouse, cold in death. Her baby boys were lying on the lounge, also dead. The indications were that the poor mother had fought desperately in defense of her life and of the lives of her little ones. A hoe and a table leg were near her, which she had probably used in her defense. A bloody axe was lying on the lounge, under the bodies of the babies.

Mr. Spicer then ran to the barn. More horror! There, inside, he found the body of Mrs. Spicer, lying on the ground. She had wounds on the head and also on the chest, having been stabbed several times with a pitchfork.

Mr. Spicer rushed to town and gave the alarm. John McCrory, J. A. Stiles and others hastened to the Spicer farm, and there found the bodies as before described.

Further search revealed the body of Thomas Spicer, partly covered with manure, in the cow-shed. His jaw was broken, his head and face otherwise brutally disfigured, and there was a gun-shot wound in his back. It is thought that he was cleaning out the stables when the shot was fired, as he had a lot of manure on the wheelbarrow. The supposition is that the shot was fired as he was wheeling the load, and then the assassin used the axe on his head, as the wounds there were evidently made by that weapon. Mrs. Spicer had been washing, and, from the appearance of things, was hanging out clothes when she heard the shot fired, and, going to the stable to learn the cause, there met her death. As no eye-witnesses are left to tell the sad tale, the exact particulars will probably never be known, unless the murderer or murderers should be captured and make a truthful confession. At present everything is conjecture. It is thought that Mr. and Mrs. Spicer first met their fate. Then the murderer went inside the house to finish his hellish work.

The only party to whom can be ascribed this diabolical deed is an Indian who was seen going from the stable to the road and then back to the barn. As Mr. Horatio Wilson, a neighbor who lives two miles north of the Spicer farm, was coming past that place, he noticed an Indian coming from the stable toward him. The Indian was approaching quite rapidly. Mr. Wilson thought he wanted a ride, and, as Mr. W. had no desire for his company, he urged his horses to a little faster gait. When the Indian found that he could not overtake the white man, he turned around, retraced his steps to the stable, and stood on the manure pile until Mr. Wilson was out of sight. The hour was about 4 o'clock Wednesday afternoon. This was certainly a very strange action on the part of the Indian. Some think the Indian was afraid that Mr. Wilson would drive up to the stable, and so he ran down to head him off, and kill him if necessary. Then, again, there are others — and there are such on the west side of the river — who do not think the bloody work was done by an Indian or Indians, but that the Indian seen by Mr. Wilson had discovered the bodies and was coming down to notify Mr. Wilson, but could not catch him. However, Mr. Wilson says that the Indian came up to within four or five rods of him, and could easily have made him understand that something was wrong. One thing is generally known, which is that Mr. Spicer was expecting an Indian to come over the river from the reservation on that day to purchase a horse from him; but whether the one he expected came, or another, is not known.

The murderer ransacked the house, taking two suits of clothes belonging to Mr. Spicer and some dresses belonging to the Misses Spicer, besides about $40 in money. He also overlooked a little more than $100. Mr. Spicer's watch he also left untouched. It had stopped at 10:11½— presumably on Thursday morning. It is thought that the murder occurred about the middle of the afternoon of Wednesday, February 17. Wednesday evening about 7:30 o'clock Miss Maggie Spicer and Mr. Frank Parks drove out to call on her people, but, seeing no light, the young folks thought that the family had gone over to Mr. John Spicer's to spend the evening. Therefore, the callers did not get out of the cutter. It is more likely that the villainous deed had been committed at that time, and that the good and kind and gentle members of this once happy family were then cold and still in death.

Major Cramsie, the Indian agent of the Standing Rock reservation across the river, has his Indian police out scouring the country for the Indian to whom suspicion points. [...]

"Major Cramsie" was John W. Cramsie, a white man who had been appointed the Indian agent at the Standing Rock reservation in 1895. The title "major," bestowed on or assumed by most agents to Indian tribes, did not indicate a military background or rank.

The news spread rapidly, including the supposition that Indians were responsible:

Grand Forks Daily Herald
Grand Forks, North Dakota
February 19, 1897

Horrible Murder

A horrible sextuplet tragedy was discovered a mile from [Winona] on the ranch of Rev. Thomas Spicer. [...] The bodies were terribly mutilated with axes and clubs, which fact is taken to at least partialy corroborate the suspicion of Indian murderers.

More details of the murders were given in the Saturday issue of the Bismarck newspaper. Some of the details, like the supposed "ravishment" of two of the women, turned out — at least to judge by the "confessions" that were to come along in the following months — to be false. Meanwhile, there were no arrests, not even any specific suspects, just the conviction that the killer-rapists must be Indians because no white man would do such things. As for a supposed motive for the killings, having ruled out the desire for money because the killers had left some behind, the journalist could posit only "some revengeful desire or more brutal passion":

Bismarck Daily Tribune
Bismarck, North Dakota
February 20, 1897

Horrible Details

There are no further developments in the Spicer tragedy except that in laying out the dead bodies it was discovered that Mr. Spicer had been shot in the back with a shot gun, twenty-six shot and a large lead bullet, which from its irregularity, was evidently home made, taking effect. Both Mrs. Rouse and Mrs. Spicer were ravished. This, however, not till after they had been stricken down as the position of the bodies and clothing indicated when found. Mr. Spicer's dress suit is missing although his watch and $3.21 was found on his person. The coroner's jury has not rendered its verdict as yet. The funeral will probably take place next Sunday afternoon. The Misses Spicer, daughters of Mr. and Mrs. Spicer, Jack Waldron and Mr. Rouse are so prostrated that it has not been thought best to let them see the bodies of the butchered ones yet. Nothing has been discovered yet giving any light as to the author of the crime.

Details of the tragedy at Winona, awful as they were upon the first report, grew more horrible with the relation and amplification of the facts of the murder. From the latest reports received, and further information of the finding and condition of the bodies, it was by far the most sickening and brutal crime in the whole history of atrocities. Six persons, representing four generations of human beings, ruthlessly slaughtered in cold blood, two women ravished, the bodies of the dead fearfully mutilated, and two harmless children with no conception of the awful tragedy being perpetrated near them, robbed of life before they were able to appreciate existence as a condition. A brutality which could be responsible for so foul a crime is almost beyond the imagination of even the most hardened sinner.

From John Eastwood, who is stage driver for Charles Kupitz, the *Tribune* has obtained further particulars of the crime. The murder was committed on Wednesday afternoon, according to the belief of all who are familiar with the circumstances. What was its object, unless it was the satisfaction of some revengeful desire or more brutal passion, cannot be said. That it was not robbery is evident from the fact that money was found in the house and in the pockets of some of the corpses. The mutilation of the bodies would indicate that the work was that of men crazed or brutalized by liquor, or whose natural instincts were those of the fiend. The theory of revenge is faulty for the reason that no one was known to harbor any feeling of enmity against any of the persons who were murdered, nor were they persons of such a disposition as would incur the enmity of anyone. Plain, simple minded, everywhere well liked, and in no way likely to incur the enmity of any person, it is difficult to see wherein the theory of revenge would satisfy all of the circumstances in the case.

The body of Thomas Spicer, the only man about the place at the time of the murder, was found in the barn, where he had evidently been doing some cleaning, as a barrow used for such purposes was found near him. He had been shot in the back, evidently the first act in the awful series of murders. His throat was hacked and cut with a knife, and there were several stabs in the region of the breast. His wife had evidently been killed outside the barn, having been attracted to the place by the sound of the shot which killed her husband. She was killed with an axe, by a blow on the head and after the killing or in the frenzied passion which accompanied it, her chin was split to the throat by a blow from the same weapon. Her breast was also perforated with little holes, as though she had been further stabbed with a pitchfork. The body was then dragged into the barn where it was found.

From the appearance of the room in which Mrs. Rouse was found there had been a struggle, the unfortunate woman fighting for her life and that of her little children, but a blow from an axe or a club had finished the struggle, and her throat was grazed, as though a hasty attempt to cut it had been unsuccessful. The bodies of the children were not mutilated beyond the blows on the head by which they had been killed. In the next room, Mrs. Waldron had been killed by a blow from a club. She was killed near the stove, and her body was then dragged to the cellar, the door of which was raised as though it had been the intention of the murderer to throw the body therein, but something had happened to prevent.

From the report brought by Mr. Eastwood of the affair, it is said at Winona that an Indian had an appointment to meet Spicer at the home on Wednesday forenoon about a matter of horse trading, but he did not come, and Mrs. Rouse, one of the murdered, was in the town in the forenoon of that day, returning about noon. That was the last time anyone of the house was seen. A settler named Wilson, the nearest neighbor of the Spicers, says that in about the middle of the afternoon in passing the Spicer place, which is about half a mile from the road, he saw an Indian come down from that direction about half way to the road, returning, after Wilson passed, to the barn. Wilson says however that he does not know whether he could identify the Indian he saw there or not. Another settler says that about noon Wednesday he was followed across the river by an Indian who wanted to trade horses and who was drunk. Efforts to trace these Indians have so far proved unsuccessful.

The six bodies of the dead were laid out in the house where they lived Thursday night. It was a scene to try the most hard hearted. Six human beings ruthlessly murdered in cold blood, their bodies slashed and cut, lying there in one room, grandmother, daughter, granddaughter and two grand sons, all of one family, flesh and blood, helpless women and children, who had been slain after the foul murder of the husband and father.

The funeral will probably take place Sunday afternoon, and the bodies will be buried on the brow of the hill just east of the house whose hearthstone has been so fearfully stained with the blood of those who have been accustomed to sit around it. Four oblong pine boxes, containing the coffins which will enclose the victims, were taken down to Winona from this city yesterday. The murdered Mrs. Rouse and her two children will be buried in the same casket.

There was, of course, intense pressure on the coroner to identify the murderer and on the sheriff to arrest him, but there was little to go on but the assumption that it was an Indian, perhaps the man, as yet unidentified, who had spoken to Thomas Spicer about buying a horse. February 21 was Sunday, the day of the funerals:

Bismarck Daily Tribune
Bismarck, North Dakota
February 21, 1897

No Verdict Yet

At the latest reports from the scene of the murders at Winona, the coroner's jury had not completed the work and no verdict had been rendered. The jury took all the testimony available, which might tend to throw light on the crime, and was still busy at last accounts. The facts in the case as they have developed since yesterday's account of the tragedy indicate that that account was a correct one, and about the only question to be solved is to the identity of the murderer, and from the account brought up by the mail carrier LeBrock last night the perpetrator of the crime is generally believed to be the Indian who had an engagement with Spicer to trade horses. From the account given by Mr. LeBrock, it appears that the Indian was at the Spicer home a day or so before the murder was committed, and wanted to make a trade, but did not have the amount of money demanded by Mr. Spicer and was not allowed to take the horse. He at that time manifested anger and went away in a bad humor. The circumstance was mentioned to Jack Waldron by Spicer, and the Indian described in such a way that it is believed he can be placed. Whether he was the one who committed the murder remains to be proven, but Mr. LeBrock says it is agreed that he is the one. The testimony given by the doctor at the inquest was to the effect that he believed that the murders were committed by the one man, and that Spicer, his wife, Mrs. Waldron, Mrs. Rouse and the children were killed in the order named. The room where Mrs. Rouse was found indicated about the only struggle which had taken place between the murderer and his victims, the curtains in two or three places in the room being stained with blood and there being pools of blood in several places on the floor. An ash stick which Mrs. Rouse was accustomed to keep about was found covered with blood, and it had been stuck in to the dead woman's throat, as though she had defended herself with it until overcome, and that then the murderer had seized it from her and plunged it into her throat in his fury.

The excitement in the neighborhood is at fever heat, and hundreds of people have visited the home where the bodies of the dead have lain, and seen the remains. The funeral will take place today.

The Spicer murders were immediately famous around the nation, but especially in the greater midwest. Almost everyone assumed that the murderer was an Indian. The possibility of a lynching, as we see below, was right from the beginning thought to be a probable outcome:

Saint Paul Globe
Saint Paul, Minnesota
February 21, 1897

Work of One Red

At latest reports from the scene of the tragedy at Winona, the coroner's jury had not completed the work and no verdict had been rendered. Testimony was taken from all sources that could throw light on the affair and doctors who were upon the scene after the murder gave evidence of the condition of the bodies and other details to show the probable manner in which the crime was committed. From the reports received here, doctors are of the opinion that the six murders were committed by one man, who shot Mr. Spicer first and then killed Mrs. Spicer, Mrs. Waldron and Mrs. Rouse in the order named, with axes. It has also developed that the Indian who wanted to trade horses with Mr. Spicer came to his house to make the trade several days before the murder, but did not have enough money to pay for the animal. He shook his fist and made threats according to reports and finally rode off. This circumstance was reported by Mr. Spicer to his brother-in-law, Jack Waldron, and the Indian described, from which it is believed he will finally be apprehended. Hundreds of people from Winona, Fort Yates and surrounding country have visited the scene of the tragedy since the commission of the crime and laying out of the bodies, and the little house has been crowded with the curious, among them several Indians, two of whom were policemen on the reservation, and even their stoical hearts were touched, and one of them wept at seeing the bodies of the twin boys among the victims. Excitement in Winona is at a fever heat and everybody is armed with a revolver, gun, or other weapon. No danger of any general trouble with Indians is apprehended, but if the murderer is captured he will doubtless be taken from the authorities and punished by the settlers, who are thoroughly aroused.

With or without precise information about the identity of the murderer or murderers, the funeral had to go forward. The local reporter from Winona described in some detail the exact nature of the various wounds and bruises. He could no doubt assume that most of his white readers would nod in agreement when he asserted that, since no white man would commit such a crime, it must have been committed by one or more Indians who, as he put it, "shed blood for the love of shedding":

Emmons County Record
Williamsport, North Dakota
February 22, 1897

The Funeral

The funeral of the members of the Spicer family, who were so brutally massacred near this village last Wednesday afternoon, occurred yesterday (Sunday) at 2 P.M. The services were conducted by the Rev. George Reed of Fort Yates. It was probably the largest funeral in point of attendance that ever took place in Emmons County. Most of the residents within a radius of fifteen miles were in attendance. The school building did not hold nearly all of the people who were present.

Sunday forenoon the bodies of the six victims were brought down from the Spicer home and placed side by side in the front part of the room, being those of Mrs. Ellen Waldron, Mr. Thomas Spicer, Mrs. Mary Spicer, Mrs. Lillie Rouse and her two twin baby boys. The bodies of Mr. and Mrs. Spicer were in the same part of the room that in life they had so often occupied while conducting religious services. The bodies, although terribly mutilated with wounds, had been carefully dressed and arranged, and the disfigurements showed but very little.

The body of Mr. Spicer was the one most mutilated. There was a gun-shot wound showing the marks of twenty-seven fine shot, and also a wound made by a leaden bullet of about fifty-six caliber in the back. The bullet had lodged against the backbone and it was easily picked out with a penknife. The throat was cut. There was a deep cut across the chin and several small cuts about the head. All except the gun-shot wounds were undoubtedly made with an axe.

Mrs. Spicer's body was not as badly disfigured. There was a deep gash just under the lower lip and several small bruises on the head. Her body had been stabbed a number of times with a pitchfork that was found near the body at the time the murders were discovered. One of the hips was broken.

The body of Mrs. Waldron, mother of Mrs. Spicer, was apparently the least bruised of any, there being but two bruises visible — one on the temple and the other on the back of the head. The left arm was broken.

On account of the tools used as weapons, and of the blood, that were found near Mrs. Rouse's body, it is thought that she had more warning of her danger than the others, and fought more desperately in defense of her life and her little ones. Her father's gun was near her which she had probably gotten to frighten the fiend or fiends away. It was not loaded, and had not been loaded for some time. A hoe was also found near the body, as well as an old table leg with which the murderer had killed Mrs. Rouse, as there was a tuft of the poor woman's hair on the weapon when it was found. It is impossible to form even a faint idea of the horror she endured during that last struggle. Her twin baby boys, nineteen months old, were found on the lounge, with the back part of their heads crushed and otherwise bruised. To the hundreds of people who have viewed the bodies, the sight of the murdered babies is the most touching.

The killing without motive of the two infant boys is one of the strongest reasons for believing that the villainous work was done by one or more Indians. No white murderer would kill little children not old enough to identify him in case their lives were spared. Not that a white assassin would not kill a babe if paid for it. But the white villain would have had a motive either of gain or revenge — and no white man could possibly have had a motive in either direction in this case. It is certain that the indiscriminate slaughter was the work of a creature who killed without motive — who shed blood for the love of shedding.

Other newspapers covering the funeral and interment of the victims gave more information about the investigation, about the history of Thomas Spicer, and about the reward offered for information leading to the arrest and conviction of the murderer or murderers:

Winona Times
Winona, North Dakota
February 25, 1897

The Funeral of the Murdered Victims

The coroner's jury have held two or three adjourned meetings, but as yet have returned no verdict. [...]

The only new feature in the case is that some personal effects of small value were taken and two or three Indians have been arrested by the Indian police as acting in a suspicious manner; but it is believed by the white people that they are not the guilty ones. [...]

Mr. Spicer was noted for his genial hospitality and had on several occasions entertained Indians at his table, and it is thought that his kind-heartedness had led to his death. [...]

Thomas Spicer was born in England, August 1850. He migrated from his native country and settled in Canada. He came to this country in May, 1892, and built the blacksmith shop on Fourth street now owned by Alexander Duncan. After working at the trade for awhile, he sold and purchased the claim just north of town in February, 1893. Mr. Spicer was an upright Christian man and in 1895 he was granted a license to preach as a local preacher in the M. E. church. [...]

$800 reward

A reward of five hundred ($500) dollars will be paid to the person delivering into the custody of the sheriff of Emmons County, North Dakota, the murderer or murderers of Thomas Spicer, Mrs. Thomas Spicer, Mrs. Waldron, Mrs. William Rouse and her twin, infant children. [...] Said reward to be paid upon the conviction of such murderer or murderers. [...] The citizens of Winona and Fort Yates have offered $300 reward for the capture of the murderer or murderers, in addition to the $500 offered by the government. This makes a total of $800 offered so far.

The identity of the "two or three Indians" who had been arrested was not revealed in that article, but it soon enough surfaced that their "suspicious" behavior involved whiskey.

3

Whiskey

It turned out that the suspicious behavior of the Indians arrested involved their killing of a cow that did not belong to them and then trading the meat to a white Winona saloon-keeper for whiskey. The article below made public their names. "Louis Agaard" was apparently a reportorial error. There was a mixed-blood Indian named Louis Agaard on the reservation, but the second man arrested turned out to be a different mixed-blood named Alec Coudotte:

Bismarck Daily Tribune
Bismarck, North Dakota
February 26, 1897

Indians Arrested

Two of agent Cramsie's wards at the Standing Rock agency are under arrest for killing a cow and disposing of it to a Winona saloon keeper last week. The hide, head and internals of the critter were found south of Winona, where it is supposed to have been killed. As yet the ownership of the cow has not been discovered.

It was reported by the stage driver, who came up from Winona last night, that the evidence given by the two Indians who were arrested on the charge related above tends to implicate them in the tragedy at Winona last week, although there is yet no proof that they were concerned in it. The two men arrested were Black Hawk and Louis Agaard, one of them a Negro half breed, who has served a term in the penitentiary. The two were arrested on Grand River some distance from the agency by the Indian police and the officers of Emmons County. They admitted the stealing of the animal and said that they were there at that time to dispose of the animal stolen, and, so report goes, admitted having bought whiskey. Since Wednesday they have been missing, and as the crime was committed that day, that fact looks as though the two facts might have been in some way related.

The face of one of the men, so it is said, was found to be scratched when he was arrested and he explained the circumstance by stating that the cow

A dance hall/hotel/brothel in Winona. Note the women looking out — beckoning? — from the upstairs windows. In the 1890s there were said to be eight or ten such establishments in Winona (State Historical Society of North Dakota 0900-030).

which they had stole had kicked him. Afterwards he said the scratches were caused from a fall on the ice. It will be remembered that it was stated at the time of the murder that the face of the murderer would likely be scratched from the result of his struggle with one of his victims.

The men are now under arrest and carefully guarded at Fort Yates. Of course there may be nothing in the fact of their reported probable complicity in the murder, and further developments may tend to throw more light on the matter.

The various reports about the likelihood that Indians, particularly mixed-blood Indians, were guilty of the Spicer murders spurred a man named H. M. Smee, who lived further north in the reservation town of Cannon Ball, North Dakota, to write a letter to the editor of the *Bismarck Daily Tribune*. Mr. Smee insisted that the Indians themselves were eager to see justice done. He quotes an unnamed "old Indian" who said that the Indians were glad that "a black man and not one of our people" had committed the murders. This Indian's reference to Fort Rice is to the first military outpost in the region (see frontispiece), established in 1864. Named for Union general James Clay

Rice of Massachusetts, killed in the Civil War, Fort Rice was the first of several forts intended to protect northern plains transportation routes and encourage settlement by European-Americans. Fort Rice had provided some of the troops who died with Custer at the battle of the Little Bighorn in 1876. Smee's "Poor Lo" is an allusion to Alexander Pope's couplet "Lo! The poor Indian, whose untutored mind / Sees God in clouds, or hears him in the wind." "Muddy River" was a term sometimes used for the Missouri River, which separates the Standing Rock reservation from Emmons County. The term "penny-a-liner" refers to journalists who were sometimes paid by the line for what they wrote. Smee was one of the first to put in print the view that the white businessmen of Winona, because they illegally sold whiskey to Indians, were at least partly responsible for the deaths of the Spicer family:

Bismarck Daily Tribune
Bismarck, North Dakota
March 3, 1897

[Not One of Our People]

Editor *Tribune*:
Will you kindly allow me through your columns to correct several foolish statements dated both from Winona and Bismarck, and going the rounds of the eastern papers concerning the tragedy. [...]

It has also been reported that white settlers are all armed and will shoot any Indian found off the reservation on sight. As a matter of fact, while it is true that settlers are for the most part going armed, they are not going to shoot either Indians or whites, unless they have cause. They are well aware of the fact that the Indians are as deeply interested in getting the criminal and universally (all over the reservation) condemn the crime, as the white people. As an old Indian fittingly remarked to a mixed crowd of whites and half-breeds the other day: "My friends, we are a poor people. We are very ignorant of the white man's ways. We killed many white men in time of war, yet never since I have been here; never since Fort Rice was built has an Indian killed white women in cold blood along the Muddy River; it is said, a man, half black, half Indian, has done this thing, and we are glad — since some one must have done this thing — that it is a black man and not one of our people. We will take a big breath of relief when we are sure the man is found and killed for bad hearts are bad." Thus spoke the old man and his sentiments represented the sentiments of the Indians.

Poor Lo is no saint. Neither is he useful or particularly ornamental, his one redeeming point — picturesqueness — departed with the buffalo. But give "the devil his due." Don't condemn the whole reservation for the probable crime of a couple of mixed-bloods and part Negro. Remember, "Mr. Penny-a-liner," that there are several educated and refined mixed-bloods on the reservation who read the papers, and who are a credit to any community. They feel hurt at these stories which are untrue and unjust and again they tell the Indians, which arouses race hatred between Indians and whites which is to be deplored.

The Indian is getting off the earth as quickly as he can. Cigarettes, pneumonia and air-tight log houses are fast decreasing their ranks. It is probably as well, for he has little to live for now but while he is here let us keep and treat him half way right anyhow.

Lastly I would say that we all believe — white, Indian or mixed-blood — that whiskey was at the bottom of this awful crime and we are nearly all agreed that the sooner Winona whiskey shops are swept away, the better for all. The best agent in the world cannot prevent the poor, ignorant Indian from once in a while slipping away to these places of (to them) alluring sin. There are always white men at these places who will sell liquor to an Indian and the result is an occasional murder and again a pitiful massacre like the present. A white man is bad enough, God knows, when he is drunk, but an Indian or a mixed-blood, with rare exception, is dangerous and should at no time be served liquor sufficient to intoxicate him, and for the most part should have none at all.

Respectfully,
H. M. Smee

Smee's idea that "the Indian is getting off the earth as quickly as he can" was a familiar one. It was based partly on the racist notion of "Manifest Destiny" — that white Europeans were destined, even obligated, to remove the Indians from the North American continent so that the land could be put to better use by smart, hard-working, and resourceful whites. But it was based in part on observation. It was easy enough to see that the history of early America was largely a history of white Europeans supplanting the Indians. It was not, of course, a matter of the Indian "getting off the earth as quickly as he can" so much as it was a matter of whites forcing the Indian off the earth as quickly as they could. The whites accomplished the task with astonishing speed. Many, many Indians had died of the white man's diseases, bullets, greed, treachery, and whiskey.

Smee's opinion that "whiskey was at the bottom of this awful crime" was shared by many, including John W. Cramsie, the Indian agent. A month after the Spicer murders, and a few days after the Smee letter appeared, Cramsie wrote a letter to state's attorney Tracy M. Bangs in Grand Forks asking him to arrest the saloon keepers who sold whiskey to Indians. Attached to his letter were documents citing specific instances when Frederick "Red" Caldwell, Scar Faced Charley, and Caldwell's "wife" sold liquor to Indians. Included here are only those instances mentioning by name the Indians eventually arrested for the murder of the Spicer family. Note that many Dakota Indians had several names. Frank Pierre and Frank Black Hawk were the same person:

3. Whiskey

Honorable Tracy M. Bangs
U.S. Attorney
Grand Forks, North Dakota
March 18, 1897

Sir:

   I have the honor to request that Frederick Caldwell, a saloon-keeper, and the woman living with him said to be Caldwell's wife, and her sister whose name is unknown together with Caldwell's bar-keeper who is known by the name of Scar Faced Charley, all of Winona, Emmons County, North Dakota, be arrested, and brought before the grand jury shortly to be in session at Bismarck, on the charges enumerated in the accompanying notes, or such of them as you may decide upon.

   The recent murders committed at Winona, if perpetrated by Indians, were doubtless the result of the whiskey traffic with Indians visiting Winona, and it is well known that these same parties have been selling liquor to Indians for a year past. It is therefore highly necessary that some prompt action be taken to put a stop to the traffic as well as for affording a possibility of obtaining some information during the examination of the witnesses in the liquor cases will lead to the solution of the murder mystery.

   The cases of sales of liquor to mixed-bloods will of course be prosecuted under the act approved January 30, 1897.

Very respectfully,
John W. Cramsie,
U.S. Indian Agent

Notes to accompany letter to U.S. attorney dated March 18, 1897:
On or about December 12, 1896, Paul Holytrack, a full blood Sioux Indian, bought of Scar Faced Charley, bar-keeper for Frederick Caldwell, one bottle of alcohol and one bottle of whiskey.

    Witness, Paul Holytrack.

On or about January 15, 1897, said Paul Holytrack bought of said Scar Faced Charley three bottles of whiskey and on February 10, one bottle of whiskey from the same party.

    Witness: Paul Holytrack.

On or about February 11, 1897, the same Paul Holytrack bought two bottles of whiskey from Caldwell's wife.

    Witnesses: Paul Holytrack, Philip Ireland.

[...]

On or about February 20, 1897, George Defender, a full-blood Sioux Indian, bought a gallon of whiskey from Caldwell, paying the latter $10 for same. The whiskey was purchased in part from the proceeds of the sale of clothing.

    Witnesses: George Defender, Alexander Codotte,
    Samuel Burguiet.

On or about February 16, 1897, Alexander Codotte, a mixed-blood Sioux

Indian, purchased a bottle of whiskey of Caldwell, and on or about the 18th February purchased another bottle of whiskey of Caldwell, paying $3.00 for the two. Caldwell delivered both bottles to Codotte.
Witnesses: Alexander Codotte, Frank Pierre.

On February 14 and 15, 1897, Frank Pierre, a mixed-blood Sioux Indian, purchased whiskey in drinks over the bar aggregating about $2.00 worth. The drinks were served to him by Caldwell and his wife at various times during the two days.
Witnesses: Frank Pierre, Alexander Cadotte.

[...]

On February 16, 1897, Caldwell's wife gave said Frank Pierre half a pint of whiskey in a pint bottle. Caldwell directed his wife to furnish the whiskey.
Witness: Frank Pierre.

John W. Cramsie
U.S. Indian agent
Standing Rock agency

It is interesting that all five of the Indians who were eventually charged with the Spicer murders had been questioned by Cramsie or his men, and that they had, within a month after the murders, given witness testimony against Red Caldwell for selling liquor to them.

The day after he sent that March 18 letter to attorney Bangs, Cramsie sent him a second, shorter note telling him that the man he was to arrest had tried to run away but had been arrested at Eureka, South Dakota. Apparently Cramsie had heard that Mr. Bangs was in Bismarck, so sent the note there:

U.S. Attorney Bangs
Bismarck, North Dakota
March 19, 1897

Letter with notes of abundant evidence to convict F. P. Caldwell and others for selling liquor to Indians mailed you yesterday to Grand Forks. Caldwell skipped the county but is held in custody at Eureka, South Dakota, awaiting arrival of proper officers to bring him to Bismarck together with his sister-in-law, who is equally guilty. Please send good officer for the prisoners. Duplicate letter mailed tonight.

Besides the parties named, Caldwell's wife, who is in Winona, and Scar Faced Charley, otherwise James Jacobs, who is in Williamsport, are both implicated and equally guilty.

Cramsie, Agent

It had long been illegal to sell alcohol to Indians. As early as 1802 Congress authorized president Thomas Jefferson "to take such measures, from time to time, as to him may appear expedient to prevent or restrain the vending or distributing of spiritous liquors among all or any of the said Indian tribes"

3. Whiskey

(*U.S. Statutes at Large* 2 [1802]: 146). Later presidents found it difficult to deal directly with such matters or even to interpret the practical implications of terms like "prevent or restrain." In 1832 the office of Commissioner for Indian Affairs was created. Two years later Congress passed a law authorizing a fine of up to $500 for anyone convicted of trying to "sell, exchange, or give, barter, or dispose of any spiritous liquor or wine to an Indian (in Indian country)" (*U.S. Statutes at Large* 4 [1834]: 729). Additional refinements of the law were made over the years as the definition of "Indian country" shifted, and as other questions surfaced. Is beer a "liquor"? Can Indians who buy liquor from a white man testify against him? Is it illegal for Indians to buy whiskey, or only illegal for others to sell it to them? Is an occasional fine sufficient to discourage greedy white men from the lucrative business of selling liquor to Indians? When and where might Indians be permitted to have a legal drink? Are "mixed-blood" considered to be "Indians"?

The Dawes Act of 1882, often called the General Allotment Act, complicated matters still further. The act provided that on certain reservations adult male Indians could take individual ownership of 160 acres of reservation land, the "excess" reservation land then to be sold to white settlers. As the General Allotment Act was put into effect, new questions arose. What was "Indian country" if the reservation was broken up and Indian families lived on their allotments next to white families on their homesteads? Was it discriminatory for only whites to be able legally to enjoy a glass of wine?

Clearly a new revision of the Indian prohibition law was needed. In an attempt to answer at least some of these questions, Congress passed a new law at the end of January 1897, just a couple of weeks before the Spicer murders. The new law to which agent Cramsie refers in his letter to attorney Bangs attempted to clarify what "alcohol" was, what an "Indian" was, and what "Indian country" was. It specified minimum jail terms for dealers who sold intoxicating substances to Indians. The law was couched in convoluted legal language. One heavily freighted sentence attempted to say it all:

U.S. Statutes at Large (29 [1897]: 506)

Any person who shall sell, give away, dispose of, exchange, or barter any malt, spiritous, or vinous liquor, including beer, ale, and wine, or any ardent or other intoxicating liquor of any kind whatsoever, or any essence, extract, bitters, preparation, compound, composition, or any article whatsoever, under any name, label or brand, which produces intoxication, to any Indian to whom allotment of land has been made while the title to the same shall be held in trust by the government, or to any Indian ward of the government under charge of any Indian superintendent or agent, or any Indian, including mixed-bloods, over whom the government, through its departments, exercises guardianship, and any person who shall introduce or attempt to introduce any malt, spiritous, or vinous liquor, including beer, ale, and wine, or any intoxicating liquor of any kind whatsoever into the Indian country, which term shall include any Indian allotment while the title to the same shall be held in trust by the government, or while the same shall remain inalienable by the allottee, without the consent of the United States, shall be punished by imprisonment for not less than sixty days and by a fine of not less than one hundred dollars for the first offense and not less than two hundred dollars for each offense thereafter.

That meandering sentence, Cramsie hoped, would allow him to put men like Red Caldwell out of business.

Cramsie's naming as witnesses against Red Caldwell all five of the men who would eventually be accused of the Spicer murders suggests that early on he suspected that at least some of them were the murderers. It also suggests that his desire to put Red Caldwell out of business was in some ways a cover for his real motive: to find out who murdered the Spicer family.

One of the duties of Indian agents was to submit annual reports at the end of June each year outlining the conditions, accomplishments, and problems on their reservations in the previous fiscal year. These reports were sent to the office of the Commissioner of Indian Affairs in Washington, D.C., where they were compiled and published annually as the "Report of the Commissioner of Indian Affairs." Cramsie's report for Standing Rock for the fiscal year ending June 30, 1897, was submitted on August 25. It is largely statistical in nature: the number of Standing Rock Indians as of June 30 (3,720; a decrease of 20 from the previous year); the estimated number of bushels of grain produced on the reservation (oats, 12,168 bushels, corn, 26,506 bushels, and so on); the number of Indian-owned cattle (11,000) and horses (6,000); the number of boarding schools on the reservation (three); the number of field matrons charged with "civilizing Indians" (four); the number of missionaries on the reservation (seventeen Catholic, twelve Congregational, one Episcopal); the number of cases brought before the reservation's Court of Criminal Offenses that year (148); the number of Indian police ("one captain, 2 lieutenants, and 44 privates"); and so on.

Cramsie's report gave a glimpse into the unusual hardships suffered by Standing Rock Indians who were trying to be farmers: "Less than the usual amount of seeding was done by Indians in the spring, as they were discouraged by the results of former years arising from droughts and hot winds." As for Indian-owned cattle in the winter of 1896–97: "Over 1,000 head perished during the protracted snows and blizzards from actual starvation. The ground was covered with snow from early in November until April. The usual winter grazing was therefore impossible. A sufficient quantity of hay had not been provided on account of its scarcity on the reservation last summer." In the section labeled "Sanitary," we find these three sentences: "Tuberculosis is by far the most prevailing disease among the Indians on this reservation. It caused nearly two-thirds of all deaths in the last fiscal year and seems to be on the increase. I don't think it is an exaggeration to say that 70 per cent of all the Indians are tubercular, either lymphatic or pulmonary, or both."

Cramsie's only mention of the Spicer murders in his report was tucked away in a section — by far the longest in his short four-page report for the year — on "Liquor Traffic," quoted in full below. A "blind pig" was a slang name for a saloon that sold whiskey to Indians. It apparently took its name from a story about an Indian who wanted to buy whiskey. The saloon keeper said, "It is against the law to sell you whiskey, but if you'll pay me to have a look at my very unusual blind pig out back, I'll *give* you a drink." The Indian, so the story goes, paid to see the blind pig and got his free whiskey. Next time he was thirsty, he would return and say, "Can I buy another look at that blind pig of yours?" The rest of the five paragraphs from Cramsie's annual report are clear enough:

> John W. Cramsie, United States Indian Agent
> "Report of Standing Rock Agency"
> Standing Rock Agency, North Dakota, August 25, 1897
> *Report of the Commissioner of Indian Affairs*
> Washington: Government Printing Office, 1897, pp. 216–20

Liquor Traffic

The opportunities for Indians of this reservation to obtain intoxicating liquors are abundant and convenient, especially in the winter time when the Missouri River is frozen over. The small village of Winona, situated directly opposite the agency on the east bank of the river, in which there are six or eight blind pigs, or properly speaking, liquor saloons, running wide open, owned by unprincipled men (for such I consider the trafficker in whiskey) and frequented by prostitutes of a very low order, affords ample and attractive temptations and opportunities for Indians to steal away from their reservation by day or night, secure whiskey by some means or other, and bring what they cannot drink in the town onto the reservation where other peaceable and well-conducted Indians become recipients of the poison, sold as whiskey, and commit acts which they never would have committed except under its influence. There are other places besides Winona, just off the reservation, up and down the east bank of the river, where this nefarious traffic is carried on.

Notwithstanding the prohibition law in this state, county or town officials have never to my knowledge made any effort to abate the sale of liquor in Emmons County. On the contrary, they seem to encourage and to throw obstacles in the way of the agent in his efforts to secure evidence against this criminal class of people for violating the law with regard to the liquor traffic among Indians.

In February last a horrible murder of a whole family consisting of six persons was committed by Indians of this reservation close to the village of

Winona, which was due to the effects of liquor purchased by the Indians from the saloon keepers in that place. I succeeded in having three of the persons who sold the liquor to these Indian murderers convicted and punished, but the punishment was very trifling compared to the enormity of the offense, as it was confidently expected that in one of these cases the punishment would be to the full extent of the law as prescribed in the act to prohibit the sale of intoxicants to Indians, approved January 30, 1897.

The law, though ample to punish these white people who surround the reservation and sell liquor to Indians, is almost a dead letter. No assistance is given the agent by the officers and citizens of Emmons County, but rather opposition, in his efforts to bring the guilty parties to justice, and hence, his hands being practically tied, nine out of every ten offenses must and do fail of punishment. Besides, the punishment meted out to these violators is so light that it is scarcely worth while to collect the necessary evidence to secure conviction. As an instance, I would state, in regard to the working of the prohibition law in that county, that during the trials for the murder before mentioned at the county town of Emmons County saloons and gambling places were run wide open under the shadow of the windows where the court was being held.

I have requested, from time to time, the deputy sheriff and others on the other side of the river to arrest any and all Indians found there without a pass, and to confine or put them to work on the streets etc., but an excuse was offered that "there were no funds to pay for their subsistence." To this objection I offered to send over rations for Indians so arrested upon receiving a notification to that effect. I have also issued instructions to the ferryman in the summer not to cross an Indian or mixed-blood without a permit from me, and have also specially instructed the reservation police to arrest and confine all Indians who are known to have been over the river without such pass. In fact everything has been done here that can be done in trying to keep Indians on the reservation, and yet I am accused of allowing the Indians to visit this wretched place, and one newspaper even ventures to remark that I am responsible for the murder referred to by not keeping the Indians at home. If the people of Winona would not hold out the tempting whiskey as an inducement, they would not be much troubled by the presence of Indians in their otherwise unattractive village.

Cramsie's frustration at the men and women of Winona who unwittingly contributed to the Spicer murders by illegally selling whiskey to those who did the actual murders is understandable enough. After all, some of the white settlers and newspaper editors accused him — Cramsie — of causing the murders by not keeping the Indians on the reservation where they belonged. As agent, Cramsie had little legal authority to insist that Indians stay on the reservation. We shall return to those accusations later. Meanwhile, let us go back to early March, when the newspapers, after weeks of having no news of arrests for the Spicer murders, suddenly found themselves with almost too much news about arrests and confessions.

4

Confessions

The authorities who arrested Alec Coudette and Frank Black Hawk were, it turned out, less interested in prosecuting them for cattle rustling than in having them serve as witnesses against the man who had sold them whiskey. Interest in Alex Coudotte and Frank Black Hawk, however, soon shifted once again, from their possible role in prosecuting Red Caldwell to their own possible role in the Spicer family murders. All too soon the newspapers were reporting that the two mixed-bloods were indeed the killers. Mandan is just across the Missouri from Bismarck:

Mandan Pioneer
Mandan, North Dakota
March 5, 1897

The Spicer Murders

The latest reports from Winona state that the authorities are certain that Alex Coudot, a French half-breed, and Black Hawk, a negro half-breed, both under arrest, are the fiends who murdered the Spicer family at that place.

From statements made by Coudot, it is probable that Black Hawk committed the murders of Mrs. Rouse and the two babies and old Mrs. Waldron unassisted, while Coudot acted as sentry outside the house. Both were under the influence of liquor when they left Winona on the day of the murder, and they went by different routes to the home of the Spicers. Black Hawk carried an old muzzle-loading shotgun, which was taken from him when he was arrested. It was with this gun that Thomas Spicer was killed. Coudot was seen going in the direction of the Spicer house, riding a gray horse. Wilson, a neighbor of the Spicers, swears that the Indian he saw at the Spicer's on the day the murder was committed, rode a gray horse.

Both prisoners are now sullen and silent, refusing to answer all questions asked them. Sheriff Shier, of Emmons county, has spent the last four days

The five accused Indians held in custody of the sheriff and awaiting their trials. From left to right, top row, standing: Sheriff Peter Shier, Philip Ireland, Paul Holy Track, and Deputy Sheriff W. B. Livermore. Bottom row, seated: Frank Black Hawk, Alec Coudotte, and George Defender (State Historical Society of North Dakota 1952–3533).

in going through the county quieting the settlers, as there were fears of an anti–Indian uprising. T. J. Reedy, chief of Indian police at Standing Rock, who captured the prisoners, refuses to turn them over to the Emmons county authorities, as he feels certain they will be lynched, and he wishes to secure the $800 reward offered for their arrest and conviction. It seems that Mrs. Rouse discovered that Coudot and Black Hawk had murdered Mr. and Mrs. Spicer at the barn, and rushed into the house to hide her babies, which she did behind the ice box. When the murderers continued their devilish work in the house, they found the babies. They reached behind the box, dealing each a terrible blow on the head with the sharp side of an axe, and then dragged their bodies out, piling them on the lounge where they were found.

After a month of questioning, the two men were removed from Fort Yates to the Emmons County jail in Williamsport, then the county seat. It is likely that they were moved to Williamsport in part to protect them from the angry, frightened, and impatient white citizens of Winona who wanted to find and punish the killers.

Bismarck Daily Tribune
Bismarck, North Dakota
March 29, 1897

[Two Indians Jailed]

The two Indians, Black Hawk and Coudot, who were brought to the city as witnesses in a liquor-selling case and were afterward arrested by the Emmons County authorities on suspicion of having been concerned in the Spicer murders, were taken down to Williamsport yesterday by Sheriff Shier and W. B. Livermore.

They will be contained in the Emmons County jail until they have a hearing and the case against them disposed of in some way. So far, there is no evidence against the men. They have been closely questioned at their former hearing at Winona, and an attempt was also made to get something out of them while here, but nothing was ascertained having a bearing on the case. So far as any evidence is concerned, there is nothing which has been brought out which throws any light on the murder.

Two full-blooded Indians were suspected, but there is no proof that they were implicated in the crime. The authorities of Emmons county and those on the Indian reservation do not agree as to a course of procedure in the case.

The decision to move the prisoners to Williamsport turned out to be a key decision because it caused Alec Coudotte to attempt to kill himself. Then, having been led to believe that he was indeed going to die of his wound, he made what he thought was a deathbed confession. The suicide attempt and the confession were reported in both the Winona and the Bismarck newspapers:

Winona Times
Winona, North Dakota
April 15, 1897

Caddotte Attempts Suicide

As a sequel to the terrible tragedy enacted here last February, Alex Caddotte, one of the half-breeds confined in the Emmons County jail at Williamsport, attempted suicide last evening. It seems that Caddotte had concealed a small penknife about him and when the officers searched him they failed to find it. With this instrument he inflicted an ugly gash in his abdomen which is thought will prove fatal. The wound was not discovered until several hours after the deed was committed and then only by the fact that spots of blood were discovered upon his bunk and clothing. Immediately a search was made when the above facts were brought to light.

The doctors, attorneys and interpreters are with Caddotte and will remain at his side all night.

The guard has been doubled and all necessary precaution will be taken to prevent any violence.

LATER — Caddotte has made a partial confession, but as the facilities for obtaining news are rather meager, the nature of the contents of his confession cannot possibly be obtained at this writing. As near as can be learned three other Indians are implicated by the confession.

Bismarck Daily Tribune
Bismarck, North Dakota
April 16, 1897

Tried to Commit Suicide

Some interesting developments in the Spicer murder case are expected soon, and it is stated that the mystery of the murder of the six members of the family near Winona last winter may soon be cleaned up. The hearing of the men was called to begin before justice Edick at Williamsport, Wednesday, last, quite a number of witnesses were subpoenaed. The officials who are engaged with the prosecution of the case have been busy with the two men under arrest, with a view to obtaining a confession if such a thing were possible, and the suspects had any knowledge of the crime, and their efforts may meet with success, according to reports from Williamsport.

There are two of the men under arrest, one of them Black Hawk, Negro half-breed, and the other Alex Coudot of French extraction. The latter has chafed considerably under arrest and confinement, and has given signs of nervousness. Wednesday night he attempted suicide by stabbing himself in the abdomen with a small penknife. The weapon was not large enough to kill him, and the wound will not prove fatal or serious unless some complications set in. The attempted suicide has a bearing on the case indicating that some sentiment of fear or other feeling is working on the man.

The officials have secured some interesting information bearing on the case, but nothing has been divulged yet, pending the efforts to secure some admission from the men as to whether or not they were concerned in the case. Black Hawk and Coudot were first arrested shortly after the commission of the murder near Winona, on the charge of stealing cattle. Certain circumstances surrounding the arrest made the authorities suspicious, and it was thought they might have some knowledge of the murder. Later they were cross examined as to their whereabouts at the time of the murder, but nothing in the way of proof could be obtained from them. They were brought to this city during the term of United States court as witnesses in a liquor-selling trial and while here were arrested by the authorities from Emmons County and taken to the jail at Williamsport.

Since their arrest they have been confined there and the confinement and the knowledge that they were to be placed on trial may have worked on them to such an extent that they may weaken.

In an effort to get Alec Coudotte to "weaken," one of the police interrogators apparently lied, telling the prisoner that he would die of his self-inflicted wound. As a result, Coudotte made a kind of "deathbed confession." All he seems to have confessed to, however, was his own innocence, as he pointed the finger at Frank Black Hawk:

Emmons County Record
Williamsport, North Dakota
April 16, 1897

The Closing of the Net

The *Record* has nothing sensational to give regarding the hunt for evidence against the men now in jail at Williamsport, under suspicion of having committed the horrible murders at Winona. Thanks to the persistent efforts of Peter Shier, sheriff of this county, to get hold of the prisoners and take them where a full investigation could be had, a point in this matter has been reached where there is an almost absolute certainty that the guilty parties will suffer the penalty by law provided for their crime.

The date set for the preliminary trial, or hearing, of Frank Blackhawk and Alex Coudotte (the way the latter signs his name) was Tuesday, April 13. By the evening of that day the town was full of people interested in the case. [...] The preliminary examination was to take place before justice Edick. In order that the case for the state might be ably conducted and the investigation thorough, the people of Winona had raised a purse and secured the services of attorney Edward Allen, of Bismarck. Mr. Allen arrived at Williamsport about noon of Wednesday and he and the state's attorney at once began an extended examination of the state's witnesses to ascertain if possible just where the state stood in the matter of evidence.

Wednesday afternoon there was a startling incident, and soon the fact became public that the night before Coudotte had attempted to commit suicide. On Wednesday the prisoner was taken out of his cell and upstairs to have a private interview with his attorney, Mr. Lynn. While he was out John Edick, the day guard, went into the cell, where he discovered pools of blood on the bed clothes. Coudotte, being questioned, claimed that his nose had bled. He was at once stripped of clothing. Two bad gashes were found, where the prisoner had tried to disembowel himself. The attempt had been made with a small penknife that in some way he had managed to conceal while being searched.

That night Coudotte, having been told that he must die, made a "confession," in which he claimed that Blackhawk had committed the murder and had told him about it afterward. The wound was at first considered to be dangerous; but, if proven guilty, Coudotte will undoubtedly remain in sufficiently good health to walk to the gallows.

Coudotte's wife and mother (both full-blood Indians) called at the jail and were permitted to see the prisoner. The poor creatures kissed him and shed tears over him; but he showed no signs of emotion. None of Blackhawk's relatives called on him.

There is strong evidence being gathered against the prisoners. Even were the exact nature of the evidence known to a newspaper writer, it would hardly be right at the present time to make it public. There is one matter, however, that was public with every one here this week. It is claimed that the evidence of two Indian boys will be to the effect that they called at the Spicer house on the fateful Wednesday; that they had called there before and had been well treated by the family, who would give them some lunch and each a cup of coffee; that when they went to the house on the day named Blackhawk and Coudotte came outside and said, in effect; "We just came here, and we find that this whole family has been killed. If you say anything about it we will be blamed for it." It is said that they finally went down in the timber with the boys, intending to take their lives; that the four were down there for some time, and that, on the boys' repeated promises to say nothing about it, their lives were spared: that being in terror of death at the hands of the two halfbreeds, they made no statement regarding the matter until a few days ago.

On account of the discovery that new evidence could be obtained from Indians who were not in town, by agreement of counsel the examination was not proceeded with, and consideration of the case was postponed until May 8th.

There is now a double guard over the prisoners at night — Tom Kelly and Frank Smith.

News of Coudotte's attempted suicide and confession reached beyond North Dakota. This article from Dodge City, however, got the order wrong, putting the confession before the suicide attempt:

Globe-Republican
Dodge City, Kansas
April 22, 1897

Spicer Family Murder

The mystery concerning the fiendish butchery of the Spicer family at Winona has been partially cleared up. Alexander Caddott, the French half-breed under arrest, has made a confession in which he implicates Black Hawk, the negro half-breed, who has also been under arrest as a suspect. After making the confession Caddott made a vicious attempt at taking his own life by stabbing himself with a pocket knife in the abdomen. The wound will not prove fatal.

On April 23, a week after the article in the *Emmons County Record* announced that "two Indian boys" had visited the Spicer home shortly after the murders, agent Cramsie wrote a letter to Peter Shier, sheriff of Emmons County, announcing that "two Indian boys" had been arrested. The letter closed with a barbed remark that if county officials had stayed away from the reservation, Cramsie and his men could have secured more evidence to use in court to convict the murderers.

4. Confessions

Peter Shier, Esquire
Sheriff, Emmons County
Gayton Post Office, North Dakota
April 23, 1897

Sir:

I have the honor to inform you that two Indian boys who are suspected of the murder of the Spicer family, or of having a knowledge of the parties who did commit the murder, have been arrested by my order and confined in the agency guard house in separate cells where they have no means of communicating with each other. Since their incarceration Mr. T. J. Reedy, head farmer and chief of police at the agency, and Mr. A. C. Wells, farmer in charge of the Cannon Ball sub-issue station, who have been working on the case since the crime was committed, have succeeded in persuading the boys to confess the part taken by themselves and their accomplices in the murder.

I have now in my possession a full and detailed history of the crime in every particular which to my mind leaves not a shadow of a doubt as to who the guilty parties are. The boys are now and will be kept separate and in secure cells and will be turned over to the proper officers of Emmons County for trial, upon demand.

I may add in this connection that had you not made the search on the reservation for the clothes and jewelry taken from the Spicer residence, as you did against my protest, the clothing would not have been destroyed as I feared and anticipated, and all the evidence we how possess would have been secured long since with the additional evidence of the clothing, without any expense to your county.

Very respectfully,
John W. Cramsie
U.S. Indian Agent

Cramsie did not reveal the names of the "boys" in the letter, but local newspaper reporters already knew that they were young Dakota men named Paul Holy Track and Philip Ireland (who was also known as Standing Bear). Their narratives of the events of February 17 caused the legal authorities to postpone the hearing at which Alec Coudotte and Frank Black Hawk were to be arraigned.

Winona Times
Winona, North Dakota
April 22, 1897

The Hearing Postponed

The Black Hawk and Cadotte hearing which was to have taken place on the 14th inst., was postponed until May 8th, to give the state time to look up more evidence, as what evidence was possessed was thought to be insufficient to bind them over.

The latest reports in the case are to the effect that an Indian by the name of Blue Boy saw Standing Bear and Holy Track, two full-blooded Indians, coming from the Spicer farm on that memorable Wednesday evening (the day of the murder) as he was watering his horse at the river. It is furthermore stated that it can be proven that Holy Track was seen with one of the victim's finger rings. This complied with the fact that Holy Track and Standing Bear have said that they met Black Hawk and Cadotte at Spicer's on the day of the murder, looks very much as though they, Standing Bear and Holy Track, were the murderers or at least accessaries to the horrible crime.

There seems to be no doubt now, but that the mystery that is shrouding the tragedy will soon be cleared up.

The next two articles give more details about the confessions of Paul Holy Track and Philip Ireland. It seems that some of the goods stolen from the Spicer home after the murders showed up in their possession. The officials conducting the investigation, confronting the two "boys" with the evidence, talked them into making full confessions. Those confessions further stimulated journalistic chatter about a possible lynching.

Bismarck Daily Tribune
Bismarck, North Dakota
April 26, 1897

Have Confessed

The confession of Alex Coudot, partially clearing up the mystery of the Spicer murders, has been supplemented by a confession from the young Indians, Paul Holy Track and Philip Ireland, which explains that gruesome affair, and reveals one of the most fiendish crimes ever committed in the history of the West, where six members of one family, from the child in the cradle to the old woman at the edge of the grave, gave up their lives to the brutish instincts of fiends. The particulars of the crime as they have been received here are most revolting and show it to have been the most heartless, cold-blooded and premeditated murder possible to imagine. The four persons who were implicated are now in jail, two of them at Williamsport and two others at Fort Yates, and it is believed that there is no doubt of the conviction of the four persons, should they live to be tried.

After the close of the hearing of the two Indians, Black Hawk and Coudot, at Williamsport, where Coudot made a partial confession accusing Black Hawk of having instigated and carried out the crime, the men who have been working on the case, including sheriff Shier and A. C. Wells, started to follow up the clue which was obtained through the Indian, Two Hearts, who testified to the authorities that he saw a ring bearing the initials "E. W." that had come from the Spicer place in the possession of Paul Holy Track. This fact revealed to the authorities that either Holy Track and Ireland, who was also known to have had some of the property that had come from the Spicer place, were implicated in the murders or could tell who were the authors of the crime by explaining how they had come into the possession of the property in question. They have been so successful in this matter as to secure from the two Indians in question a full confession of the crime, giving the details.

No direct report has been received here as to the details of the confession, but from the story which comes from Winona through those who have come up from there in the past day or two, the crime was prearranged at the instigation of Black Hawk, who appeared to be the leading spirit. Thomas Spicer was the first member of the family to be killed, and that was done by Black Hawk, who shot him in the back with a shotgun. Mrs. Spicer was called out of the house by Coudot, who met her with a pitchfork and stabbed her, afterward cutting her throat. In the meantime the Indian boys had killed Mrs. Waldron with an axe, and when the other men reached the inside of the house were struggling with Mrs. Rouse, who fought desperately, as it will be remembered appeared from the indications about the room in which she was found, but who finally succumbed to the common fate of the others of the family, and perished with her children. The four then rifled the premises and fled. They secured $62 in money, some clothing and the jewelry which led to the detection of the younger Indians. As the report comes from Winona, the boys have confessed everything, admitting their complicity in the affair.

The boys are now in the guard house at Fort Yates under a strong guard, and the authorities are endeavoring to get them to Williamsport or some other place where they can be kept. The residents of Winona are intensely excited and if they get the murderers into their hands it is thought they will not live to be tried for the crime.

This confession clears up the mystery of the murder and all that remains to be done is to try the murderers and establish their guilt by a court. The officers of Emmons County and A. C. Wells have been indefatigable in their prosecution of the case, and are deserving of the greatest credit for having unearthed the perpetrators of one of the most terrible murders in the history of the state.

Confronted with the direct evidence of his guilt — a witness who saw him and Philip Ireland leaving the Spicer farm, the discovery in their possession of certain items stolen from the Spicer home — Paul Holy Track caved in and confessed. He made the following statement in the Standing Rock agency guardhouse on April 23, 1897, but it was not published until June, just after the trial. By then it had been superceded by a second, and then a third, "confession":

Emmons County Record
Williamsport, North Dakota
June 25, 1897

Holy Track's First Yarn

Personally appeared before Thomas J. Reedy and Aaron C. Wells, Paul Holytrack made the following voluntary statement:

"On the 17th of February, 1897, I left home in the morning and came to the agency, in company with Philip Ireland. Between 11 and 12 o'clock on the same day I asked Philip Ireland to go to Winona with me, and we started from the agency office.

"From the office we went through the timber on this side of the river and to a point opposite Spicer's house, and just before we crossed the river we heard the 11:45 A.M. whistle blow. After crossing the river we hunted rabbits for a short time in the timber near Spicer's house, having nothing to hunt with but sticks. We then reached the stage road and went to the well near Spicer's house.

"While we were going to the well we saw an old man hauling manure from the stable.

"When we reached the well we stood drawing water to drink, and we heard a peculiar sound, as though a gun had been discharged inside of a house or under ground, the noise being very dull. The man who had been hauling manure was then coming out of the stable, and when we heard this noise he disappeared, as though he had fallen. Philip Ireland remarked that the man who had been hauling manure fell when he heard the noise. We then saw a man come from the stable and go toward the house. He wore a black overcoat and brown duck trousers, similar in appearance to the clothing issued to the Indians. Another man then came from the stable, and from his actions we judged that he was dragging a heavy object back into the stable. This man wore blue trousers. We could not distinguish the object he was hauling on. We could not see from which door in the stable the man who had been working at the manure came, but the man wearing the blue trousers came from one door of the stable and dragged the object back into a different door and then returned to the door from whence he came.

"We then saw the man wearing the brown trousers and black overcoat returning from the house accompanied by a woman who followed close behind him. They went into the part of the stable where the man with the blue trousers had gone shortly before. In a short time the brown-trousered man came out of the stable and motioned to us to come toward him. Philip and I started for the stable. I was in the lead, and I went toward the door into which the object had been dragged. Philip went toward the door into which both men and the woman had gone. To go to the door for which I had started I had to pass the other door, and, while passing, I recognized Alec Coudotte as the man who wore the brown trousers and black overcoat. He stood leaning against the door jamb, with a pitchfork in his hand. When I reached the part of the stable later into which the object had apparently been dragged, I looked around, but, as the room was dark, I could see nothing but a calf.

"I then returned to the part where all the others were, and, as I drew near, Alec Coudotte and Frank Blackhawk, whom I now saw was the man with the blue trousers, came outside.

"Frank Blackhawk then approached me and said that we had discovered he and Alec in the act of committing a great crime, but that if we would keep the matter quiet he, Blackhawk, would give me a gray horse. Alec Coudotte then spoke out and said that he would give Philip Ireland a bay horse with bald face and white feet.

"Frank Blackhawk then went back into the stable and brought a gun and powder-horn, which he asked me to hold. He and Coudotte then went toward the house, but before they reached it Coudotte turned and called to Philip and I to follow them, which we did, leaving the gun and powder horn outside the stable.

"When we all reached the house, but before entering, Coudotte told Philip to remain outside on guard.

"Blackhawk entered the house first, with an axe in his hand. Coudotte went in second, and had in his hand a club, while I followed last without anything. We saw the young woman inside the house, with a hoe in her hand, and the old lady sitting by the stove with a pipe. The young woman was standing before an entrance to an inner room, and Coudotte handed me the club and told me to strike her with it. As I approached her she struck at me with a hoe, cutting through my hat and making a gash in my forehead, just over my left eye. I then dropped the club and went back to the door, where I stood wiping the blood from my face. Before I dropped the club the woman struck at me a second time, but the hoe caught in the wire supporting the stove-pipe, so that it did not reach me, and the hoe remained suspended from the wire. Blackhawk now went up to the young woman and pushed her down to the floor with his hand. He then struck her on the side of the head with the back of the axe, while she was attempting to get up. By this time the old lady was very much frightened, but was not making any noise. She rose from her seat and started to go out the door, just as Philip Ireland was entering. Coudotte threw him a stick and told Philip to strike her. Ireland struck her first across the small of the back, and she fell face downward, on the floor. He struck her again on the upper part of the right arm.

"Blackhawk then threw the axe over to me and told me to strike the old woman with it. She had turned on her side when Ireland struck her on the arm, and I struck her first on the back and then on the breast, with the poll of the axe. I then dropped the axe. I then turned from the old woman and saw one of the babies lying, dead, on the floor. Coudotte at that time picked the other child up by the feet, swung it around and struck its head against the wall."

Mr. Wells now asked Holytrack if any whiskey had been drunk during all this time. Holytrack stated that, before leaving the stable, Blackhawk and Coudotte had produced a bottle holding about a pint, of which they drank about half, handing the bottle to Philip Ireland, telling him — Holytrack and Ireland — to finish it between them. Holytrack further stated that, while they were speaking about the horses and before drinking this liquor, he judged from the talk and actions of Coudotte and Blackhawk that they were under the influence of liquor.

"Blackhawk now told Ireland and me to search for money. As he spoke about searching he also said that the old woman was not dead yet.

Coudotte went up to where she was lying, picked up the axe which I had dropped on the floor beside her and struck her upon the head. Blackhawk now pushed a trunk toward Philip and me and told us to search it. We did so, throwing the contents on the floor. He then pushed a second trunk toward us; but, before we had emptied it, he directed us to go outside and look around.

"We remained outside quite a time, and then re-entered the house. Philip Ireland and I then continued the search for money among the contents of the trunk which we had emptied. I found a package about ten inches long and eight inches wide and about an inch thick. I said to Blackhawk that it might contain the money; but he, upon looking at it, said that it was papers relating to the land, and he placed it on the table. We finished searching, but found no money. Blackhawk then said that perhaps something of value might be in the cellar, and as the old woman was lying with her legs over the cellar door, he directed us to move her away. Alec Coudotte took her by the legs and I took her by the shoulders, moving her over beside the stove. Blackhawk then raised the cellar door, went down and looked around in the cellar. When he came up he told us that there was nothing down there.

"We then went into the other room, and Blackhawk gave me a white silk handkerchief, mother-of-pearl breastpin in the shape of a horn, the clasp for the pin being broken." The pin was then produced, and Holytrack stated that it was the pin, but that the clasp had been repaired.

"[Blackhawk also gave me] a coat and vest, with a red paper-covered pencil in the vest pocket, and a watch-guard which Mr. Wells showed me yesterday.

"Alec Coudotte gave to Philip Ireland two baby rings, one large ring and a necktie. Frank Blackhawk gave Philip a suit, consisting of coat, pants and vest.

"Now we all left the house and went toward the stable after the gun and powder horn. We went into the stable, and, as the ammunition was scattered about, we picked it up. The sack containing the ammunition was then given to me by Blackhawk, to hold. Philip had by this time stepped out of the stable, and he reported that some one was passing on the road with a team and a sleigh.

"Blackhawk told us that he would go and fetch them to the stable, and for us to grab the little boy while he killed the man, and he started to go toward the people in the sleigh. He got as far as the little sod house when the man drove fast and left him. He turned then and came back to where we were. We remained in the stable until the team was out of sight, when we started for the road, taking the path leading by the well. Blackhawk cautioned us to follow the beaten track and to be careful not to step out of it. I think that this was about two o'clock in the afternoon.

"Just after we left the house and before reaching the stable Coudette took hold of his left hand with his right hand and said, 'I nearly broke my hand.'

"We followed the stage road to the south for a short distance and came upon the tracks of two horses, one following the other. These tracks led toward the timber. Blackhawk took the lead and, stepping into the footprints of the horses, we proceeded single file until we came to Alec Coudette's team and sleigh and Frank Blackhawk's saddle horse, concealed in the timber. We had left the horse-tracks on the edge of the timber. Upon reaching the sleigh we all took a drink of whiskey. We followed an old road, after hitching the team and starting, until we came to the wood road. We had been traveling toward the north. The wood road was followed until it forked, where we again drank whiskey.

"Frank Blackhawk then handed me the gun and ammunition and asked me to take them home and take care of them, telling me that he would come for them very soon. I took both, but handed the gun to Philip to carry.

"We parted then, Coudotte giving us a quart bottle of whiskey. Blackhawk's horse was facing north; and he said that he was going some place when we left them. I would judge that the time was then about 3 P.M. The road which forked where we separated is the one over which wood was being hauled to the military post, and the forks of the road were about half a mile from the point where the horses were concealed in the timber during the time the murders were being committed.

"Just before we reached the river we spoke of putting on the clothing which had been given to us. Philip removed his overalls and put on the trousers, then put the overalls back on. He then put the coat and vest under his overcoat. Some papers which were in the pockets were thrown on the ground by Philip, and, as I had no watch, I threw the watch guard there also. The suspenders were also thrown down with the rest of the articles, by Philip.

"We then uncorked our bottle and took a drink. Before we went out on the ice we looked up and down the river and saw that Coudotte had almost crossed the river south of us. He was alone.

"We crossed then, and stopped at the watering-hole on this side and took another drink of whiskey. When we got about 150 yards from the river we met John Blue Boy, who was driving his horses to water.

"After reaching my home I hid the gun in the stable. About 12 o'clock on this same night, while I was on my way home from the house of a man named Bear Shield, I was passed by a horseman, who turned after going a short distance and asked me in English, 'Is that you, Paul?' I replied, 'Yes.' He then said, 'I have come for my gun.' We went to my home together, and I took the gun from the stable and gave it to him. That horseman was Frank Blackhawk. Upon going into the house I saw Philip and told him that Blackhawk had come for his gun."

Although the exact wording of the confession was not published until after the trial, there was wide media coverage of Paul Holy Track's April 23 confession (and the "me-too" one of Philip Ireland). Often embellished for sensational effect, news of the confession made its way around the nation. A Washington, D.C., newspaper reported that the Indian murderers, true to stereotype, had raped — the euphemism used was "outraged" — two of the white women:

Evening Times
Washington, D.C.
April 27, 1897

Indian Fiends Confess

Two Indian boys, Paul Holytrack and Philip Ireland, have confessed to the authorities that they were at the Spicer place on the day of the murder of the Spicer family. The boys implicate themselves, as well as the two half-breeds, Black Hawk and Caddotte, who have been under arrest. The Indian boys are closely confined to the guard-house at Fort Yates, and will be brought to Williamsport to testify at the preliminary findings of the other two men.

The boys state that the murders were planned some weeks before it was committed, and that Black Hawk was the leader. The four went to the Spicer home on the day of the murder, Black Hawk and Caddotte going to the barn and the two boys to the house. At the barn the two men found Spicer, and Black Hawk shot him and then split his head open with an axe. Caddotte then ran to the house and told Mrs. Spicer that her husband was sick at the barn.

As soon as Mrs. Spicer appeared at the barn door Caddotte stabbed her through the heart with a pitchfork. Caddotte then went to the house and found Holytrack engaged in a terrible struggle with Mrs. Rouse. He said to Holytrack: "Why don't you brain her with the axe?"

Holytrack replied: "I cannot, as the children are bothering me."

Caddotte then picked up the axe and dealt each of the twin babies a death blow. The two fiends then had no trouble in killing Mrs. Rouse. After she was killed she was outraged by Holytrack. Black Hawk had outraged Mrs. Spicer at the barn. About $62 in money was found and divided by the four wretches after the completion of their bloody work.

An almost identical article appeared that same day across the country in *The Record-Union* (Sacramento, California) on April 27, 1897. The headline was "Murder of the Spicer Family." The main difference was the addition at the end of one sentence: "Public sentiment is at fever heat, and it is more than probable that all four implicated will be lynched." Still another nearly identical article appeared on April 28, 1897, in *The Roanoke Times* (Roanoke, Virginia) under the headline "Awful Crimes Confessed." Instead of the word "outraged," however, this article uses the term "feloniously assaulted." The closing line is: "Excitement is at fever heat, and it is more than likely all four will be lynched." A somewhat different article appeared in *The Grand Forks Daily Herald* on April 27, but it also spoke of a lynching: "If residents of Winona get hold of the boys there will be a lynching." The writer of the next short article alluded to Sheridan's phrase "the only good Indian is a dead Indian":

Princeton Union
Princeton, Minnesota
April 29, 1897

[More "Good Indians"]

The Indians who murdered the Spicer family in North Dakota in February are in custody and the confession of a couple of their accomplices leaves little doubt of their guilt. There will probably be a couple more "good Indians" before the snow flies again.

No sooner had the people of North Dakota begun to digest the implications of Paul Holy Track's April 23 confession than they began to hear news of a second confession. This new one seriously contradicted the one he had just made. Like the first confession, the second was not published until just after the trial. Originally made on April 24, 1897, it appeared in print on July 2, 1897. In addition to the text of the confession itself, I reproduce here the introductory paragraph, in which the editor of the *Emmons County Record* provides a context for the second confession. The reference to a third confession is apparently to the one that Paul Holy Track gave in the course of the trial itself, which had been completed a few weeks earlier. The name "Scare the Eagle" derives from Paul's biological father, whose name is more accurately translated as "Eagle That Scares."

Emmons County Record
Williamsport, North Dakota
July 2, 1897

Holy Track's Second Yarn

Last week the *Record* presented the first so-called confession of the murderous villain, Scare the Eagle, or Paul Holytrack. In that confession he sought to throw the chief blame on Blackhawk and Coudotte. This week we give the second "confession" of Holytrack. The young scoundrel again goes into the minutest details of the murders, and tells how he and Standing Bear (Philip Ireland) slaughtered the Spicer family. In the confession he states positively that Coudotte and Blackhawk were not present, and that he and Philip alone planned and committed the murders. He claims that he and his shadow, Ireland, first murdered his unsuspecting friend Thomas Spicer by shooting him in the back. Then Mrs. Spicer was lured to the spot and from the darkness of the stable the bullet that took her blameless Christian life was sent. With the husband and wife out of the way, the only person left who was at all able to resist was the young and gentle mother,

Mrs. Rouse. Whether or not this — of Holytrack's three stories — is the true one, it gives further evidence, by its point-blank contradictions of his other yarns, that the monster's ability as a plausible liar is something phenomenal:

"On Tuesday February 16th, 1897, Philip Ireland and myself started for Spicer's house reaching there about noon. We made a bargain for a horse for which we were to call the next day and close the deal. We then went to Winona and sold an overcoat to Red Caldwell for one dollar and a half, for which amount he gave us a bottle of whiskey. This bottle held about a quart. It was blueish glass, the bottom being telescoped.

"I had also 25 cents for which Red sold us a drink of whiskey each. We then started for Spicer's house with the intention of murdering Spicer and his family. When we arrived there circumstances and surroundings were not favorable for the execution of our designs, so we hid the whiskey in the woods, and started for home. It was our intention to return on the following day and do the job. While on our way home we met John Blue Boy and wife, on the east side of the river gathering wood.

"Just about sundown we arrived home and fed the stock and did the other chores.

"On the morning of the 17th we got up and did our chores. Between ten and eleven I took my gun and we started again for Spicer's. We arrived at the point where we had hidden the whiskey on the previous day. We drank about half the whiskey and loaded the gun. It was a single-barrel gun. The load consisted of shot and ball. The family was at dinner when we arrived at the house and we chatted with them and remained about two hours in the house. Mrs. Spicer then started to do some washing and Mr. Spicer went down to the stable and commenced to clean it out. We accompanied him to the stable. He used a wheelbarrow in taking the manure out of the stable. Philip and I took turns in helping him with the work. Just about the last barrowful was being taken out by Spicer. I stood inside the stable and shot him in the back as he was going out. Philip was standing on the outside. Philip started to run but went only a short distance when he returned and took up a spade with which he finished the man, striking him in the breast and mashing his head. Spicer said something in a loud voice as he fell but we could not understand it.

"I told Philip to go to the house and tell Mrs. Spicer to come out to the stable, but he refused to do so. Upon his refusal I went myself and told Mrs. Spicer that her husband had called her. I also told Philip to shoot her when she returned with me, to which he agreed. Before I went to the house we took another big drink of whiskey. When I got to the house Mrs. Spicer came out and emptied some water and went back in. When I told her her husband wanted her she asked me if we were going to take the horse. I replied that we were. She then said it was a fine horse and that they wanted seventy-five dollars for it. I told her we were willing to give more than that, but of course it was my intention to kill her when she got out to the stable. As we approached the stable I walked very fast and told Philip she was coming. He said that his courage had failed him and he could not kill her,

4. Confessions

so I took the gun and went back in the stable to just about where the calves were standing. When Mrs. Spicer got to the stable she asked Philip, who was standing just outside the door, where Mr. Spicer was. I could not distinguish what he said in reply. She came on and when she entered the stable I threw up the gun and fired at her. The muzzle pointing between the breast and mouth. I fired without taking any aim. Philip then came in with a pitchfork with which he stabbed her in the breast. We then wanted to shut the door but as she was in the way Philip took her by the leg and dragged her to one side. We then came out of the stable and while I was closing the door Philip mounted the pile in front of the door and said that a man was passing on the road in a sleigh. I told Philip to cover up the blood where Spicer had fallen and that I would go to the road and see if I could recognize the man who was passing. By this time I was very drunk. I had gone as far as the root house when the man whipped up his team which had been going very slowly and it started off at a trot while I stood there. I remained at this point until the man disappeared over the hill, then I returned to the stable.

"I asked Philip to go to the house with me. We left the gun at the stable. I picked up an axe at the woodpile on our way to the house. When we went into the house Philip had a cottonwood club but I do not know where he got it.

"When we entered the house I was in the lead with the axe in my hand. I had just passed the cellar door when the young woman pushed me back towards the door. She went into the inner room and I followed her striking at her with the axe, just as I was at the door. The axe caught over the door so that the blow did not reach her. I drew down the axe and went into the room. By this time she had a hoe and as I went in she struck me with it cutting through my hat and making a gash in my forehead over the left eye. She aimed a second blow at me but the hoe caught in the wire supporting the stovepipe, and hung on this wire. By this time I noticed that Philip was killing the old woman.

"I then struck the young woman on the left shoulder and on the side of the head with the poll of the axe. She fell on the lounge breaking it. The young woman had been crying ever since we entered the house. She raised up from the lounge and staggered towards a large box with white handles which was in the corner of the room. I struck twice with the axe and she fell against this box, in a leaning posture. I then turned from her and saw that Philip had killed one of the babies and was at the second which he finished as I was pulling out a trunk. He came to help me and I said that the young woman was still alive and told him to finish her. He took the axe and struck her two or three times when she fell over to the floor.

"We then searched the house for money but found none. I took the following articles which we had come across in our search. One coat and vest, one white silk handkerchief, one mother-of-pearl breastpin shaped like a horn, and one lead pencil. Philip took one suit of clothes, two baby's rings, one large ring and one necktie.

"Then we went back to the stable and finished the whiskey. Philip had the empty bottle and we started for home. I do not know what he did with it. I had the gun which had been left at the stable. Going from the stable we went westward along the field and into the timber. We followed an old road through the timber until we reached the river's edge. At this point Philip removed his overalls, put on the trousers he had taken, and over them put on his overalls. From the pockets he took some papers which he threw on the ground, together with the suspenders which had been attached to the trousers. In the pocket of the clothing I had taken was a watch guard. This I threw down with the other articles on the ground. I then put on the coat and vest which I had taken and we started out to cross the ice.

"After we had crossed the river and gotten about one hundred and fifty yards from it we were met by John Blue Boy. He asked us if we had drank it all up. No answer was made to this question and we passed on.

"Leaving Blue Boy, we proceeded a short distance into the timber and hid all the clothing we had brought with us, except the trousers which Philip had put on under his overalls. Shortly after we left Spicer's I turned the gun over to Philip who carried it the rest of the way home. After hiding the clothing we went on to my home."

Q.-"What did you do with the stolen property?"

A.-"On Sunday I went to where the clothing was hidden and took it home, and commenced wearing the coat and vest which I had originally taken. I traded the handkerchief and breastpin to Philip, for which he gave me one baby's ring and one large ring. We now heard that the people from the other side of the river were coming to search the Indians' houses, so I took the coat and vest and the two rings and the pencil down to the river bank and hid them under a big log. Since then you know that I went with you and Mr. Reedy and made a search for these articles, but found that the rise of the water had washed log and all away."

Q.-"Who dragged the old lady from where she was knocked down to where she was found?"

A.-"I did for the purpose of opening the cellar door."

Q.-"What was this door opened for?"

A.-"For the purpose of looking for money and other valuables."

Q.-"How many went down into the cellar?"

A.-"I alone."

Q.-"Were you not sorry for having killed these people?"

A.-"Well, when I sometimes think of it, I feel sorry for the babies. We would not have killed them if we had not been drunk."

Q.-"Whose knife was used to stab these people?"

A.-"There was no knife used. The cutting was done with the corner of a spade and an axe."

Q.-"Who covered up Mr. Spicer's body in the stable?"

A.-"Philip Ireland."

Q.-"Why did you kill this family?"

A.-"For the purpose of getting money."

Q.-"Whose gun was used in the killing?"

4. Confessions

A.-"Mine."
Q.-"Were you not friendly with the Spicers?"
A.-"We were friends."
Q.-"Had you not been there a great many times."
A.-"I had been there four times."
Q.-"You said you were friendly with them, then why did you kill them?"
A.-"For the purpose of obtaining money."
Q.-"Why did you not shoot the people instead of killing them by beating them?"
A.-"We were afraid the report would draw attention."
Q.-"Why then did you shoot two of them?"
A.-"That was in the stable where the report could not be heard far."
Q.-"Who threw the children on the lounge?"
A.-"They were asleep there when Philip started to kill one. The other was crying and I do not remember just how they happened to be left on the lounge."
Q.-"Who took the hoe into the house?"
A.-"I do not know. It was there when we went in."
Q.-"Who threw the axe onto the lounge."
A.-"I do not know. Philip used the axe last."
Q.-"Where did you first see the table leg?"
A.-"I did not notice any table leg."
Q.-"Who stabbed Mrs. Rouse in the breast?"
A.-"She was not stabbed in the breast."
Q.-"Then what made the cut in her breast?"
A.-"It is possible that I struck her there with the poll of the axe."
Q.-"Did you find any money?"
A.-"Yes."
Q.-"How much?"
A.-"Twenty cents, all in coppers in a baking powder can."
Q.-"Who found this money?"
A.-"Philip."
Q.-"Where was it found?'
A.-"In the trunk."
Q.-"Who took the money that was found?"
A.-"Philip."
Q.-"How many horses were there in the stable?"
A.-"Three."
Q.-"Were there any cattle in the stable?"
A.-"I only saw three calves in the stable."
Q.-"Were any of the women ravished by either you or Philip?"
A.-"No."
Q.-"The doctor states that the women were ravished."
A.-"The doctor must have formed this opinion from the fact that the woman in the stable had been drawn by the legs which were spread apart in doing so."
Q.-"Are you not trying to deny this heinous offense?"

A.-" Why should I deny this when I have acknowledged to committing murder. I tell you the doctor is mistaken."
Q.-"What did you hear Mr. Spicer say when he was shot?"
A.-"He said something in a loud tone that I did not understand."
Q.-"What did you hear Mrs. Spicer say?"
A.-"She said nothing."
Q.-"What did you hear the old lady say?"
A.-"I heard her crying and screaming."
Q.-"What did you hear Mrs. Rouse say?"
A.-"She was crying and screaming also."
Q.-"Did you hear the children cry?"
A.-"I heard only one cry. The other was killed before it could cry."
Q.-"Where did you get the balls with which your gun was loaded?"
A.-"Two I got from Patrick Yellow Lodge. I think he has the mould yet in which they were cast. The other four we have had for a long time."
Q.-"Which of the balls did you use in killing Mr. Spicer and which in killing Mrs. Spicer?"
A.-"I do not remember."
Q.-"What was the difference, if any, in the size of the balls?"
A.-"The two I got from Patrick Yellow Lodge were smaller than the others."
Q.-"Who was struck in the corner of the room by the ice chest?"
A.-"I struck Mrs. Rouse there. Philip struck her there also."
Q.-"Why did you try to implicate Frank Blackhawk and Alec Coudotte?"
A.-"These men were accused and arrested for this crime, and, as the evidence was so strong against them, I thought that they might be convicted and that we would get off."
Q.-"Did you and Philip ever talk about casting the blame upon these men?"
A.-"Yes. We talked about it and had arranged all we were to say; but, as you questioned me so closely, I thought that you were aware of our plans."
Q.-"Why do you suppose that Alec said he knew these people were to be killed and for that reason went home?"
A.-"I cannot account for it. I never talked with him about it, and he was not with us."

On April 24, the same day as Paul Holy Track's second confession, Philip Ireland also made a confession. It, too, was not published until after the trial. There is no need to reproduce it here, but the opening paragraph effectively conveys the editor's disdain for the "murderous whelps":

Emmons County Record
Williamsport, North Dakota
July 9, 1897

Philip Ireland's Story

Last week the *Record* gave Holytrack's second written "confession," in which he asserted with minute detail that he and Ireland — and they alone — committed the murders. This week we print a "confession" by "Me-Too" Ireland, which is supplemental to the one made by Holytrack and printed in our last issue. The *Record* has stated that three so-called "confessions" were furnished by the pair of young scoundrels who make little distinction between actual murder by their own hands and legal murder through their perjured testimony. But it appears that their "very first" statement was not reduced to writing. In that statement, the *Record* has been informed, the young villains asserted that they happened at the Spicer residence after the murders had been committed, and that Blackhawk (whom we now know was not present) and Coudotte were there and had killed the Spicer family, and that Blackhawk took them (Holytrack and Ireland) down into the timber, and, under threats of death, made them promise to say nothing about the perpetrators of the crime. It is a knowledge of the facts that these self-confessed assassins have told four separate and distinct stories regarding the murders that has caused a good many people in this county to doubt whether the villains lied or told the truth at the Coudotte trial. And the least that can be said is that there are many people who would have felt better satisfied of Coudotte's guilt had there been something in the shape of evidence to corroborate the stories told by the murderous whelps in the witness stand. Our readers can believe this story or the one told before judge and jury, as they may see fit. True, the assassins were under oath when in district court, but is it not an insult to any one's intelligence to ask him to believe that men who would commit the greater crime of murder would have any qualms of conscience over the lesser crime of perjury?

The puzzlement, the confusion, and the anger of the editorial staff of the *Emmons County Record* were echoed by the staffs of other newspapers. Although they had not yet been published, the word was out about the general details of the new confessions.

Bismarck Daily Tribune
Bismarck, North Dakota
April 27, 1897

Still Another

Sensation appears to crowd sensation in the Spicer murder case. The latest report from Fort Yates is that the written confession of the two Indian boys has been taken and that in that they take the whole crime of the murders upon themselves, and completely exonerate the other two men, Black Hawk and Coudot. This bit of intelligence is startling if the truth, and reports from Fort Yates indicate that it is reliable. According to the reports that have been latest received, the boys were drunk and at the Spicer house assisting Spicer with his work about the place, taking advantage of an opportunity when his back was turned, to murder him. The other members of the family were then murdered, the boys having a desperate struggle with Mrs. Rouse who defended herself with a hoe until overpowered.

No definite news can be obtained from Yates, and the only reports that are received are those that are brought up from there by persons who have come up. According to these, the boys say they were so drunk when the crime was committed that they do not know whether they used an axe or a spade to mutilate the bodies. Ireland is said to have always borne a good reputation on the reservation, but the other boy was a bad character.

The excitement about Winona is said to be indescribable and there are prospects of a lynching bee, if the boys are secured.

Over against this story stands the confession of Coudot, but it is said that he was so frightened at the possibility of suffering for the crime that he would have told anything to exonerate himself. Then again there is his attempted suicide, and altogether, in the absence of reliable and definite reports, the whole matter is in doubt, as is the exact nature of the confession made by the boys.

The version of events that Paul Holy Track and Philip Ireland told about their involvement with the Spicer murders varied significantly over several months. Which of the versions — if any — was the true one? That was a question many citizens and reporters were asking. In fact, the editor of one of the newspapers went to Fort Yates to interview Paul Holy Track and Philip Ireland in their cells. His report is interesting for several reasons. First, it clarifies the family connections of Paul Holy Track — that his father was from Montana, and that his mother had at some point married a man named Siyaka, who thus was his stepfather. Second, the age given for Paul Holy Track was apparently wrong. His own testimony at the trial of Alec Coudotte and tribal records made him nineteen, not twenty-two. Third, it tells us — perhaps accurately, perhaps not — that Paul Holy Track was motivated in part by his desire to kill some white people. And fourth, it states that other Standing Rock Indians were angry about the murders and would, if they'd had the chance, have put Paul Holy Track and Philip Ireland to death themselves:

Mandan Pioneer
Mandan, North Dakota
April 30, 1897

The Spicer Murders

Your correspondent has just returned from Fort Yates, where he has interviewed two of the murderers of the Spicer family. Paul Holy Track, aged twenty-two years, and Philip Standing Bear, or Ireland, aged nineteen years and six months, have made three confessions. In the first confession they charged Black Hawk and Coudot with the actual deed. Secondly, they claimed the half-breeds instigated the affair, but in their third and last confession they take all the blame on themselves. Paul appears to have been the leader in the whole affair. He is step-son of Siyaka or Rushing Eagle. Paul's own father lives at Poplar Creek, Montana. He was trying to make his way there when captured. Rushing Eagle is a chief of a band of Indians living a mile or two this side of the agency. Ireland belongs among the Cannon Ball Indians, and worked through haying for Mrs. Parkins all last summer. Both boys speak good English.

Paul killed Mr. and Mrs. Spicer, and Mrs. Rouse. Ireland killed the two babies and old Mrs. Waldron. Paul says, in substance, as follows:

"Since last July I wanted to kill some white people. For a long time since I had no opportunity, but I heard of these white people, and thought it a good chance to kill. So I went to Winona with Philip and we bought whiskey to make our hearts strong, and we went up and killed them shortly after dinner time. Now I am satisfied, I have killed three white people. Let the white people take me and do as they want to with me." He states that he shot Mr. Spicer first, then Mrs. Spicer, and that he attacked Mrs. Rouse with a club. "Mrs. Rouse had a hoe and hit me a blow on the forehead with it, and the blood ran down my face so I could hardly see. A second time she raised the hoe to strike me, but it caught in a wire holding up the stove pipe, or she would have [done] away with me. I got a hit at her with a club, and that settled her. Philip killed Mrs. Waldron with a club, as she was rocking in her chair. I wore my hair in a fringe over my forehead, so that nobody would find the scar. We wore the clothes under our overalls for several days and finally hid them in the brush with the ring." [...]

The day after the murder Paul Holy Track took the temperance pledge. They bought five bottles from Caldwell (now serving a term in jail) the day of the murder. Paul was captured near the "Circle M" ranch on the Cannonball River. He could not swim the river, or he might have got away. The Indians are wild with anger at the murderers, and if they could get hold of them they would meet with justice swift and sure. White people are quiet but there is a strong undercurrent of feeling that bodes no good for the prisoners. Philip Ireland appears to be somewhat ashamed, but Holy Track greeted your correspondent with a "How, friend" and a smile, and seemed quite unconcerned. [...]

Feeling was high against the liquor men, and it will probably go hard with any man found selling liquor to Indians from now on.

Both Holy Track and Ireland are slight boyish-looking fellows, and it is hard to realize they have committed such an appalling crime.

The news that Paul Holy Track and Philip Ireland now said that only they two were responsible for the murders, and that Black Hawk and Alec Coudette were entirely innocent, was of special interest to the editors of a newspaper called *The Appeal*, which billed itself as "A National Afro-American Newspaper." The editors were clearly pleased to note that Black Hawk, who was part black, had been suddenly exonerated:

The Appeal
Saint Paul, Minnesota
May 1, 1897

Confessed

Several confessions have been made by suspects under arrest regarding the murder of the Spicer family at Winona, North Dakota, and tonight from Fort Yates news was received of a full confession by the two Indian boys, Paul Holy Track, aged twenty, and Philip Ireland, aged seventeen, both full blooded Sioux. In the last confession, which seems to be sustained by every circumstance surrounding the crime, the boys say that they committed the murders unassisted and completely exonerate Black Hawk and Caddotte. The confession explains in detail the fiendish massacre of a family of six, comprising four generations — great-grandmother, grandmother, mother and the twin babies — and shows the crime to have been premeditated and one of the most heartless and cold-blooded ever committed in the West. The confession was taken by a stenographer and has been sworn to by both of the Indians.

[...]

Both of the Indians state positively that the women were not criminally assaulted and that the doctor who conducted the post mortem is wrong regarding this.

After having completed their bloody work they dragged the body of Mrs. Waldron into the house where she was found. They went to the barn and dragged Mrs. Spicer's body into that building, covered Spicer's body with refuse found in the barn, and returned to the reservation. Both boys state that they had been drinking and that they carried a bottle of whiskey to the house with them. Ireland says he was so drunk that he does not remember whether an axe or spade was used to mutilate the bodies. They have been kept apart since their arrest and both tell the same stories.

All the talk of Indians murdering white people, mutilating their bodies, and possibly sexually violating their female victims further enraged the white settlers. Now that the sheriff had in his custody two Indians who had confessed to murdering the Spicer family, he had the responsibility of keeping his prisoners safe from the angry settlers who might want to take justice into their own hands. In the end the sheriff had to whisk Paul Holy Track and Philip Ireland out before dawn and sneak them, shackled and well guarded, to a more secure jail at Bismarck.

Bismarck Daily Tribune
Bismarck, North Dakota
May 10, 1897

Indian Boys Here

Paul Holy Track and Philip Ireland, the self-confessed murderers of the Spicer family, who have been confined in the jail at Fort Yates since their

4. Confessions 79

arrest on suspicion of having been concerned in the murders, were brought to [Bismarck] last night and placed in the jail here. Sheriff Shier of Emmons County has been awaiting a favorable opportunity to get the two boys away from Standing Rock since their confession of the murders, but it has not offered itself till now. The awful details of the crime as confessed by the leader of the two boys, Holy Track, has aroused the anger of the settlers in the vicinity of Winona to such a degree that it was feared violence might be attempted if they could get their hands on the murderers. Under these circumstances, the sheriff has been watching for a chance to get the boys away without the knowledge of the settlers, so that any possibility of an encounter with a mob might be avoided. He succeeded in doing this yesterday, and last night the two were turned over to sheriff Taylor and securely locked up in the jail here, where they will remain until the time comes for their trial.

The trip from the jail at Standing Rock was begun at 3 o'clock yesterday morning. At that time the boys were taken out of the jail there after having been securely handcuffed, and shackles placed upon their legs to prevent any possibility of an attempted escape. All preparations for the trip had been made secretly, and before anyone knew that the boys had gone they were miles away.

The trip to the city was an uneventful one except for the fact that the sheriff had to dodge around by unusual paths, whenever there was danger of meeting a party of settlers. At Cannon Ball, William Rouse, husband of one of the women who was killed by the young fiends, was crossing some cattle and he was seen there by the sheriff, who drove into a thicket with his prisoners and waited until the road was clear. Had he come upon the men who were with Rouse it is not possible to state what action the sight of the murderers might have caused them to take, and the sheriff was not taking any chances. He succeeded in passing this place without exciting suspicion and the rest of the journey to the city was uneventful, the prisoners being safely lodged in the jail here at about 9 o'clock last night. The sheriff was accompanied by Billy Welch, one of the agency officials at Standing Rock. The prisoners were securely shackled and they were locked up in the jail, where they now are.

Both of the boys were glad to get away from the jail at the agency. It is a small place, and not so comfortable as their present quarters. Then it is probable they have a feeling of greater security where they are now. Ireland, the younger of the boys, is confined in a cell on the first floor of the jail. He is a typical Indian, and does not look at all like such a murderer as he has admitted himself to be. Of medium height, he is rather light complexioned for an Indian, but he has all the features of a full blood. His age he says he does not know, but he is about eighteen or nineteen. He is an athletic looking young fellow and has been educated at an Indian school, knowing how to read and write some English. The other man, Holy Track, is a larger fellow, coarser featured and taller. He understands English but does not talk very much, and is a more treacherous looking man than the other. He says he is nineteen years of age.

The sheriff says the boys do not seem to be troubled by the knowledge of their crime, and laugh and joke as though there was nothing of the kind to worry them. It is probable that neither of them realizes the horrible nature of the crimes they have confessed. Ireland, it seems to be the general opinion, was drawn into the matter upon the persuasion of the others who were concerned.

Almost three months after the murder of the Spicer family, agent Cramsie thought that it was time that he inform the Commissioner of Indian Affairs in Washington, D.C., about the Spicer murders. The letter tells us that the saloon owner Red Caldwell had confessed to two of the half-dozen charges against him and was given the sentence mandated by the new law regarding selling intoxicants to Indians. Also found guilty were Caldwell's "wife" and his bartender Scar Faced Charley (James Jacobs):

Honorable Commissioner of Indian Affairs
Washington, D.C.
May 12, 1897

Sir:

I have the honor to report that on February 17 last a white family of six persons, (one man, three women, and two children) who were living on the east side of the Missouri River in Emmons County, North Dakota, about two miles from the agency, were murdered by Indians of this reservation. Soon after the murders a negro Frank Pierre and a French half-breed Alexander Cadotte were arrested on suspicion and taken to Williamsport, the county seat of Emmons County, confined in the jail, and are held awaiting trial on June first.

When the crime was committed and when indications showed these Indians were the murderers at hand, a meeting of the police and others connected with the agency have tended increasingly to discount evidence which would have led to the arrest and conviction of the guilty parties. It was learned from an Indian that he saw the two Indian boys crossing the river on the ice from the direction of the house where the murders took place on the evening of the murders.

Detectives (Indians) were engaged to watch and discover whether or nor these boys had in their possession any of the jewelry or clothing which had been taken from the house, and it was learned that one of the boys showed a ring to his comrade; this ring answered to the description of one taken from the house where the Spicers were murdered.

I had the boys arrested immediately and placed in the agency guard house where we succeeded in inducing them to confess their crime. The names of the boys are Paul Holytrack and Philip Ireland, full-blood Indians aged twenty-three and nineteen respectively. They are now in jail in Bismarck, as there are but two cells at Williamsport, which are now occupied by Pierre and Cadotte.

The two boys have made four or five statements, all contradictory. The

4. Confessions

first statement implicated themselves, Pierre and Coudotte. The second exonerates Pierre and Cadotte and implicates the two boys only. These two statements were made to Thomas J. Reedy, chief of police, and A. C. Wells. Additional statements were taken down by the typewriter using the same clerks.

The third and fourth statements were made to Mr. Armstrong, the county attorney of Emmons County and typewritten by himself. In the fourth statement they implicate an Indian by the name of George Defender, who has been arrested and placed in the agency guard house and who will be delivered to the Emmons County officials on demand for trial.

Paul Holytrack and Philip Ireland were under the influence of liquor (bought of F. S. Caldwell) at the time the murder was committed. This man, Caldwell, runs a saloon in Winona, as is well known, directly opposite the agency on the east side of the river about a mile and a half from the scene of the murder. He has sold liquor to the Indians and mixed bloods all winter. On March 18 I made complaint to the U.S. attorney for North Dakota against Caldwell and others and they were afterwards indicted for selling liquor to Indians at various times. To two of the indictments against Caldwell he pleaded guilty and was sentenced to imprisonment for sixty days and a fine of $200.00. Caldwell's wife (or rather a prostitute kept by Caldwell) was indicted for two offenses and pleaded guilty, receiving a sentence of $200 fine and one day imprisonment. A bartender of Caldwell's named James Jacobs pleaded guilty to one indictment and was sentenced to imprisonment for thirty days and one dollar fine. [...]

To my mind there is no question as to the guilt of Holytrack and Ireland, but there is no evidence against the others.

I respectfully suggest that counsels be furnished to the defendants to insure a fair trial and that none but the guilty parties are punished.

The feeling in the county is very strong against the prisoners. It would require very little to stir up the people to a lynching point and it will be doubtful whether a county jury can be procured who will afford each and every one of the prisoners a just trial based on the evidence.

I am, sir, very respectfully, your obedient

John W. Cramsie

The white settlers were generally convinced that agent Cramsie had been unreasonably resistant to allowing civil authorities to come onto the reservation to conduct searches and to question and possibly arrest the Indians who were his wards. He seemed particularly to resist the seizure of George Defender, the fifth Indian accused of involvement in the Spicer murders. The next two articles deal with the arrest of Defender and his trip from the jail at Fort Yates to Bismarck.

Emmons County Record
Williamsport, North Dakota
May 14, 1897

The Latest Facts

In a quiet manner, last Sunday, the confessed murderers Paul Holytrack and Philip Ireland were taken from the Fort Yates prison and escorted to Bismarck. Besides sheriff Shier, there were in the party Charles Welsh, assistant chief of police on the reservation, and two Indian policemen. The prisoners were taken up on the other side of the river as far as the Cannon Ball ferry, and the rest of the journey was made on this side. In Bismarck the young fiends were placed in the Burleigh County jail.

George Defender is still imprisoned at Fort Yates. Whether he is held as a principal or as a witness, the *Record* has been unable to ascertain. Major Cramsie, the Indian agent, still has his gall with him. With his usual high regard for civil laws and civil officers, he condescended to inform the Emmons County officials that, after he had had an interview with Defender, they might see the prisoner. The *Record* learns from good authority that, if the pompous Indian agent had done his duty, the murderers would have been arrested within forty-eight hours after they committed the crime. Possibly some very interesting facts regarding reservation methods will be elicited during the trial.

Early in the week state's attorney Armstrong returned from Winona and Fort Yates, bringing with him Steve Burke, an interpreter. An interview with Coudotte produced no results, as the prisoner refused to talk of the murders. Mr. Burke asked him if he might call again. Coudotte told him that he might call if he wanted to, but that he would not talk on the subject.

Last Saturday — the day set for the examination of the prisoners — Justice Edick postponed such hearing until Saturday, May 29th. Court opens the following Tuesday.

Racism and racial profiling surface frequently in the various accounts included in this book. The article below, for example, shows that Paul Holy Track knew that the authorities would assume that Frank Black Hawk was involved in the murders because he was part black, and "the black man in the country to the south often did these things." The "temperance pledge" referred to below was a written promise, usually signed in front of witnesses, to abstain from alcohol. The reporter was sub-agent Wells. The speaker of the quotations is Paul Holy Track:

Mandan Pioneer
Mandan, North Dakota
May 14, 1897

The Spicer Murders

"I knew right along that you thought Blackhawk had done this thing, because I heard the Indians say that you said the black man in the country to the south often did these things, and the white men all said the same thing. So I told Ireland that if Blackhawk did not tell on us we were all right. But it seems people had seen us that we knew nothing of and finally, when you put this thing and that together, and, worst of all, found the scar on my forehead, I knew that I must be killed by the white people for this thing and did not care much, for I am ready to die any time now. But Defender is, as you know, my near relative, and I would not have him killed. He does not like to die yet, so I told that only Philip and I did this thing, hoping that Blackhawk and Coudotte would not tell on Defender, as I did not tell on them, but took all the blame on myself and Philip Ireland. But again you have found out too much from me, and I cannot save Defender; so I may as well tell the truth, and we will all die soon, which is better than to be shut up like this, for we must die anyway and we are dead, yet living in this place. Now, I will tell the truth, and no more and no different if you ask me a thousand times, or the white men either I have no more to tell.

"I have known Blackhawk since I was a little boy. I was there when he said — took that Indian man up Porcupine and killed him. I heard his cries and screams as they dragged him to death with their horses, and I ran away, for I was only a boy and was afraid. I will tell you where his bones are, and, if you do not find them, then I lie. (Some bones of the man have been found.) That day I drank my first whiskey, and I liked it.

"On the 20th of last December, Blackhawk, Coudotte, Defender and I stole and killed two cattle. We traded a quarter of each to Caldwell for whiskey and the rest we sold to farmers. We stole altogether nine head of cattle and always traded some for whiskey to Caldwell, and the rest we sold. Finally we could get no more cattle. They were too poor and Blackhawk suggested that we kill some white people and get some money. We planned to kill a family below Winona, but there were too many men there and we were afraid. Blackhawk said: 'I know a man with lots of money near home, and they are all women there but the one old man. We will kill them Tuesday.'

"Tuesday was very stormy, and Blackhawk said we will put this off till next Monday. But Blackhawk had not been dividing the cattle money fairly, and I said to the others when he had gone. 'Let's fool him and kill them ourselves and get the money.' They agreed and I said: 'I think I can get Philip Ireland to help us instead,' which I did." [Then follows Holy Track's story, as given while in jail at Fort Yates.]

Such is the awful, sickening, tale of horror told to Mr. Wells by this fiend incarnate — a tale almost unparalleled in the annals of crime. To one who knows or has seen these, to all appearances, mere boys (for they do not look to be more than sixteen or seventeen years old, though they are really over twenty), it seems scarcely creditable. But Mr. Wells, as I said, is thoroughly satisfied their last confession is the true one, and sheriff Shier says the same thing. Agency officials, state's attorney Armstrong and the sheriff have all tried to trap the boys into altering the last statement, but could not do so. Philip says but little. He has been afraid of Paul all along. Mr. Wells says that both he and Major Cramsie were to be victims of this murderous band at a favorable opportunity. Mr. Wells has received a threatening letter without a postmark signed, "Half-breed," threatening him with death for the part he has taken in tracking the murderers. There are still others, who, though not connected with the Spicer murders, are hand in glove with the gang, and these may be run to earth after a while. Sheriff Shier says Paul said to him before he took him away: "I have one thing to ask of you when you get the rope around my neck." "What is that?" said the sheriff. "Give me one last good, big drink of whiskey," replied the scoundrel, who took the temperance pledge the day after the murder.

Paul Holy Track and Philip Ireland were brought up to Cannon Ball on Sunday, and shipped across the river and taken to Bismarck, under the guardian of sheriff Shier and Deputy Welsh. The steamer Cannon Ball was run down to a point in the heavy brush on the reservation side of the Cannon Ball river, and the prisoners, heavily ironed, were taken on board and transferred to a landing in the brush about a mile up the Missouri. The job was neatly done, and nobody but the guards and officials and boat crew knew that the murderers were being taken away.

It was curious to note the action of these desperate scoundrels while on board the boat. The Indian officials, who transferred the keys of the prisoners' big chains to the sheriff, got into some dispute about the key fitting, and the boys were convulsed with laughter at the idea of not being able to get the irons off. They were highly interested in watching the machinery of the boat in action, and the waves made by the paddle wheel. There was no long, lingering look at their old reservation home, fast fading out of sight, which they would probably see no more; no regrets of any kind; apparently no dread of the future; just the ordinary curiosity of an everyday passenger on the boat; and yet the very thought of the horrible crime of those striplings makes the ordinary man's blood boil. In olden times such a crime done by Indians might not have caused surprise. But these young fellows are all well educated, all know a little English, are all what one would call civilized Indians. Now the old Indians who have been in wars and massacres in early days are appalled at this crime, and, as they say themselves, "It makes our own hearts sick to even think of it." They are ashamed — bitterly ashamed — to think that members of their own tribe, full-blooded Indians, are the guilty ones. And there is no hypocrisy about it. Their shame is genuine, as any one who knows them can easily tell.

The title of the next article was an allusion to James Fenimore Cooper's most famous novel, first published in 1826, *The Last of the Mohicans: A Narrative of 1757*. Uncas is the son of Chingachgook, who says of the imminent death of his son, "[W]hen Uncas follows in my footsteps, there will no longer be any of the blood of the sagamores, for my boy is the last of the Mohicans":

Bismarck Daily Tribune
Bismarck, North Dakota
May 19, 1897

Last of the Mohicans

The Indian Defender was brought up from Winona last night. He has been in the guard house at Fort Yates since his arrest and as there are few accommodations there for prisoners, he has been brought to the jail in this city, where his comrades Holy Track and Ireland are, to pass the time until his trial, which will take place next month. Defender was the last of the Spicer murderers to be arrested, upon the confession of Holy Track. He is a married man and has a wife living on the reservation. According to the story of Holy Track, Defender was the man who killed the twin children of Mrs. Rouse, while Holy Track was killing the mother. Defender was last night lodged in the jail here and will remain with the other Indians in the custody of Sheriff Taylor.

Defender is not an old Indian, being somewhere in the twenties. He speaks English, and talked freely yesterday with W. B. Livermore and Jerry Hart of Winona, the men who brought him to the city. He says the story of Holy Track so far as it concerns him is a lie, and that he had nothing whatever to do with the murder of the Spicer family. The officials, however, are inclined to the belief that he was implicated along with the other Indians, and believe there will be testimony enough at the trial to convict all the men of the murder.

Defender was brought across the river at Winona at 5 o'clock yesterday morning and taken directly through the town of Winona. He was seen by a large number of citizens, but there was no evidence of any desire to commit violence. The citizens of that place know that all of the men have been held for trial, are satisfied to leave the matter to the courts and feel satisfied that the men will meet the punishment they deserve.

When used as a legal term, an "examination" is an analysis of the facts of a case in advance of a formal trial. It provides both the prosecution and the defense a chance to talk with potential witnesses and to plan their trial strategies. In the following account of Paul Holy Track's testimony in a pretrial examination, the rich man who lived "on the other side of Winona" was not Thomas Spicer, who lived north of Winona, but probably a man named Jack McCrory, who lived on the south side and had several hired hands:

Winona Times
Winona, North Dakota
May 20, 1897

The Examination

The preliminary examination of Frank Black Hawk and Alex Kidote, the two half-breeds who have been incarcerated in the Emmons County jail for the murder of the Spicer-Rouse families here last February, was held at Williamsport last Friday and Saturday.

The two men were held to the next term of the district court without bail on the testimony of Paul Holy Track, an Indian, who was made a witness for the state. His testimony is substantially as follows:

"On the morning of February 11th, I started to go to Winona for the purpose of getting some whiskey, getting drunk and get some Indians and then charge the white people, but when I got into the timber I met Frank Black Hawk and made the above proposition to him, but he did not answer. After a while he said there are lots of cattle around, let's kill some and sell them and later on Frank said let us go to someone's house and kill them and get all the money they have. He then gave me a bottle and I went home and did not go to Winona.

"On February 13th, the Saturday preceding the murder, I went to the agency with Philip Ireland and while there I met Alex Kidott who said that he wanted to see me, we went down under the hill from the agency and had a talk, and during the conversation Alex asked me did Frank Black Hawk say anything to me. I asked him about what? Oh, anything, he said. I answered yes. Then Alex wanted to know what I thought about it, and I replied that it was all right, that I would do anything. George Defender then came over to where we were and asked Alex if I was satisfied. Alex said yes. Defender then laughed at me and said that if it was a cross dog he did not believe that I could kill it. I told him to shut up. We then talked about who we would kill, and Alex said there was a man who lived on the other side of Winona and he was rich, but we all thought that there were too many men there, and then we decided to go on this side of Winona where there was only one man and two women living and we would kill them. We then went home.

"On Monday evening I went to Bad Horse's place where I met Black Hawk and Kidott. Frank told me to get a gun and we would kill a steer. I got a gun and we went into the timber below Spicer's where we found a steer tied up. We sat there a long time and talked about it, they wanted me to shoot the steer, but I was afraid that the report of the gun would be heard in Winona. Finally I did shoot it and waited a long time but nobody came, we then loaded the steer on to a sled and hauled it to town and sold it. Black Hawk then told me to go to Spicer's and find out how many persons were there, and that is the last I saw of Black Hawk.

"On Tuesday night Philip and I went to Red's and got some whiskey. We then went up in front of the *Times* office and drank some of it and talked, then we had our plans arranged and went home.

"On Wednesday Alex Kidott, Philip Ireland, George Defender and myself went up in the timber below Spicer's and talked. After awhile Philip and I went up to the house and told Mr. Spicer we wanted to buy a horse, and we talked for awhile and then Alex and George came up. We were all in the stable, and the gun too. Mr. Spicer was wheeling out manure. He wheeled out several loads before we killed him because none of us could shoot him, and every time he would go out with a load we would go behind the door and take a drink and debate as to who should shoot him. I then said I would. I then took a big drink and the next load he wheeled out I shot him and the others struck him. Mrs. Spicer then came down to the barn and I shot her and the others struck her. We then went to the house and found the women crying and wringing their hands. I struck at the young woman and missed her, she in return struck me with a hoe and cut a hole in my forehead. Alex then hit her with a club and Philip hit the old lady. I do not know how George killed the babies, but suppose he killed them with our custom by catching them by the feet and knocking their brains out against the wall."

It is presumed that the preliminary examination of George Defender, Paul Holy Track and Philip Ireland will take place at Williamsport, on Saturday, May 20th.

A somewhat different account of the same "examination" or preliminary hearing was published in a Minnesota newspaper. Note that Paul Holy Track unequivocally denies the reports that he and Philip Ireland had "outraged" Mrs. Spicer and Mrs. Rouse:

Princeton Union
Princeton, Minnesota
May 20, 1897

A Terrible Tale

The preliminary hearing of the five Sioux Indians who murdered the Spicer family at Winona in February is in progress at Williamsport, Emmons County. Holy Track, one of the accused, took the witness stand, and told the terrible story of the crime, implicating Black Hawk and Cadotte, the two half-breeds, and Standing Bear, Defender and himself, full-blood Sioux. This is Holy Track's story:

"On December 20 Black Hawk, Cadotte, Defender and I stole and killed two cattle. We traded a quarter of each to Caldwell for whiskey and the rest we sold to farmers. We stole altogether nine head of cattle and always traded some for whiskey to Caldwell and the rest we sold. Finally we could get no more cattle, they were too poor, and Black Hawk suggested that we kill some white people and get some money. We planned to kill a family below Winona, but there were too many men there and we were afraid. Black Hawk said: 'I know a man with lots of money near home, and they are all women there but one old man; we will kill them Tuesday.' Tuesday was very stormy and Black Hawk said: 'We will put this off till next Monday.' But Black Hawk had not been dividing the cattle money fairly, and I said to the others when he was gone: 'Let's fool him and kill them ourselves and get the money.' They agreed, and I said: 'I think I can get Standing Bear to help us instead,' which I did.

"On Wednesday we killed them all. I first shot Mr. Spicer and Standing Bear pounded him with a shovel and then Defender stabbed him as he fell with a pitchfork. I then went and shot Mrs. Spicer and stabbed her with a pitchfork and Defender hit her with an axe. Cadotte attacked Mrs. Rouse, but she hit him with something and knocked him senseless. Then she went into another room and got a hoe to defend herself with. I went to kill her then with the butt end of the gun, but she was quick and hit me with the hoe, but maybe she would have killed me with the hoe if it had not caught in the stovepipe wire. I knocked her onto the lounge and she lay there, as I thought, dead, but Cadotte, who had come too, said: 'She is not dead yet,' so I finished her with an axe. Defender meantime killed the two babies. Standing Bear killed old Mrs. Waldron with a club as she rocked in her chair. We got altogether about $5 in money, besides the clothes and jewelry. There was no outraging of women. The doctor was wrong about that."

The officials are satisfied now that they have the story of the murder as it happened. It was believed all along that the four Indians were implicated, and the man Defender had been under suspicion. They have all been held for trial in the district court, which convenes June 1.

5

Trial

Each of the five defendants was to have his own trial by jury, though it was assumed that Paul Holy Track and Philip Ireland, after having given sufficient testimony to convict at least Alec Coudotte and George Defender, and possibly Frank Black Hawk, would plead guilty and so have short trials. In fact, however, only two trials were actually held, those of Alec Coudotte and George Defender. This chapter focuses on the murder trial of Alec Coudotte, which started June 1, 1897, in Williamsport, then the county seat of Emmons County. Because the courthouse in Williamsport was deemed too small to accommodate the crowds that were expected, the trial was held in a larger room in the schoolhouse. The term "venire" below refers to the list of potential jurors from which the actual panel of jurors would be selected. Because of the sparse white population of Emmons County, it would have been virtually impossible to come up with five such lists:

Bismarck Daily Tribune
Bismarck, North Dakota
May 29, 1897

The Spicer Trial

Judge Winchester, stenographer Tuttle and the attorneys who have business before the term of court in Emmons County will leave for Williamsport next Tuesday, when the term of court begins. The principal business of the term will be the trial of the men implicated in the Spicer murders, and if all of them are tried there the term of court is apt to be a long one. A jury of forty-eight persons has been called and if the men demand separate trials, it is likely that separate venires will have to be summoned to try some of them. The defense will be conducted by attorney Lynn — at least the defense of Black Hawk and Coudot. It is not likely that Holy Track will do other than plead guilty after the confession that has already been made by him. It is stated that attorney Lynn is firm in the belief that Holy Track and Ireland alone committed the murders, and that Black Hawk, Defender and

Alec Coudotte's trial took place in the large classroom in the Williamsport School in June 1897. In this makeshift courtroom Coudotte was found guilty and sentenced to be hanged for murdering Thomas Spicer (State Historical Society of North Dakota 1952-3536).

>Coudot had nothing to do with the crime. He says he can prove that, from the Sunday before the murder until the Thursday after it, Defender was sixty miles from the scene of the crime; that Dr. Ross was at Coudot's house the afternoon of the murder, and that Alec was there; that no steer was killed in the timber near the Spicer place as Holy Track related; that Holy Track and Ireland were seen crossing the river together, and not separately, as stated in the testimony before the justice; and that Holy Track's detailed statement of minor incidents before and after the murder will prove to be largely drawn from his imagination.

The second defense attorney was R. N. Stevens. It turned out that Stevens did most of the actual defense work in the trial. The judge was Walter H. Winchester. The jury selection was challenging because it was difficult to find a sufficient number of citizens in Emmons County who did not already have firm opinions on the case. The following article shows what the defense was up against in selecting the jury.

Winona Times
Winona, North Dakota
June 3, 1897

Murder Trial Begins

A challenge to the jury panel was filed by the attorneys for the defense, going to the question as to the method adopted in selecting the jury. Clerk of court Streeter stated that the method was strictly in accordance with the law as far as he knew. The motion was overruled.

Herman Backhouse was the first juror called. On his examination he said he was a brother of a man who was murdered in the county some years ago, and he thought it was about time that there was a hanging in the county, but he would only hang a man on sufficient evidence. He also stated that he was a Lutheran, but he was not excused.

S. F. Wright was next called and excused as he had formed an opinion that would be hard to alter by evidence. [...]

John Jackson came next. He had heard of the murder and said he was not prejudiced, but would a little sooner believe a white man than an Indian. The defense tried to get him off but failed.

J. I. Roop had formed an opinion that was unchangeable by evidence or anything else and was excused in a hurry. [...]

William Derr had formed an opinion from what he had read in the newspapers, but if accepted as a juror he was positive that he could weigh the evidence as fairly and impartially as though he had never heard a word about it. He said he would believe an Indian as quick as a white man. The juror was challenged by the defense which was denied, and he was passed.

Olaf Thompson did not think he could believe an Indian or any other race whose customs and habits he was not familiar with, and not having a very thorough knowledge of the English language, he was excused. [...]

And so on. Finally a jury was accepted, but only after running through all forty-eight names on the venire. No Indians were on the jury. A fair number of the settlers were excused because, having come from Europe not long before, they did not understand English well enough to follow the proceedings. The writer of that last article included a section of "Notes." Here are three of them: "Holy Track says that he is ready to die and the quicker they hang him the better it suits him"; "Aaron Wells says that he has received a letter from Paul Holy Track's father, stating that if Paul is hung he will roll the heads of Mr. Wells's children in at the door sometime"; "There has been no talk of lynching. All the people want is justice, and the general sentiment seems to point toward the gallows. It would not be safe for the defense to ask a change of venue as the taxpayers think they have been to enough expense already."

The term "information" as used in the next article is a legal term for the formal statement accusing the defendant of the crime for which he or she is to be tried:

Emmons County Record
Williamsport, North Dakota
June 4, 1897

The Great Trial

The great murder trial has begun. Promptly at 2 o'clock last Tuesday the June term of court for the third subdivision of the sixth judicial district was opened by proclamation of the sheriff, as provided by law.

[...]

The first criminal case on the calendar was that of the *State of North Dakota vs. Ruby Caldwell*, accused of assault with intent to kill, but the state's attorney elected to take up the more important case of the *State vs. Alec Coudotte*, one of the men accused of the Spicer murders. Coudotte was in court, seated between deputy sheriff Livermore and Harry McLaughlin, who had been selected and sworn as interpreter. Coudotte was asked if he could speak English and he replied in the negative. The information was then read by state's attorney Armstrong, and defendant was asked if he was ready to plead, and he replied in the affirmative. He was asked his age and gave it as being about thirty-three. The information—a lengthy document—was read. As the attorneys for the defense had just been served with a copy of the information, they were given until 9 A.M. Wednesday to plead thereto.

The murder charges against the defendant were fivefold, though he was accused of murdering only Thomas Spicer, not any of the other five in the household. Armstrong's official "information" stating the accusations against Alec Coudotte:

> On the seventeenth day of February in the year of our Lord one thousand eight hundred and ninety seven at the county of Emmons in the state of North Dakota, one Alec Coudotte, late of the county of Boreman and state aforesaid, did commit the crime of murder in the first degree committed in the manner following, to wit:
>
> That at the said time and place the said Alec Coudotte, with force and arms in and upon the body of one Thomas Spicer, then and there being, willfully, feloniously, unlawfully, deliberately, of his malice aforethought, and with the premeditated design to effect the death of him the said Thomas Spicer, did make an assault; that the said Alec Coudotte a certain single-barreled muzzle-loading shotgun, then and there loaded and charged with gun powder and a number of small shot and one leaden bullet, then and there, willfully, feloniously, unlawfully, deliberately, of his malice aforethought and with the premeditated design to effect the death of him the said Thomas Spicer, did discharge and shoot off, to, at, against and upon the said Thomas Spicer; that the said Alec Coudotte with the small shot and the leaden bullet aforesaid, out of the shot gun aforesaid, then and there, by the force of the gun powder aforesaid, by the said Alec Coudotte discharged and shot off as aforesaid, then and there willfully, feloniously, unlawfully, deliberately of his malice aforethought and with the premeditated design to effect the death of the said Thomas Spicer, did strike, penetrate and wound the said Thomas in and upon the back of the said Thomas Spicer. [...]

And so on, for five verbose and repetitious pages. The shooting of the "aforesaid shot gun" was just the first of five counts against the "aforesaid Alec Coudotte." The second was that Coudotte used an axe to strike Thomas Spicer on the head. The third was that he used a shovel to lacerate Thomas Spicer's throat. The fourth was that he repeatedly stabbed Thomas Spicer with a pitch fork. The fifth was that he used a knife to "strike, cut, stab, and thrust, giving unto the said Thomas Spicer then and there with the knife aforesaid, in and upon the left breast of the said Thomas Spicer, one mortal wound of the length of one inch and of a depth unknown." Whether or not Alec Coudotte was able to ferret out the meaning of all that verbiage, he pled not guilty to the charges.

Armstrong explained to the jury that several different weapons were used against Thomas Spicer, and that it was not clear which one had actually killed him. He told the jury that if they found that the defendant had attacked Thomas Spicer with any one of the five weapons, they should find him guilty of murder in the first degree. He asserted that Coudotte was in any case the leader of the attack on the Spicer family, and that Paul Holy Track and Philip Ireland were little more than pawns following his lead and taking orders from him.

Many witnesses were called, both by the prosecution and by the defense. I reproduce in this chapter a selection of their testimony, those portions that have the most direct bearing on the actions of the five accused murderers on the day of the actual murders, February 17, and on the days just before and after.

The transcript was made by court stenographer R. M. Tuttle. Because the appeals process would require readable copies, Tuttle was paid by the county to type from his handwritten transcript three copies of the court proceedings. His transcription was all in English, though we should keep in mind that some of the actual testimony would have been given originally in the Sioux language, but rendered into English by Harry McLaughlin, court-appointed translator. Tuttle's typescript is more than 150 pages long — mostly double-spaced legal-size pages, but with some sections single-spaced. I present in this chapter only about a quarter of the actual typescript. For those interested, the rest of the typescript is available, on faded and blurred onionskin carbon copy, in the archives of the North Dakota State Historical Society in Bismarck.

In the interests of making the transcript more accessible to modern readers, I have taken certain liberties with the text as typed by Tuttle. I have divided the longest paragraphs into shorter ones; I have adjusted Tuttle's erratic spacing and punctuation; I have corrected obvious typographical errors; I have removed the period that Tuttle sometimes placed after the name "Alec" as if it were an abbreviation; I have sometimes altered the spelling and capitalization of words ("didn't" for "did'nt," "county" for "County," "state" for "State," and so on); I have made more consistent Tuttle's inconsistent practice of placing in parentheses information about the case — for example, "(Witness continues his narrative)"; I have removed a few phrases that seemed to be Tuttle's notes to himself, such as "More cross examination." Where I have added a word, I use square brackets. The bold, italicized, and centered section headings identifying the witness in or the subject of the following section are my own additions to guide the reader.

Apparently court stenographer Tuttle did not write down some of the leading questions asked by the attorneys, and so has presented much of the testimony in narrative rather than dialogue format. When dialogue is indicated, it is not always clear who is asking the questions. I have made no attempt to alter the sometimes choppy and disconnected testimony that has resulted.

Because they had confessed to their own part in the Spicer murders, Paul Holy Track and Philip Ireland were called as state's witnesses against Alec Coudotte. Frank Black Hawk denied having been at Spicer's but was called to verify what he knew of the whereabouts of Alec Coudotte at other times. The other accused man, George Defender, was not called on to testify in Alec Coudotte's trial, presumably because his own trial was to follow right after Alec Coudotte's.

In what follows, I have for the most part kept the order in which the various witnesses were called. I move a few of the shorter testimonies so that they follow the longer testimonies that they are meant to refute, clarify, or verify. Paul Holy Track was the first and most important witness called by prosecutor Armstrong. At the very start he was asked to read something and write something in English. Because he did well on both tests, he began his testimony without benefit of a translator, though the services of Harry McLaughlin were used for certain parts of his testimony.

Because Alec Coudotte was charged in this trial with murdering only Thomas Spicer, not the other five victims, Paul Holy Track's testimony focuses on the events in the stable and barn. For this trial the prosecutor was not interested in determining how or by whom the other murders, the ones in the house itself, were committed. Paul Holy Track, then, says little more than this about the murders of Mrs. Waldron, Mrs. Rouse, and the twin infants: "We then went to the house and all went in. After the people in the house were all killed, Alec told us to look for money."

Testimony of Paul Holy Track

Paul Holy Track had made several contradictory confessions about the Spicer family murders. Part of what both the prosecuting and the defense attorneys wanted to accomplish was determining which version of what hap-

5. Trial

pened to Thomas Spicer was the accurate one. Of course, they had different motives in doing so. Armstrong wanted to prove that Alec Coudotte was guilty of murdering Thomas Spicer. Stevens wanted to prove that Alec Coudotte was innocent. Apparently led by the questions of one attorney or the other, Paul Holy Track spent much of his time on the stand reconstructing, often somewhat confusingly, the events of the several days before February 17: the killing of the steer, dealings with Red Caldwell for whiskey, hunting rabbits, plans to kill and rob a white settler, his movements on both sides of the Missouri River, discussions with his accomplices, the way he loaded the shotgun, the kinds of livestock in the stable and barn, and so on. The trial proceedings sometimes give Frank Black Hawk's name as "Blackhawk," and sometimes refer to him as "Pete," a derivative of "Pierre," one of his names. I have allowed these inconsistencies to stand.

> Q.-What is your name? (Defense objects to the testimony of the witness on the ground that by the records of the court he confesses himself a codefendant in the commission of the crime for which this defendant is to be tried, and for the further reason that under the information filed in this case the testimony of this witness is incompetent, irrelevant and immaterial. Objection overruled, and exception granted the defendant.)
> A.-Paul Holy Track. I am nineteen years old. Live at Standing Rock Indian agency, and have for about thirteen years. I was born at Poplar Creek, Montana. Know Alec Coudotte and have for about twelve years. I knew Thomas Spicer. He lived this side of Winona about a mile and a half. Last saw him February seventeenth at his place. Saw him on the sixteenth of February, the day before. On the seventeenth of February when I saw him at his house he was cleaning out the stable. He was at it about half an hour. He was alive. Don't know what county Winona is in or in what county Thomas Spicer's place is.
> On the morning of the thirteenth of February I went to the agency about nine o'clock from our place, which is about three miles from the agency, southeast. Philip Ireland went with me. Started to go to the agency about nine o'clock. Got there about half past ten. Went on foot. After arriving saw Alec Coudotte at the agency office. By Alec Coudotte I mean that man there (pointing at the defendant). Nobody was with him when I saw him. Philip was with me. Stayed at the agency office about half an hour that morning. Went from there under the hill. Alec Coudotte went with me. First said he wanted to see me. I said all right. Don't know where Philip went when Alec and I met at the office. Didn't go with me. Left him at the office. After we went down under the hill and had a talk with Alec. Can't say what he said very well in English. (Harry McLaughlin sworn as interpreter. Witness continues.)
> When I first saw him he asked me if I had seen Frank Blackhawk, and if he had told me anything, and I said yes. He asked me what I thought of it. I said all right. We talked about different things, and finally Alec said we will go over to Winona. The other side of Winona there is a rich man liv-

ing there, and that is where we will do it. Before he said that, George Defender arrived. When he arrived there George Defender said to Alec, is he satisfied? Alec said yes. George then said he would not be able to kill a cross dog if he was told to, so Alec said we would go to the rich man's place the other side of Winona to do the killing. George spoke up and said, no the Indians come there often and besides he has a man working for him.

Then George asked me if I ever went to this house of Spicer, and I said yes. He asked me how many men there were there, and I said two women and one man was all I had ever seen. Then he asked me if I thought they had money and I said yes. George and Alec and I were there together. Then George said that will be the place we will do it. We talked it over quite a little while and then I left and went home.

[...]

Had a conversation with Frank and Alec at that time. Frank told me to go and get a gun and we would kill an animal, a steer. He did not state where it was. Told me to go where the big tree was across the river under Spicer's. I went home and got my horse and gun and two knives and went over to the tree. Not meeting them there, I left the gun there and rode on to Winona.

When I arrived at Red's stable I saw Frank Blackhawk and Alec Coudotte. They were getting on their horses. We all three rode back, then we rode to where I had the gun and we rode through the brush to Spicer's and came upon the steer that was tied a mile or a little less maybe from Spicer's house. One of the steer's horns was broken and he was tied around the neck to a tree with a rope. Frank knew before I went there that I had a gun because he saw me hunting rabbits that day, and also that was the gun we used killing cattle. When I went home after the gun I stayed a little over an hour. Got to Winona near midnight I think.

While at the steer Alec and Frank and I talked quite a good deal. Spoke of killing this man and arranged it that we would divide up the money equally. Blackhawk spoke first. He asked how many people were there and I told him three. Alec said nothing aside from talking about the killing. Said we would kill those people and divide the money equally. Frank Blackhawk said that. I said all right.

Alec said he did not want Frank Blackhawk to be in it for fear he would take all the money.

Q.-Was that said at that time?

A.-It was that evening.

Q.-State what was said right there where the steer was.

A.-Alec asked him if he would be able to join them in killing those people, and he said yes. That is all I can remember that was said at that time about killing these people.

We talked a little about different things. We had some whiskey. We all had some of that to drink, and also smoked some. They then wanted me to shoot the steer and I was afraid the report would be heard, so we waited until just about daylight, and then I shot the steer with a shot gun, a single barrel muzzle loader, loaded with shot and a ball. It was a red steer with white legs behind, about three years old. After I shot the steer and he fell down, Frank Blackhawk took an axe and hit him on the head. I shot him right in his forehead between the eyes. Alec said he would go and get his sled.

After Blackhawk hit the steer in the head, I had the knives so I gave one to Coudotte to skin with and Blackhawk had a pocket knife of his own. I had two butcher knives, regular skinning knives, issue knives. I brought them from home. We butchered the steer and quartered it, and threw the hide over the meat and Coudotte said he would go and get his sled and Black Hawk told me to go home and return about the same time, and help Coudotte — about the same time Coudotte would return with his sled, so I should be sure to help him load the beef. [...] I walked on to where they had killed the steer and I saw Black Hawk and Coudotte, and they had the beef all loaded up except one quarter and the offal and hide. Also the head had not been loaded. So I put in the head, and the hide and offal was loaded also. While we were standing there I saw a man on the hill and recognized Philip. Blackhawk said, you go and get Philip and go up to Spicer's house and see how many people there are there. So I said all right and got Philip and went over to Spicer's house with him.

We went over and saw Mr. Spicer hauling manure and we helped him. [...] After we got through hauling manure he hitched up the mare that Philip had talked of buying and said he was going to see a man that lived the other side of the post. After that we followed him on foot toward Winona. [...]

Tuesday it was windy, not a very pleasant day. Tuesday night we stayed at home, and the next morning about ten o'clock we started. We were slow going over. We took a gun with us, the one we used to shoot the steer with. I left home on foot. We went to Spicer's house. They had finished their dinner. We first put the gun in the barn and then went to the house. When we went in we saw Mr. Spicer and his wife and a young woman. I did not know at that time what the young woman's name was, but I now know that it was Rouse.

We talked with the people there half an hour. After we had been in the house a short while, Mrs. Rouse looked out the window and said, two Indians have arrived. Shortly after that they came into the house, and it was Alec and George Defender. When Alec came into the house he said in quite a loud voice, is that you, Paul, and I said, yes.

Then he asked me if there was anyone else in the house, if that was all the people living there. I said yes, and he then said wait and I will go down and take our horses in the brush and then we will return and do it. I said all right. Then Mrs. Spicer said when they were gone out, it looks as though they are pretty full, and I said, yes. Mrs. Spicer asked what they were saying, and I said they thought of eating, but you were through dinner and that is as far as I went. She said if you had told me that I would have given them something to eat.

Then the old gentleman walked out and went to the stable and we followed him, Philip and I. The old man went to the stable and went in. The gun was on the outside and I took it inside. Then we helped him haul manure out. Philip and I were doing that when George and Alec came. Alec Coudotte and George Defender were there in the stable and Philip was on the outside. We three were inside and talked about different things. When the old gentleman would wheel out manure we would take a drink of whiskey. They gave me three bottles of whiskey. They had sold some meat and they gave me that for helping kill that beef.

Alec told me to shoot the man first. I told him I couldn't do it. Then Alec told George to shoot him, and he said he could not do it. Then he was going to do it himself and he couldn't do it. So I said, hand it here, I will do it. Alec had had the gun but George had taken it. George handed me the gun and I went into the corner and took some more whiskey. When Spicer had filled his wheelbarrow with manure and wheeled it out I shot him from the inside of the barn. At the time I shot him he was wheeling the wheelbarrow.

Alec was inside but I did not notice how close he was to me. I just took aim and shot at the man. I think he was a little this side of that door (pointing), about the door or a little nearer. About five or six yards. About as far as from the shed door as from here to that window (pointing). He was nearer to the shed door than the stable door. After I shot, Philip started to run away, but he returned to the shed. George Defender took a pitch fork and went to the man I had shot, and Coudotte took a shovel and gave it to Philip and told him to come and help him. He did go but returned shortly, and Coudotte then took the shovel and went out. I told Philip to reload the gun and took another drink of whiskey. I did not see Alec strike Mr. Spicer with the shovel.

Shortly thereafter we returned to the stable and shed, Alec and George Defender. Alec wanted Philip to go up after Mrs. Spicer. He would not do it. Then I told George to go, and he would not go. Then Alec told me to go and I said, all right. I then went and told Mrs. Spicer. We went down to the stable together. We walked part of the way down together and I started on a little run and told George she was coming. Alec and the others were all inside. I told George Defender to shoot her. He said he could not.

At the time I shot Mr. Spicer he fell. He must have been alive after the shooting because they took out the pitchfork and shovel. At the time he was shot he yelled, but that was all I heard, but Philip said he was still alive. I did not see them hit Mr. Spicer's body, or see him dragged into the stable. I went back into the stable into the corner and therefore did not see his body. When I shot him I saw him fall and that was all. I did not see his body the second time. Did not go into the shed. I hit him in the back somewhere. Somewhere in the center of the back. I did not look at it and therefore can't tell exactly where it was.

I shot him with shot and ball. In loading the gun, I first put in the powder and used shawl for wadding, then the shot and another wadding with a piece of shawl. The shawl was an issue shawl, red with black stripes. I would recognize the wadding if I saw it. (Witness is shown a piece of cloth.)

5. Trial

Q.-Does that look like the wadding you put into the gun?
A.-Yes. (Bullet shown witness.)
Q.-Does that look like the bullet?
A.-Yes.

There was in the stable at the time two blue horses, a bay mare and some calves. The calves were tied in the corner next to the door, and two grays tied in the stall on the other side and the bay in the stall on this side. The grays stood in one stall together. After we got through at the stable, Alec told us to look for some clubs and we walked up to the house. Alec took the axe and George took a cottonwood stick. Philip and I, we had nothing. Before going up to the house we drank two bottles of whiskey, bottles you would pay fifty cents for. Philip had one and Alec and George had the other.

We then went to the house and all went in. After the people in the house were all killed, Alec told us to look for money, and we commenced to look for money but found none. We pulled out the trunks and went through the trunks, Alec, George, Philip and myself. Alec got a suit but gave me the coat and vest. I took a pencil, handkerchief and breastpin and earrings. Alec took a pair of pants, some writing paper and envelopes. He gave me the writing paper and envelopes, and also a pocketbook. The pocketbook was a long one you fold over. There was also taken from there at that time a suit of clothes, three rings, a little red box and a long necktie. Philip took these. There was also taken a white shirt, pair of pants, three neck ties, handkerchief, a six-shooter and a pocketbook belonging to the old lady. George took these.

I don't know the name of the old lady, but she was quite old. She was the one in the house. After we got through in the house we went down towards the road and down the hill to the mail road. George Defender and Coudotte said they were going up to sleep at Pete Blackhawk's, and Philip and I then went down into the brush where we had hid a bottle of whiskey. Alec had taken the road, so had George. We went into the brush.

I received a cut that day on the forehead. I told Alec in the house that the young woman had struck me. Alec said the young lady nearly knocked his chest in. After getting our bottle of whiskey we went to the edge of the bank and Philip took off a pair of overalls and put on a pair of pants, then put the overalls on over the pants. At that time Alec had taken the mail road so I don't know where he was. Then we drank more whiskey and crossed the ice to the water hole where they watered ponies, took another drink of whiskey, went through the willows and met Blue Boy, John Blue Boy, and then went home.

After that I was in the guard house at Fort Yates with the defendant Alec and Frank. I talked with Alec about the murder of the Spicers. They were to have me up there that Saturday and have me tell what I knew. Alec told me to stick to it no matter what they did or said. For me not to give it away. I saw Alec give Frank Blackhawk five dollars in the guard house. As long as I was in the guard house Alec and I used to talk together. Nearly every evening we talked about the killing and also the killing of cattle. I heard Alec tell Philip not to give it away and he would give him a horse.

I was afterwards taken to Bismarck as a witness before the U.S. grand jury. We went in a stage. There was in the stage, besides myself, Alec, George, Patrick Yellow Lodge, Philip and Peter Blue Shield. I talked with Alec about the Spicer murder on the way up. He said, this will be the same thing. They will take us up here and try to find out what they can but no one saw it. Be sure not to give it away. No one knows it. Then he gave me ten dollars.

After he said that I said I was going to tell it anyway. Then he gave me ten dollars. I had no money when I left Winona. I remember the time Alec was taken out of the stage at Bismarck. We stayed at Livermore while in Bismarck. I gave five dollars of the money Alec gave me to George.

After I had been arrested the last time and placed in the guard house, I made three statements to Mr. Reedy and Mr. Wells. In the first statement I said Alec and Frank killed Thomas Spicer, and Philip and I. In the second statement Philip and I alone. In the third, George, Alec, Philip and myself. The reason I included Frank Blackhawk in the first statement was that he was the man that made it. I did not include George Defender in the first statement, because when we were going to Bismarck he cried, and that is the reason. There were a good many other reasons. We were very good together. The reason we left out Frank, Alec, and George in the second statement was because they were each to give us a horse apiece and also for the reason that I gave an account of George before. The reason we left out Frank and included George and Alec in the third statement was because they had found out all these things taken from there and it was known, and that is why we told. Besides, it is right and that is the reason I told it that way.

(Cross examination by defense attorney R. N. Stevens.)

While I was in the jail at Bismarck I did not say or threaten to swear on the trial that Frank Blackhawk was present and helped to do the killing. I did not say anything like that except to a man by the name of Bill. He asked how it was done and I told him. He wrote Frank's name on the paper and likely that is what it means. I don't remember telling that Frank Blackhawk did it or that I had tried to help him out, and would now tell it because he was trying to lay it to me.

Q.-Is that your writing? (Paper produced.)
A.-Yes.
Q.-What does F. B. H. mean there?
A.-Frank Blackhawk. (Paper marked defendant's exhibit "2" for identification.)

On April 24th I made a statement in the Standing Rock Indian agency guard house to Thomas J. Reedy and Aaron C. Wells, and in answer to the question, "Why did you try to implicate Frank Blackhawk and Alec Coudotte?" I answered that these men were accused and arrested for this crime and as the evidence was strong against them I thought that they might be convicted and that we would get off. They told us to hide it and they would give us horses.

I expect to be hung for this offense. My mother would have the horses. I live with my mother. This is the only offense I have ever been accused of. I was accused of forging my father's name to orders for goods at the store.

Q.-Were you ever accused of stealing carpenters' mittens and found out at it and had to give them up?

A.-I was playing there, fooling and took the gloves and skipped off with them and they thought I had stolen the gloves. I put on the gloves and we were boxing. He saw me take the gloves.

[...]

Bought some whiskey of Red Caldwell, the man that keeps a saloon in Winona. That is Red Caldwell standing over there — that's the man I bought the whiskey of on Tuesday the 16th day of February at four o'clock in the afternoon.

Nobody said anything to me about buying whiskey of a man called Scar Faced Charley while I was in the Bismarck jail, but when I went to Bismarck they asked me what I was taken there for and I said it was for having bought some whiskey from Scar Faced Charley. I appeared before Thomas J. Reedy and Aaron C. Wells on the 24th of April, 1897, at the guard house, Standing Rock Indian agency, and made a statement as to my connection with the murder of Thomas Spicer.

Q.-Did you at time say the following?

[...]

At this point the defense attorney, Stevens, read to Paul Holy Track almost the whole of the statement made on April 24 and printed in chapter 4 as "Holy Track's Second Yarn." Stevens's aim was apparently to call the witness's credibility into question by reminding the jury that he had earlier made quite a different statement. He also wanted to remind the jury that according to Paul Holy Track's own earlier statement, Alec Coudotte had played no part in the murders. Paul Holy Track admitted that he had made that statement:

A.-Yes. (Testimony of witness resumed. [...] Here witness was shown state's exhibit "B" for identification.)

I know that is a piece of shawl. I have seen a piece like it before. I think that is the piece but it was square when I last saw it. I think it is the piece of shawl I used in loading the gun to shoot Thomas Spicer. (Witness examines leaden bullet marked state's exhibit "A." Continuing, he says:)

That looks like the ball that Patrick Yellow Lodge gave me. I last saw it the time I loaded the gun on the 17th of February. I shot Thomas Spicer with it. That is the identical ball I shot Thomas Spicer with. The way I recognize it, I got two just like it from Patrick Yellow Lodge with that little ridge. The ones I had of my own did not have that little ridge. Am certain that is the ball with which I shot Thomas Spicer. The only way I identify it is the little ridge. Don't know whether there are any other bullets with ridges on them or not. I carried the balls quite a while and looked at them a great deal. The balls I have did not have indentations on them like that one. I recognize it on account of the ridge. I account for the marks on the ball by guessing it flattened when I shot the man. I never shot a man before, but I know from shooting cattle. When you shoot cattle like that the bullets flatten. This piece, if it is the piece I think it is, is an issue shawl. It was an old shawl that was at home, and I tore it off to use as wadding.

Went to Spicer's on the 17th of February after they were eating dinner. We were going that same day hunting rabbits with sticks. We had the gun but still used sticks. There was only one hole we dug in because we saw a rabbit go in there, we did not go around other brush piles, we just went off the road a little way and then back into the road. I mean we went through the timber with sticks that little time we went off the road.

Q.-Did you say this?: "On the 17th of February, 1897, I left home in the morning and came to the agency in company with Philip Ireland between eleven and twelve o'clock. On the same day I asked Philip Ireland to go to Winona with me and we started from the agency offices. From the offices we went through the timber on this side of the river to a point opposite Spicer's house and just before we crossed the river we heard the 11:45 whistle blow. After crossing the river we hunted rabbits for a short time in the timber near the Spicer house, having nothing to hunt with but sticks."

A.-I said that at the time, but I meant chasing rabbits, what little time we were off the road.

On the 17th after hunting rabbits we went to the Spicer house a little after dinner. After shooting Mr. Spicer I went to the house and got Mrs. Spicer. Came round the barn to get in at the door. There is a little path that bends around the outside corner of the fence. She followed that around. Shortly after she was shot I walked outside and saw this man on the mail road I think about two hundred yards or less. When I saw him he was going towards Winona. I started towards him. Went a little past the root cellar, then the man drove up. Did not know him. I may have seen him when at the agency, but I don't know the man or that man's name. After the man passed I went back to the stable. Shot Spicer I think at nearly three o'clock. Shot Mrs. Spicer very soon after. Stayed around the place I guess less than half an hour after that. Think I left the place about half past three.

When we left, went down past the well into the brush and struck the path in the brush and followed that to the bank. Philip changed his clothes and I threw away a watch guard. I did not stagger across the river, didn't have a bundle of clothes. Philip had nothing tied up. Did not stagger. When we got across the river Blue Boy was driving horses to water. We were not staggering at that time. Philip had the gun.

When I was taken to Bismarck after my arrest I was taken by a man by the name of Charles Welch. One time we were driven into the brush to avoid a man by the name of Rouse who was crossing with some cattle. Had a conversation with Welch in the timber about this murder. We were waiting for this man Rouse to get out of the way. I told him then Alec, Philip, George and myself were in it. Told him Frank was not in it. I told him that Alec had $15 dollars. He gave Frank five and me ten. I said he gave me the ten in the stage. I gave five of it to George. Bought a few articles and some whiskey with the other. (Here witness was shown exhibit "2" and said:) Yes, I write that F. B. H. means Frank Blackhawk. When I wrote that it was a lie. (Exhibit offered in evidence and received without objections. Witness continued.)

Red was bothering me all evening. He asked if Frank was in it, and to get rid of him I told him he was. It was on the 25th of May. Red Caldwell left the jail the next morning.

Q.-Did you not write the following language on a piece of paper or this in substance?: Then when you come to hang, all you want to do was to have a big drink of whiskey and say "Go ahead you sons of bitches" and dance?

A.-Yes, I said that. I did not say I would dance or tell anyone to get away, but that I would like to have a drink of whiskey, take a smoke, sing and say a few things.

Q.-Did you use the term "sons of bitches?"

A.-Yes, if they ask me to say something, that is what I would say.

It seems to me it was the 25th when Lynn called on Red. He went down stairs with George and was going to have him do the interpreting for him. Red was to be the interpreter for George Defender. Red brought up these sheets of paper. Then Red asked me how this affair happened down here and I told him the whole thing and we wrote it down, and he spoke about Blackhawk and I finally wrote what you see on that piece of paper which you have shown me. (Defendant exhibit "2.") Red said for me to say nothing about George Defender being in it, as people could account for where he had been from the 13th to the 18th and I had better not say anything about him. Also not to say I had got any whiskey from him, but to say I got it all from Scar Faced Charley.

Q.-Where did Red tell you all this? (Objected to as incompetent, irrelevant and immaterial. Objection overruled and exception allowed the defendant.)

A.-Upstairs in the cell. There were three cells in the jail, but we were out in the hallway passage. We went to sleep I think just about midnight. He asked me to write and I wrote about the Spicer murder.

[...]

Testimony of Philip Ireland

Philip Ireland was one of the "boys" whose confessions helped the authorities understand, or think they understood, who was involved in the Spicer murders on February 17th. Although he was perhaps a couple of years older than Paul Holy Track, he was shyer and tended to follow his friend's lead in his various confessions and testimonies. He came to be thought of as Paul Holy Track's "me-too" follower:

> My name is Philip Ireland. Live in Cannon Ball. Guess I am 20. Know the defendant, Alec Coudotte. [...]
> After returning home that night, Paul went somewhere. He returned quite late, then he said they told him that he and Philip were to take a gun

and go over to the white man's place. I asked him who said that and he said Coudotte. We slept there that night and the next morning at eight o'clock we went over to the white man's house, Spicer's. We put the gun outside the stable and Paul and I went in the house.

Then George Defender and Alec Coudotte came to Spicer's. Tied their horses to the root house. They walked up into the house, and Coudotte said in a loud voice, Paul is that you? and Paul said, yes. Then Coudotte said, is this all there is in here? Paul said, yes. Then Coudotte said, we will take our horses down into the brush and then we will do it. Later they went out.

Mrs. Spicer said, he is very drunk, and Paul said, yes. Then Mrs. Spicer wanted to know what they had said, and Paul said they wanted to get something to eat and they were through dinner so they were going home. She said, if you had told me they wanted something to eat I would have given them something.

The man went out about half an hour afterwards. We went down to the stable where Spicer was working. I helped him clean out the manure. Then Alec and George came up. There was a stall there where there was a horse standing and another stall where there was a horse standing and another stall empty. Paul, George and Alec were in the empty stall. Spicer wheeled four wheelbarrows of manure and somebody shot him. Although I did not see who it was I think I saw Paul with the gun in his hand after the shooting. I started to run, but Paul called me back. Also one of the others called me.

George struck him with the pitch fork, Coudotte hit him with the axe and I hit him with the spade. Coudotte hit him on the head more than once — more than three times. Held the axe in both hands and George and Alec laid him in the shed. The axe was the one they cut wood with. I would know the axe if I would see it. The man used it to chop away the ice. I saw Spicer use it. The axe was inside and I guess Alec got it from there. I struck Spicer with the spade twice across the neck. I guess I hit him after Alec did. Spicer said something, I don't know what, when he was shot. When I started to run away I looked back and saw him just as he fell. When he was shot he was close to the stable. I did not see very well how he fell but when I got there he was lying on his back. He fell to the right hand when he was shot.

(Witness being shown an axe, is asked to state if he can recognize it as the axe used in killing Thomas Spicer, marked state's exhibit "C," and recognized the axe, also recognized the spade that was used at the time, spade marked state's exhibit "D." Also recognized pitch fork, state's exhibit "E." The state then offered in evidence state's exhibit "C," "D," and "E," all having been testified as being used in the killing of Thomas Spicer. Witness continuing said:)

George and Alec took Thomas Spicer by the feet and drug him into the shed. He was dead at the time. The wheel barrow did not upset when Thomas Spicer fell on it. We next went into the stable and Paul wanted George to go up after the woman. George wanted Coudotte to go and he would not go. Then Coudotte wanted me to go and I would not go. Paul told me to load the gun and I did so. He went up to the house and I loaded the gun. I stood the gun up inside the stable and walked outside. Then Paul came along with the woman. He was the first.

I don't know who shot the woman. There was in the stable some cows, one bay mare, two grays. When the woman was shot [...] I was on the outside looking around. When she was coming down she bowed to me and I also bowed. They told me to cover up the man with manure so I did so using a pitch fork in doing so. The pitch fork you have there. Paul then pulled out a half-dollar flask of whiskey and drank out of it and I had some, about that much (indicating). Coudotte also drank out of the same flask. Then they said we would go to the house and kill the people.

Coudotte took the axe and Defender took the club. We went to the house. I had nothing. I stood outside. George and Coudotte went in. Stayed there quite a little while. When they were going for them I went inside and the old woman was standing on that side and I hit her. I saw there besides Alec and George and Paul, the old woman. Saw her in the kitchen just as you go in the first door. There are two rooms there.

When we had killed them all I went into both rooms. Besides Alec and Paul and George, there were two boys and a young woman there. When I first entered the room the young [woman] was on the right hand side of the chest that was there with bright handles on it — white knobs. After the people were all killed we commenced picking up articles. I got two small rings, one large one. Blue necktie and a package and Paul gave me a suit of clothes. The package was red. It opened but there was nothing in it. It was so long and so wide (indicating). It was made of thin leather. Don't know what it was used for. George got a black pair of pants, a white shirt and three neckties, a six-shooter and a pocketbook. Don't know where he got the pocketbook. Alec got a pair of blue trousers and a yellow pocketbook. One that folds. Think he got it out of one of the trunks. Did not see him get it. Saw it in his hand. He did not say anything about the things he got. He got the pants in the left hand corner of the last room. I did not notice the color of the pants. They were not real black, appeared to have little stripes. There was also taken a coat, vest, earrings, breast-pin, pencil, writing paper. I did not see where they found the earrings. Saw Paul have them after we returned home. Paul had the breastpin. Don't know where he found the handkerchief. Saw them after we returned home. There was twenty cents in coppers which I forgot and left at Paul's. No other money that I know of.

When we went to court Paul had ten dollars — court at Bismarck. He gave five dollars of it to George Defender. I saw him give it to him. Didn't see Paul get the ten dollars and don't know who gave him the money.

I was in the guard house at Fort Yates a short time after the murder. There was in the guard house at that time besides myself, Paul, George, Coudotte, Blackhawk, Lewis Agard, Peter Blue Shields. While in the guard house had a talk with Alec Coudotte about the murder. I told him Paul and I were going to tell about it and Coudotte told us to hide it. I said if we tried to hide this we would suffer for a long time for it. He said that is all right and if they find it out themselves it will be all right. Coudotte said he would give me a horse. Paul heard it.

Saw Coudotte have money while in the guard house a few times, that is all. Did not hear Paul and Coudotte talking about the money while in the guard house. In the latter part of April I made some statements to Reedy and Wells in regard to the murder. In the first statement I said there was in the murder Blackhawk, Coudotte and George Defender, just those three.

That was not the first statement I made to Reedy and Wells. In the first statement I made that the man wrote down, I said it was Blackhawk and Coudotte alone. In the second statement I said George and Coudotte was in it, and started to tell it and Mr. Wells would not believe me. I said no. I was right. The second statement that a man wrote down on the typewriter, I said Paul and myself did the murder. I wanted to tell those fellows, George and Alec were in it and Mr. Wells doubted me and he started to go, and I said why do you want to help those people? If you want to help them I will say we did it alone.

What I told in the last statement was exactly right. I told it to Mr. Armstrong. I included Frank Blackhawk and not George Defender in my first statement because I felt sorry for him, that is why I kept him out. Put Frank Blackhawk in because he was the first man to start this thing, and I said Paul and I did it alone just because I was vexed. [...]

We arrived at the Spicer house the day of the killing in the afternoon. Don't know what time we left but I guess about four. I just happened to guess that. Didn't see any watch. I did not see any watch or clock at Spicer's. Don't know whether they had one or not. I think it was about four o'clock. I think we left Spicer's house about an hour and a half before dark. Got to Paul's house before dark, stopped on the road and changed clothes, threw some things away and then walked across the river.

Don't know how far it is from Spicer's to Paul's. After we got there we ate supper. It was nearly sunset. Quite light. Wasn't dark for quite awhile after we got through eating supper. First thing we did on arriving at Paul's house was to feed the horses. Cut some wood. Cut a pile about three feet high. We were nearly drunk while we were cutting the wood.

When I saw the man come along the road at the time of the tragedy, I was outside the stable door. You could not look from the stable door and see the road towards the river. I stood on the left hand side of the door quite a little ways back from it. When I saw the man coming I was looking east. When standing facing the rising sun I am facing the east, and when looking east my right hand would be south. I now say the man was coming from the north traveling south. I told Paul there was a man coming. Paul came outside. I stayed out some time and then I went in. I don't know whether Paul went to meet the man or not. He went down that way but he didn't say anything to me. While he was gone I went in and out again. When I came out I stood on a snow pile until he got back and then we both went in the barn. That was after we had killed Mrs. Spicer. Paul was gone about one minute. There are sixty minutes in an hour. Twelve hours in a day. The same in a night. Might have been two minutes Paul was gone.

After the man had gone by and passed over the hill, was the first time went to the house after the killing of Mrs. Spicer. Could see the road along which this man passed from the house. I only heard the old lady crying inside. I hit her. Don't know whether she was weakly or strong. Never saw her walking around. I hit her on the back and she fell down.

After killing the two at the stable, Paul pulled out a fifty-cent flask and gave me about that much (indicating) and he gave me some more when leaving, and some more when we were going home on the road. That is all I had.

I know Thomas J. Reedy and Aaron C. Wells. I made a statement at the Standing Rock agency guard house, but I don't remember the date.

Q.-At that time did you or did you not say as follows?: "On the morning of the 17th of February, 1897, I started from the home of Paul Holy Track and came with him to the agency office. As nearly as I can remember it was shortly after nine o'clock when we arrived at the office. Paul asked me to go to Winona with him and we started, I think about 11 o'clock. We went northward through the timber on this side of the river until we got to a point opposite the Spicer house. When we reached the other side of the river we chased a rabbit for awhile. We then went through the timber, and when we reached the open ground Paul asked me to go to the well at the Spicer house. After reaching the well, we drank water from it and Paul asked me to sit down. We sat down on the south side within a four post enclosure about the well. While sitting there I heard a dull report, and upon looking around saw a man who had been hauling manure disappear as though he had fallen down. I then saw a man come out of the stable and drag something back into the stable, but not into the same door whence I saw him come. Shortly afterwards this man appeared again and entered the door from which I saw him come first."

A.-Yes, I think I said that.

Q.-Was this question asked you?: "Could you see the door from where you sat?" and did you answer?: "I could only see the tops of the doors. I then saw a man come from the door into which the other had just gone and start towards the house. He wore brown duck trousers."

A.-Yes.

Q.-Were you asked the following questions, and did you give the following answers? "Are you sure that he wore brown duck trousers?" Answer: "That is the way I remember it. This man entered the house and shortly afterwards went back to the stable with a woman. This woman entered that part of the stable from which the first man came, and the man who had gone to the house returned with her and followed her in. In a few moments two men came out of this same door and motioned us to come up to them. We went up to the stable and I saw Alec Coudotte standing in the door and Frank Blackhawk just inside. Frank was buttoning up his trousers. I saw the woman lying dead with her clothes up a little above the knee."

"What did Alec have in his hand?" Answer: "I do not remember. We then were asked into the stable and the four of us drank up two bottles of whiskey. The bottles held about one pint each. The three others started for the house while I remained on guard outside the stable. Blackhawk had an axe in his hand. From where I stood I could not see who entered the house first."

"Where did Blackhawk get the axe?" Answer: "I do not know but think he picked it up between the house and stable. I now remember that Blackhawk picked up the axe at the woodpile. I started for the house, and when I got part way I heard a great noise, yelling and screaming. Before entering the house I heard someone crying in Indian 'Strike. Strike.' Upon entering the house I met the old woman who was coming towards the door and at the same time she was screaming. Frank Blackhawk was standing near the inner door. He threw a stick to me and told me to strike the old woman. I took a stick and struck her across the small of the back knocking her down, when I again struck her, this time on the upper part of the arm or right shoulder. Paul now came up and hit her about the head with an axe. He struck her two or three times."

"Who else hit her besides you and Paul?" Answer: "None else besides Paul and I."

"Did she die from the effect of the blows inflicted by you and Paul?" Answer: "Yes. About this time Paul and I were asked to go out and act as a guard. We were outside quite a while when we were called in again. Coudotte, Blackhawk and Holy Track were ransacking things when we went back in. Frank then gave me two pairs of pants and a coat and vest, all of rough texture and dark color. I did not take both pairs of trousers with me upon leaving. Left one pair in the house. We all now left the house and returned to the stable. While at the stable Frank gave me one large ring, a baby's ring and a necktie. Alec Coudotte told me I must be careful and conceal the clothing, so I put it under my overcoat which I buttoned up. We then drank another small bottle of whiskey, and Alec Coudotte told me this affair must be kept a secret and nothing told to any person. Also that he would give me a horse. He did not say what kind of a horse he would give me. While Alec was cautioning me about keeping the affair secret, if we were all caught and when the worst came then was the only time to tell but not before. To this I replied, I would never tell, and with that came out of the stable. At that time a team was coming along the road. I called to the others about it and Paul came out and started towards the team. I told him not to go, but he went, but as the team did not stop he came back and we all went into the stable again. We waited until the team disappeared. This was about two o'clock."

A.-Yes, sir. I said that. [...]

(Witness here shown state's exhibit "A" for identification and asked what it is.)

A bullet. Paul gave me one like it that I loaded. It may be the same one but I don't know. Not in every respect it was round. Paul gave me one like it, and I don't know whether that is it or not.

(State's exhibit "B" shown witness and asked what it is.)

When Paul told me to load the gun I used a piece like that for wadding. The gun was fired off after that. I don't know who fired it. I loaded the gun both times the same. When Mr. Spicer was killed I put the shot in. Then afterwards loaded it again when they killed Mrs. Spicer. After they had killed Mr. Spicer, Paul went to the house after Mrs. Spicer and I loaded the gun. The first load that shot Mr. Spicer the gun was loaded by me in the brush. I was going to shoot a rabbit. The gun was loaded but Paul put the bullet in after we got to the barn. That is all Paul put in.

Paul had an overcoat that day. I don't know whether he left it at the barn when he went after Mrs. Spicer or not. Paul had the powder horn and gave it to me about two o'clock. He took the powder horn when we left.

I saw Coudotte at the Standing Rock Indian agency on February 13th. I guess it was about 11 o'clock. Saw George Defender at Spicer's house on February 17th. I am positive of that. It was about two o'clock when the man passed Spicer's house on the road. Don't know what time it was they were all killed. It must have been considerably after two o'clock when we left. Quite awhile. I guess it was half an hour after Mr. Spicer was shot before I saw the man going along the road. I set the time at which Spicer was killed at half past one. By saying in my examination that Frank was the first man started it, I meant that Paul said Frank was the man he had first talked with. I did not talk with Frank.

[...]

Testimony of Horatio M. Wilson

Wilson happened to drive past his neighbor's farm on the afternoon of February 17, just after the Spicers were murdered. He says that he saw a man in "government-issue" clothing—that is, in clothing given out on ration day to reservation Indians — and from that deduced that the man must have been an Indian. Wilson was not, however, able to make a positive identification of the man who followed him:

I reside near Winona about a mile and a half north of Thomas Spicer's. On the 17th of February I passed Thomas Spicer's driving two horses to a bob sleigh with a box on. While passing the Spicer place — before reaching there — I saw a person. At that time I was about half a mile north and saw a person walking from the barn to the house. I took it to be a man but could only see the top of his head. There was another one went from the barn and that was a man.

I did not see the person who went from the barn enter the house. The door to the house is on the east side, and I was northwest, therefore could not see. The man I saw coming from the house went in front of the barn and stood up on the manure pile. I was traveling south. As I got near the place, Spicer's place, he started from the barn to the road. It proved to be an Indian. He came to within six or seven rods of me. Wasn't carrying anything, had on government-issue clothes, overcoat and cap, one that turned up around the edge. Don't know whether it was government-issue or not.

I drove by pretty fast. I saw it was an Indian and I thought I would hurry him up a little. I thought I would make him get a move on him if he wanted to ride with me. He did get a move on but not fast enough. He went towards the road on a fast walk but did not run. He stopped about the time I got even with him. He stayed about half a minute and then returned to the manure pile from which he started. When he started he was twelve or fifteen feet, I should think, south of the stable door. When he returned to the manure pile he went to about the same spot.

There were cattle all round him. The last I saw of him when I got to the foot of the hill he was still standing there looking. I went on to Winona. I think I got to Winona about fifteen minutes of four. I had only been there a short time when the whistle blew and it blew at four o'clock at that time. There was a discussion about the time of day and I was informed that the whistle blew at four o'clock. It is near a mile and a half from Spicer's to Winona. I drove fast and it probably took me seven or eight minutes to drive it. I was not over ten minutes driving it. If the whistle blew at fifteen minutes of four, then I would say it was half past three when I passed Spicer's house. As near as I can recollect, my wife said it was about three when I left home. [...]

I don't know that I can say who it was. I can't say it was Paul Holy Track. It looked to be too small for him. He had an overcoat on and stood on the brink of the hill. Possibly it might be him. Neither he or I said anything. When he returned he went back as fast as he had come.

[...]

Testimony of John Blue Boy

Blue Boy saw Paul Holy Track and Philip Ireland, both acting drunk, crossing the river not long after the Spicers were murdered:

I live outside of the agency at Fort Yates. I know where Paul Holy Track lives. I heard of the Spicer murder on Thursday the next day after it was committed. I saw Paul Holy Track and Philip Ireland the Wednesday the murder is supposed to have occurred. Saw them down at the river. I was taking my horses down to water. Previous to that while taking my horses down I saw two men on the ice coming towards me. I afterwards ascertained who these two were. After they came off the river they came close to where I was. They were about three steps off the road when I went by them. They were Holy Track and Standing Bear or Philip Ireland. Holy Track had on an issue overcoat, black hat. I didn't see him carrying anything. He might have had something under his overcoat but he had it buttoned up so I could not see. Philip Ireland had a gun along and a horn to carry powder in swung across his shoulder. I don't know what was tied to the horn but there was something tied to the two ends which were swung over his shoulder. I think they were drunk. When they were going over the ice they were staggering. They went apart and then came together, and that made me think they were drunk. I didn't say anything to them.

[...]

5. Trial

Testimony of Patrick Yellow Lodge

Patrick Yellow Lodge was one of several Indians who saw Paul Holy Track and Philip Ireland together around the time of the murders. He testified that he had seen Paul heading off to Winona to buy whiskey the day before the Spicer murders. He said that the day after the murders the two had shown him some of the pieces of clothing and jewelry they had apparently taken from the Spicer home after the murders:

> I didn't know on the day the Spicer murder was committed, but I heard of it on Thursday. I heard that it happened the day before that, on Wednesday. I know Paul Holy Track and Philip Ireland. I saw them Tuesday the day before the Wednesday on which the murder was committed. [...] I asked him [Paul Holy Track] where he was going and he said we are going across the river, and I asked him whereabout they were going and he said to the store across the river. I asked what the were going there for and he said I am going over there to buy whiskey. [...]
> Joseph Twin told me about the murder. Paul and Philip came to our house on Thursday the day after the murder. They did not tell me anything about the murder, but they had two rings, a coat and vest, breast-pin and handkerchief, which Paul showed me.

Testimony of Charles Welch

The prosecutor called to the stand Charles Welch, who said that he had seen Alec Coudotte and George Defender the evening of the murders heading towards Alec Coudotte's home. He sounded pretty uncertain about it, though:

> Q.-Do you remember on the 17th of February last of seeing the defendant, Alec Coudotte?
> A.-I do.
> Q.-Will you state where and at what time upon that day?
> A.-It was in the evening after six o'clock. I think it was dusk. I could not swear positively it was Alec, but I took it for Alec and George Defender.
> Q.-Where did you see them?
> A.-Going towards Alec's house on the back road.
> Q.-Near what place?
> A.-Near the mule corral. They were riding along and stopped at the end of the corral and one got off his horse, and I noticed one of the horses had a white face. I should judge I was about two hundred yards from him. [...] Could not say positively that it was the defendant. After we heard of the murder I mentioned it. Not positive whether it was them or not. I mentioned it to the agent Thursday or Friday after the murder. I think Friday.

Testimony of Aaron C. Wells

Wells was the "boss farmer" on the Standing Rock reservation. He was part Mohawk. As boss farmer, his job was to teach the Standing Rock Indians about farming: preparing the soil, fertilizing, planting, weed control, harvesting. Because he had direct contact with many Indian households, he had a pretty good idea what was happening around the reservation. He served as a kind of reservation detective, and was from the start closely involved with the investigation of the Spicer murders. His testimony dealt primarily with Alec Coudotte's suicide attempt:

> I reside on the Standing Rock Indian reservation, northern part. I hold the official position of farmer in charge of a district. The farmer has police power. I am acquainted with the defendant.
> [...]
> As to the defendant's physical condition at that time, he was not well. He had tried to stab himself, tried to commit suicide — that is what he told me. He told me he had stabbed himself.
> Q.-Did he tell you that he had tried to commit suicide?
> A.-Yes, sir. (Defense moved to strike out answer. Motion denied and exception granted defendant.)
> Q.-Tell all he said about that.
> A.-He said he was afraid they would bring him out guilty in this crime, and he felt badly, and thought he would commit suicide and it was for that intention that he stabbed himself. I am quite positive that this was stated in the presence of Mr. McLaughlin, Corrigan, and Reedy. He stabbed himself in the stomach. I saw the stab wound. [...]
> I tried to make him understand that if he was guilty — my intention was to find out the facts as he understood them. At the time, of course, we were not certain that he was guilty. I wished him to understand it would be better to tell the truth. He said he thought he would not recover from the wound, and it was for that reason he would tell the truth. That statement was made I think in the presence of McLaughlin and Reedy. [...]
> I have been very active in tracing the perpetrators of this crime, and have been constantly on the lookout for anything that would pertain to the conviction of any person who committed this crime. Have spent a good deal of time in the last three months on this case. I had police power on the reservation, authorized to arrest without a warrant any Indian I might find on the reservation and take him to the agency for any offence I might see fit.
> I was the cause of Paul Holy Track's arrest, but did not arrest. I think there is a reward for the conviction of these murderers, but I have not any promise of it. I have not looked after the reward. I am an officer on the reservation. When I find an Indian doing wrong, I tell him to do right. They understand they are to obey me, that when I speak to them I speak with authority. [...]
> He had attempted to commit suicide before I talked with him, and told me he thought he would not recover from the wound. He believed he was going to die and it was under these circumstances he made the confession. Though expecting to die he at no time and in no manner said he had anything to do with the commission of the crime. He denied that portion. He said he did not commit this crime. I think McLaughlin, Corrigan and Reedy questioned him a little. I don't know whether any of the persons

stated to him they believed he would recover or not. The confession was made without any inducement being held out to him.

Testimony of Dr. Ralph Ross

Dr. Ross was employed by the Standing Rock agency to see to the health of the Indians living there. He took the stand again later in the trial to defend his attempt to provide an alibi to Alec Coudotte, but in this first appearance he was questioned mostly about Alec Coudotte's self-inflicted wounds. We are left to speculate about why he lied to the prisoner about how dangerous the wound was:

> I reside at Fort Yates, Standing Rock Indian reservation. I am the agency physician. I was in Williamsport on the 14th of April last, at which time I was called upon to visit the defendant Coudotte. After being called I was told he had stabbed himself. I found a wound about half an inch deep and between a quarter and half an inch long in the abdomen, right below which there was a little one a quarter of an inch long just through the skin. The large one looked as though it was through the abdominal wall, and as though it had been made about twelve hours before I saw it. I saw it I think along in the evening after dark, of the 14th of April. I don't think it was a very dangerous wound.
>
> I stated I did not think it was dangerous, but I did not tell Coudotte so. At the time I saw it was oozing a dark blood a little. It had been covered with tobacco. He had a handkerchief tied around him. I took it off and it bled quite a little bit. It was swollen. I didn't probe it. It was made with some sharp instrument like a knife. I believe I said that peritonitis might happen. I thought it possibly might happen, but did not think it would happen. I told the defendant it was a dangerous and serious wound, although really I did not think so. [...]
>
> I think the defendant was under the impression that it was dangerous. At the time I dressed the wound the sheriff was there and I think Mr. Livermore. I should think the sheriff might have heard what I said to him. The sheriff and I had talked it over. Think it was understood I was to tell Coudotte it was a dangerous wound. I do not think now it punctured the abdominal wall. I talked to the defendant in Indian. [...]
>
> The first time I dressed the wound I did not say anything about its being dangerous. Next time when I said it was dangerous, Dr. Muench was there. I think I said it was a pretty dangerous wound. No one translated this into the Indian language. I don't think he said anything. Would not swear he understood it. I think the last time I saw it was the evening of the 15th. It — the wound — was better.

[...]

Testimony of Harry McLaughlin

Harry McLaughlin, who served as translator during the trial of Alec Coudotte, was also asked to serve as an expert witness. He was the son of

James McLaughlin, the previous agent at Standing Rock, and was part Indian himself (through his mother, Marie McLaughlin). Because of his long and intimate knowledge of Indian ways and language, he was asked to testify about the probable causes for Alelc Coudotte's attempted suicide:

> I live at the Standing Rock Indian agency. Have for fourteen years. Am a son of Major McLaughlin who has been the Indian agent at Standing Rock. Previous to that I lived at Devils Lake on an Indian reservation. Lived there ten years or a little over. Lived among the Indians all my life, but about three years. Am acquainted with the habits, customs and manners of the Indians and talk their language. Have been engaged in business which brings me in contact with them. Have been Indian trader. That is, I keep a store at which they trade. Have also acted as interpreter for my father. I am well acquainted with the habits and customs of the Indians.
>
> Q.-State whether or not there is any habit, custom or predisposition among the Indians as a rule, to do anything in particular when they are confined either for grave or trivial offences? (Question objected to by the plaintiff as incompetent, irrelevant and immaterial. Objection overruled.)
>
> A.-There is.
>
> Q.-Please state what it is. (Same objection. Objection overruled.)
>
> A.-If an Indian is put in the guard house for any little offense I have known them to cut themselves, and try to commit suicide in many different ways. That seems to be a predisposition among them when in confinement.
>
> Q.-Where they are confined for any supposed offense, and where they commit injury to themselves, is it considered among those acquainted with the Indians, their habits and customs, as any evidence of their guilt of the offense with which they are charged? (Question objected to by the plaintiff. Objection sustained and exception granted the defendant.)
>
> A.-I have frequently known of Indians attempting suicide because they were in confinement. I talk the Indian language. I was present at a conversation with Coudotte in the Emmons County jail. He spoke in my presence in relation to his attempt to commit suicide. I think Mr. Wells asked him why he did it, and he said he could not stand to be confined, and he would just as soon be dead as to have to stay in there and stand the confinement. This was in Wells's presence and so he could have heard it. [...]
>
> Could not say the number of Indians I have seen in confinement. I would say from five hundred to a thousand. Majority of them would attempt to but not succeed. I don't believe that I know of any succeeding. As to how many I know of mutilating themselves, I know a majority of them always attempted something of the kind. I could not say whether or not it is a trait to mutilate themselves rather than to attempt to commit suicide. I know they have all tried it and lots of times if they had not been found out in time they would have succeeded. I am pretty sure Frank Blackhawk has been confined as long as Coudotte. I know that Paul Holy Track and Philip Ireland have been confined a considerable length of time;

also George Defender but not so long as the others. Don't know of any difference between the different tribes as to this trait.

Q.-Do you know whether there is any difference between Indians and white men in regard to this trait.

A.-Yes, indeed.

Q.-As a rule the white men succeed and the Indian does not? Is not that so as to suicide during confinement? (Objected to by the plaintiff as immaterial. Objection overruled and exception granted to the defendant.)

A.-I don't know about that. [...] I have not heard of Indians killing themselves that I remember because they have been found out in time in order to save them. The method they generally adopt is hanging or stabbing themselves. That is about the only two ways I know of. He is found out in that time quicker than the white man. I do not think that of the Indians that have been confined in the guard house in the last two months any of them have attempted to commit suicide except in this case. I would not consider it an exceptional and out of the ordinary trait for Alec Coudotte to attempt to commit suicide when he had been confined less than two months, and during that time had been at liberty some of the time.

I do not consider this an exceptional trait because it is so common among the Indians. An Indian may be confined two days and try it. I have not kept track of how many were confined in the guard house in the last two months, but I should say there had been over twenty, none of whom have attempted to commit suicide that I know of. I would not like to guess at what proportion of the Indians have been in the guard house in the last fifteen years proportionate to the whole population. It is one of the traits of the Indians when they have committed murder to commit suicide on the spot; that is in cases where murder is committed for revenge. It is not a fact that those who commit suicide or attempt it are confined under serious charges as a rule. I think there is a slight difference between late years and former years. They are not so apt now as formerly to attempt to commit suicide. The trait still sticks to them but not in so great proportions. I could not say whether the trait is the same in the half-breeds and wholebreeds or not.

[...]

Testimony of John W. Cramsie

John Cramsie was named Indian agent at Standing Rock in 1895 when James McLaughlin left the post to take up a position in the Indian service in Washington, D.C. Cramsie was criticized by many people for his handling of the investigation following the Spicer murders. Feeling that it was his duty to protect his wards from the angry white settlers who wanted to send local police onto the reservation in search of evidence and revenge, he at first refused to let them onto Indian lands, preferring to let his own Indian police handle the investigation without outside interference. His defensiveness was evident in the way he gave his testimony:

I am Indian agent at Standing Rock reservation, North Dakota. Remember the time Thomas Spicer was said to have been killed, Wednesday, February 17th. I was called upon by some parties to go over and assist in the search. I am pretty certain that was on Saturday they went over. I left for Washington the next day. I was at the house where the murder was committed. I was not in the timber at the time. I was at Mr. Spicer's house. Thirty or forty people had been all over the premises before I got there.

I went for the purpose of discovering if there was any evidence of the crime having been committed by Indians. I took two of the smartest Indian boys to assist me and sent for our chief of police who went over there. The Indian boys were High Eagle and William Burke. Standing Soldier also went and I left him there. He was there trying to ferret out the crime. The reason I took them over was I know they could take a track and follow it. There had been so many tracks I was anxious for them to use what skill they had tracking. I instructed them to take a large circle and see if there was any tracks leading to or from the house, which they did. [...]

I don't know if any of the police went over on Saturday. Don't know who applied to me for the police to go over. It was on ration day and I was very busy. At the time I was at Spicer's I examined the house closely; so did Standing Soldier and the other Indians. After the crime was discovered, before the bodies were removed by the coroner and doctor, I was under the impression the crime had not been committed by an Indian, but after I learned of the nature of their wounds there were evidences and circumstances that would make me willing to swear the crime had been committed by an Indian.

I know the way an Indian is in the habit of loading his gun. They load with a small charge of powder and a small charge of shot. They usually get very close to their game and it requires only a small charge of powder or shot. They are in the habit of having bullets, carry them in their pocket, and if they see large game they roll a bullet in on top of the load of shot. I was satisfied that if the charge had been shot into Mr. Spicer's body as it would have been loaded by a white man, the bullet would have went through his body, as they would have loaded with a charge of powder sufficient to put the bullet through his body at close range. The Indian's charge would have had about the effect that the shooting of Spicer had. I did not learn of Spicer's being shot in the back until after he had been dressed for burial, and that satisfied me an Indian had committed the crime.

Q.-What steps did you take on the reservation to ferret out and ascertain who the guilty parties were? (Objected to as improper cross examination by the defendant. Objection overruled and exception granted.)

A.-We have a captain of police, Mr. Reedy. I told him to call to his assistants, the policemen of the reservation, and any others he had confidence in that would work on this case, without making any particular noise or display, and to use all means in his powers to ferret out who the parties were that committed the murder; to be very careful and do it slyly, and excite no suspicion in their minds that we suspected they committed the crime.

I did not tell anybody that I supposed it was Indians who did it because I did not want to arouse their suspicion for I was satisfied if they had taken the clothing, jewelry and other things from the house they said was missing, it would be but a short time till we discovered it if we worked on it quietly. I told Mr. Reedy to go at it in this way. That was on Thursday. Friday we could not do much. Saturday was ration day and a very busy day.

Then I heard there was a man from Winona they suspected. That was the man who had visited Spicer's house to buy a horse. They gave me his name. On my way to Bismarck I stopped at Mr. Wells's place and told him I had learned that a man had been there to buy a horse, and I thought the young woman that was killed had put up a fight, and for him to assist Mr. Reedy in any way he could. Mr. Wells did so and sent for this man but found it was a mistake. This man was not the man that was at the house. He told where he was all the time. I went to Washington and did not return for some time.

About three weeks after my return I learned what steps had been taken to ferret out the murderers. They had some little clues that did not amount to much. It was not long after my return that we got a clue I thought was worth following. Any clue we did get was run down, until finally we discovered that Paul Holy Track had been seen with a suit of citizen's clothes on and that he had shown a ring to an Indian. That was the first positive evidence we had. The Indian described the ring. I then sent for and arrested Paul Holy Track and Philip Ireland and confined them in separate cells as soon as I found this clue.

Q.-Was Coudotte arrested before that time?

A.-That was done while I was away. I understood he was arrested for killing a beef. Mr. Reedy was instructed to send out and get anybody he wanted. I understood he was arrested for killing an animal and selling beef in Winona. On my return from Washington I said at Bismarck I did not think the Indians had committed the crime. I said it all the time for the purpose I have explained. I was not expressing my real opinion at the time. I heard Coudotte was arrested and released, and re-arrested. I sent him as a witness before the United States grand jury at Bismarck.

[...]

Further Testimony of Dr. Ralph Ross

Dr. Ross was called to the stand once again, this time not to talk about Alec Coudotte's self-inflicted wound, but to explain and defend his having provided Coudotte an alibi by stating that he had seen him at his — Coudotte's — mother's house on the afternoon of February 17th, when the Spicer murders were taking place. The testimony is crucial, for of course if Coudotte was known to have been elsewhere, then he could not have participated in the murders at the Spicer farm in Winona. The prosecutor, Armstrong, questioned Dr. Ross closely in an effort to challenge his testimony. Armstrong was especially skeptical about the sudden discovery of a notebook in which Dr. Ross had made a notation about visiting Alec Coudotte's mother on February 17th, but the notation makes no mention of Alec Coudotte's having been present during that visit:

> I reside at Standing Rock Indian agency, North Dakota. I am a graduate of the University of Georgetown, Washington, D.C., medical department. Am a regular practicing physician. Have been for six years. I am employed by the government on the Standing Rock Indian agency as agency doctor. I remember there was a dance at the agency in the month of February. It was on Tuesday night the 16th. I know Alec Coudotte. I saw him on the 16th day of February in front of my office. He asked me to come to his house and see his mother.
>
> I know where he lives. It is between three and three and a half miles, a little bit southwest — more south than west — of the agency. I should judge it was about five o'clock in the afternoon of Tuesday when I saw him. On the next day, Wednesday the 17th, I went to his house. I cannot remember the exact time of day but it was sometime between two and three o'clock. I drove there with a pair of horses and a sleigh. It wouldn't take me over half an hour I think to go there. Would arrive there about three or a little after, I think. I remained there about half an hour.
>
> When I got to Coudotte's I found Alec Coudotte, his wife and child and mother. His mother was sick and I went to see her. I had a talk with her. Alec partially interpreted for her. I can talk a little Sioux but not very much, and he can talk some English. I am positive that this man here (indicating) was the man that acted as my interpreter on the 17th day of February last. I should think I left there between half past three and four. I went from there directly home. I made a written memorandum of this visit which I have here. (Witness hands book to Mr. Stevens.)
>
> The book you hold in your hand is just a memorandum of the distance I traveled with my team during January, February and a part of March. I lost it towards the last of March and did not keep it up any more.
>
> Q.-I see on the first page under the date of Sunday, November 1st, 1896, written "January 7, 1897, Fort Yates to St. Elizabeth's — 48 miles." Tell what that means.
>
> A.-I must have called at St. Elizabeth's that day. It was a school [at] Oak Creek about that far from the agency. I drove that far in one day and put it down.
>
> Q.-I will ask you to examine the book for February 17th, please, and read what you have there written. When did you write that?
>
> A.-I wrote that the night I returned or the next morning. I am not positive which.
>
> Q.-Please read it.
>
> A.-"February 17th to Alec Coudotte's and back, six miles."
>
> Q.-What does it mean?
>
> A.-It means I went to Alec Coudotte's that day. I called the distance six miles. Must have been about seven but I called it six. In summertime it is six miles. (Book admitted in evidence, marked defendant's exhibit "3." Narrative continued.)

5. Trial

By the book I see on January 8th I was at St. Elizabeth's. The 23rd I drove from McLaughlin's ranch to the agency. If I had not driven the team I drive I would not have put it down in this book. If I had gone without a team I might have made a memorandum of my visit but I would not have put it down in this book. I am positive that I made the memorandum on February the 17th or the morning of the 18th, 1897, and that it records the fact, and that Alec Coudotte at his own house on February 17th acted as my interpreter in talking with his mother. I am pretty sure it was between half past three and four o'clock and Coudotte was there. In coming from Alec's house to the agency or to Winona I think I would take the same road most of the way. Only a broken path in winter. If Alec Coudotte followed me I did not see him. I think I would if he had been very close.

Q.-When did you find out you had this memorandum?

A.-I found it out a week ago Friday. Until that time I was not positive of it. I did not tell Armstrong on or about the 22nd day of April that I had seen the memorandum. I deny telling him I had seen the memorandum. I don't deny telling Mr. Armstrong at that time that I thought I was at Alec Coudotte's that day. I may possibly have told him that I could not remember seeing Coudotte. I was not sure I saw him there at that time because I was then under the impression it was the second or possibly the third visit I was there. I knew the first visit this year he was there, but I was under the impression it was the second or third visit I made on the 17th of February.

The reason I now swear from the memorandum that that was the day I saw Coudotte is because that was my first visit there this year. I did not know that when I was talking with Armstrong. I have the other visit down there (indicating). I can't remember the conversation I had with Mr. Armstrong. I know I saw Alec there the first visit. I can recall the first visit. I could recall the first visit before I saw the memorandum but I didn't know the date. He was not there the second time I went. He was then I think in jail.

I went to see his sick child who died, the exact date I don't know. I have not got it down, the child was not dead when I was there. Week after this visit was made I knew Alec Coudotte was arrested. Knew that Shier and Armstrong were over there investigating Alec Coudotte, and I said nothing to them about it. Knew that he was arrested and having a preliminary trial April 14th. Sat in Armstrong's office and heard Mr. Wells and Harry McLaughlin interpret a statement Coudotte made at that time. In that statement I believe he made certain statements about me being at his house on Wednesday afternoon. I didn't say anything about it, wasn't sure that I was there at that time.

Since that time my servant girl found this book in among some old papers in the wood shed. This book is one used for 1897. It is really an 1896 book but was used in 1897. I omitted to put in the year. I remember Armstrong was over at Fort Yates soon after the murder. I don't know the exact date. There several days. Armstrong and Shier. Conversed with both of them frequently about the Spicer murder. Knew that Coudotte and Blackhawk were placed under arrest for the murder. This was a week or so after I had made the visit. There was nothing to call it to my mind that I was down there on the 17th. It escaped from me entirely. I never thought of the fact. Did not know what I was called for in the middle of April. I think Alec was placed under arrest some time during the week following the murder.

I talked about the murder with different parties. Didn't suggest to anybody that on the 17th, the time the murder was supposed to have taken place, that I was at Coudotte's. If you, Armstrong, on the 22nd and 23rd of April were again at Winona and Fort Yates, I think I saw you there, the time the boys made their confession. Talked with you at different times during the week. I think I used this language to you in telling you that I had been to Coudotte's that afternoon: "but I don't know whether Alec was there or not." I told you I had thought about the matter but had not found my record at that time. That is all the record I have during January, February and a part of March of my outside visits with my team. That is all I kept it for. I have a record of each patient visited but don't put down the date. I sometimes do. I don't think I did in this case. [...]

I asked you at Fort Yates what they expected me up here for and you told me Alec Coudotte said I was at his house that day. Then I attempted to find this book but could not find it until very recently. I think I told you that I had been to Alec's but did not know whether Alec was there or not. I think you asked me and I think I told you I was not positive of it at that time. That was before I found the book.

Q.-You told Mr. Armstrong you did not know whether Alec was there on your first visit or not?

A.-I told Mr. Armstrong distinctly that if it was my first visit Alec was at home. I remember that. I was under the impression that I had made more visits to his house than I had until I found this book. I had made so many visits around there I had the impression I had made more visits to his house than I really had.

In our conversation I am pretty sure there was reference to more than one visit. I didn't know myself how many visits I had made. As I found my records there on March 1st and the only other visit I made there was on the 17th of February.

Q.-Have you been in Winona since the 22nd of April in the store of Mr. McCrory, and in conversation with different persons there have you made statements concerning this murder, and the defendant and others? (Question objected to as not definite enough. Objection of defendant overruled, and exception granted.)

A.-I don't remember that at all. I don't remember anything about that. I don't think I have.

I was in Winona with Dr. Cochrane one day. I found him there in the store. In there something like five minutes. Think there was a general talk there at the time and I have forgotten what about. Don't recall anything that was said. I don't recall that Alec Coudotte or Frank Blackhawk were there mentioned in reference to the Spicer murder. I might have made remarks about it myself, but I don't recall them. My memory is fair. I don't have any trouble in remembering things a week.

The entries in that book represent the drives I took with my team. No one drove my team but myself. Every entry represents my individual riding.

Q.-You think your memory is fair, and yet a week after the murder you could not remember that you had been at Alec Coudotte's on the day of the murder because you did not look at your book, and you now say you can remember when you look at your book and the only entry in it is February 17th. Alec Coudotte's six miles, and you said then you had been to Alec Coudotte's but could not remember seeing him. Please explain this. (Question objected to as incompetent, improper cross examination and futher assuming that the witness has heretofore made statements which he has not made. Objection overruled and exception granted defendant.)

A.-I never stated at that time I had been to Alec Coudotte's. My attention was not called to the matter, and I don't know what other kind of answer you wanted.

I think my memory is fair. The book was sent to me by the people who manufactured it. I have a number of them. The book was lost from about the time of the last date in it, March 20th I think, until the 28th of May. I did not start another book. Only kept this record to March 17th. I have plenty of other books like it. The reason I quit keeping the book is because I lost this one. I know this is [my book] by my writing. I suppose that is the only way I know it. I know I know my writing.

I remember close around the dates mentioned in the book. Monday the 15th I can remember. I can remember that date without the book, and I can remember the 17th I was at Coudotte's. I remembered it but not until my attention was called to the fact that I was there. I would not know it from this book if somebody substituted my handwriting, I saw that is my handwriting and the same as that of March 1st. If I have spelled one name "E. C." and the other Alex it was probably done hurriedly. I don't know why I spelled the name in two different ways. It is both the same handwriting. I wouldn't swear they were both written with the same pencil. I made the entry the evening of February 17th in my house. Can't swear to the exact room or whether I was standing or sitting, but I remember writing it that evening. I started quite early the next morning, and did not write it the next morning. I think that is the only way I remember I wrote it the night before. I don't remember the exact occurrence. I am sure I did it the night before or next morning. [...]

I am as sure as I could be of anything that that is the book I kept from the first of January up to the time stated. It is all in my writing. I am positive the leaf which records the 17th of February was in the book up to the time you tore it out yesterday, and that the writing thereon was done either on the 17th of February or the morning of the 18th. My attention was first called to my being down there by Mr. Armstrong after the April hearing — the first it had been suggested to me. Remember no other associations of the case previous to that time. I suppose he made the inquiry to find out if it was so. I think at that time I told him that I had been down there but I was not certain whether it was my first visit or my subsequent visit. Told him I kept a book in relation to the matter and I would hunt it up. I did hunt the book up. Found it on the 28th of May. Had a talk with Mr. Lynn about it. Showed him the book and explained it to him.

I think I told Armstrong that I had a book that was lost and would look for it. That is a decided impression of mine. I am positive that I told Armstrong about the first and second visits.

[...]

Testimony of Spencer Chilcot

In an effort to undermine Dr. Ross's testimony that he had seen Alec Coudotte at his mother's house on February 17th, the prosecutor called as a witness a man who testified that he had heard Dr. Ross say, shortly after the Spicer murders, that he could not provide an alibi for Alec Coudotte:

> I live near LaGrace, Campbell County, South Dakota. Know Dr. Ross. He was down to my place in Campbell County I think the 14th. My wife was sick, we sent for a doctor and he came. While we were at dinner the conversation naturally turned to this tragedy, the Spicer murder. Several heard that Coudotte was going to prove an alibi by the doctor. He said, "He can't prove it by me." He said he was there on two occasions, but it was his impression he was not there on that particular day, that he would not swear positively he was not, that he couldn't prove an alibi for him was the purport of it.

[...]

Testimony of Henry A. Armstrong

In an unusual move, defense attorney Stevens called to the stand the prosecuting attorney in order to question him concerning his skepticism about the testimony of Dr. Ross. He got Armstrong to admit that he had lied to Dr. Ross when he told Dr. Ross that Alec Coudotte had told him that he saw the doctor at his mother's on February 17th. Armstrong's motive in telling that particular lie is not clear. Armstrong's reference to Moses Martin was to a relative of Alec Coudotte who had testified about the whereabouts of Alec Coudotte three days before the murders. I have not included Moses Martin's testimony here because it had no direct bearing on the Spicer murders:

> I am state's attorney of Emmons County, and as such made an investigation in connection with the Spicer murder. I heard the testimony of Dr. Ross. It is true he had a conversation with me about being at Alec Coudotte's house. He said nothing to me about a book. I would say here that at the time I spoke to him I told him for the purpose of ascertaining what he knew that he said that he, Dr. Ross, was at Alec's place on the 17th. He said, "yes, I was there but I don't know whether Alec was there or not. I don't know whether I saw Alec or not." I am not certain as to his exact words. I asked him the question simply for the purpose of ascertain-

ing whether or not he was there on the afternoon of the 17th. Dr. Ross had been at Williamsport on the 14th of April. After he had gone to Fort Yates I saw him there. I made a statement to Dr. Ross that Alec said that he, the doctor, was at Alec's house on the afternoon of the 17th. He did not say anything about his first visit or second visit. I know Moses Martin who testified in this case. He informed me that Alec Coudotte was not at William Coudotte's on the 14th of April. I had heard that Alec claimed that Dr. Ross was there near that time, and I fixed in on the 17th to test whether or not Dr. Ross was there.

I do say I told Dr. Ross that Alec claimed he, Dr. Ross, was down there on the 17th of February.
Q.-You did a little lying yourself.
A.-Stretched it that far.
Q.-Did Alec tell you that he was there?
A.-He did not.
[...]

Testimony of William Coudotte

The defense attorney called to the stand Alec Coudotte's brother William. William's testimony goes on for several pages, but since it has to do mostly with his brother's whereabouts several days before the Spicer murders, I reproduce here only small portions of it. Its relevance for Alec is that it explains why he had blood on his pants and what happened to the pants. It also corroborates his mother's sickness and confirms that Alec was with his mother, at least on the Sunday before the Spicer murders:

> I live at Oak Creek, twenty-four miles south of the Standing Rock Indian agency. I am a brother of the defendant, who lives four miles south of the agency. In going from my house to the agency I pass quite a ways from his house. On the 13th of February I was at home, there was also there at that time Alec, Grey Eagle, Moses Martin, my wife, Alec's wife, and my father and mother. [...]
>
> On Saturday the 13th day of February I killed a beef which belonged to my father. I had to go to the agent to get the permit on Saturday, February 13th. Alec Coudotte was with me when I got the permit, and the animal was killed not half an hour afterwards. There was present at the time the beef was killed Alec Coudotte, Moses Martin and Grey Eagle. [...]
>
> I got a pair of pants from Alec Coudotte that had blood on them. A pair of blue pants. Got them from the stable. Got some corn also on the 25th of February when I went after the sleigh. Took the pants and put them on over my other pants. They were just like these (indicating). When I sent to his house I had a pair of drawers and a pair of issue pants on. Nobody told me to take them. I thought they were mine. I have them at home yet. I have not washed the pants out. Wore them to the agency just as they were. They had some blood spots on them and offal marks. Pieces of hay frozen on the pants down on the front of the leg. I haven't washed them since but

> I dusted them up. At the time of high water I used them crossing the creek and there is no blood on them now. [...]
>
> Alec Coudotte left my house on Sunday the 14th day of February. With him was my mother, Alec's wife, and three children. They left in a sleigh I think about nine o'clock. [...]
>
> The agent gives permits to kill beef. My mother was sick at the time we killed the beef. We didn't have anything to eat. [...] The steer was a two-year-old and had two horns. Killed him about three o'clock. I caught the steer and Alec killed it with an axe. Alec and I skinned it with issue butcher knives. [...] My mother was sick was the reason the judge gave me permission to kill the steer and Mother went with Alec.
>
> [...]

Testimony of Thomas Martin

The defense called Thomas Martin to the stand. Martin had nothing to say about Alec Coudotte, the man on trial, but much to say about what George Defender was doing at the time of the murders. Defense attorney R. N. Stevens apparently wanted to undermine the credibility of Paul Holy Track and Philip Ireland by showing that they could not have been right about George Defender's role in the murders. He hoped to suggest, by implication, that they were probably wrong also in what they said about Alec Coudotte's role:

> I live thirty-five miles from Standing Rock agency, south, and south of the big school. I know George Defender and where he lives. Lives north of me and south of the big school. [...] Monday was the 15th, Tuesday was the 16th, and Wednesday was the 17th day of February. It was the 17th day of February, 1897, I am speaking of. My sister, brother, and I stopped at George Defender's who is now under arrest in connection with the Spicer murder. We arrived at George's place about 12 o'clock. George's wife and Smell the Bear's wife were there. We stayed there about half an hour. Had dinner. Before we went away Charging Eagle came. We had been there about a quarter of an hour before they came. He arrived before we had finished dinner. Before we left George and Leo Smell the Bear came. We had been there about a quarter of an hour before they came. They came from the south with a load of wood on a sleigh. [...] We arrived at George Defender's about four o'clock where we remained all night. We found there George, Leo Smell the Bear. Charging Eagle came a little later than we did. George wasn't doing anything. Left there about seven o'clock next morning. George was not away from the place from the time we got there until we left next morning at seven o'clock. I can swear positively that George Defender was at his house between twelve and one o'clock and at his house at about five o'clock in the evening, and the rest of the night of the 17th of February until seven o'clock the morning of the 18th.

5. Trial

Testimony of Charging Eagle

The defense called Joseph Charging Eagle to the stand to verify Thomas Martin's testimony about the whereabouts of George Defender on the day of the murders. The prosecutor in cross-examination challenged Charging Eagle's statements by asking him many detailed questions about his visit to George Defender's house. That visit, we should recall, had happened four months earlier:

> I reside on the Indian reservation south of the agency. George Defender lives twenty miles from the agency. I live about fourteen miles south of him. Services were held at Father Martin's church on the 14th of February. I was there but I left right away. The 16th of February I remember was stormy in the afternoon. I went after cattle on Wednesday. A little after noon I went to George Defender's house. Leo Smell the Bear and wife and George Defender and wife were there. Besides those there was Thomas Martin and his brother and sister at the house. I remained there about half an hour. By George Defender I mean the man who is now in jail connected with the Spicer murder. I saw George Defender there. Left there about one o'clock. I was out hunting for my cattle. Returned to his house about six o'clock, after sun down. At that time George and his wife, Leo and his wife, and Tom Martin and his brother were there. Slept at George's house that night. George Defender could not have been at Thomas Spicer's house two and three-fourths miles from Fort Yates at any time from twelve o'clock on the 17th of February until the morning of the 18th without my knowing it. At one o'clock on Wednesday, February 17th, he was at his house. Also at six o'clock in the evening, twenty miles south of the agency. [...]
>
> (Cross examination.)
>
> Saw him half an hour, maybe less. Don't remember anything we talked about. We were in the house talking and I forget what we said. Said nothing to me. May have said something in my hearing but I don't remember what it was. [...] Did not see anybody to tell I was hunting the steer from the morning I left home on the 17th until that night, except I may have mentioned it when I first got to George Defender's, and if I did that I have forgotten it. I was hunting for my steer and came there to his house, and I don't remember the conversation we had that day. Don't remember any other words we used except just "how" and I said "how."
>
> [...]

Testimony of Mrs. George Defender

The defense called on Mary Defender to verify the statements made by Thomas Martin and Joseph Charging Eagle. Again, since her husband George Defender was not yet on trial, the defense attorney called her to help establish the whereabouts of her husband and by doing so to suggest to the jury that if Paul Holy Track and Philip Ireland were wrong in implicating George Defender as being at the Spicer home at the time of the murders, they by implication they were perhaps wrong about Alec Coudotte's being there also:

I am the wife of George Defender. I know where the mission school is. Know Thomas and Frank Martin and where they reside.

In going from Thomas Martin's house to the mission school they pass our house. I know Thomas Martin's sister and Mad Bear's youngest son were at my house as they came back from the mission. I saw her again a few days afterwards, with her brother Frank and Tom coming from home taking her back to school. Had dinner at our house. That night after they had eaten at my house they stayed there. There was there that night George and myself, Leo Smell the Bear and his wife, Tom and Frank Martin and Joseph Charging Eagle. From the noon hour to the next morning of that day that Thomas and Frank Martin came and stopped to dinner, George Defender was at our house. Could not have been away at any time as far as Fort Yates. [...] Day before the Martin boys came there, George Defender, my husband, was at home, and at home most of the day before that. [...] George stayed at home all the next day. I am positive of it. If he had gone away I would have known it, but he was at home.

[...]

Testimony of Charles White Bull

Alec Coudotte's defense attorneys were eager to explain how their client had damaged his left hand. They did not want jurors to assume that he had damaged it while murdering the Spicers on February 17th. Charles White Bull's testimony was important because it indicated that Alec Coudotte's hand had been wounded the day before the murders:

I live at Grand River thirty-six miles south of the Standing Rock agency. Have known Alec Coudotte twelve years. On the 16th of February I saw Alec at his home about six o'clock. I went first to my father's and then to Coudotte's. That was on Tuesday. Alec was not there when I got there. Alec arrived there about ten minutes after I got there. It was after dark when he and I both got there. Dark about six o'clock. Nobody came with him. Don't know whether he had been away on horseback or on foot. Don't know where he had been. [...]

Alec and I are not chums or together a great deal, and haven't been. I never went there before nor since. The way I came to go there that night, Father told me his [Alex's] mother was sick and I went over to see her. [...] I am a very good friend of Alec's and went over to see his mother because she was sick. It was pretty stormy that night is the reason I didn't go back to my father's. Had hard work to get to Alec's. On the night of the 17th I was at home. I am sure I went to father's on the 16th and not the 17th, by the weather. It was storming on Tuesday and not Wednesday. One of my cattle died on the 16th. It was a black one. Alec was not pretty drunk when he came home. He had his left hand done up. That was not Wednesday night, but Tuesday night. [...] I told my father that Alec came back with his left hand tied up and told my father about Alec's mother being sick. I told him that Wednesday morning. I asked Alec what was the matter with his hand and he said he cut it. He had it done up with tobacco and I didn't see it.

[...]

Second Testimony of Paul Holy Track

Near the end of the trial the prosecutor asked Paul Holy Track to return to the stand to answer just one question about Alec Coudotte's wounded hand:

> Alec Coudotte told me he hurt his hand inside the Spicer house on the 17th of February. Didn't tell me how he hurt it.

[...]

Testimony of Andrew Slater

The defense attorney called Andrew Slater, who was apparently an owner of one of the saloons in Winona, to testify about Alec Coudotte's wounded hand:

> Q.-Did you give this man Alec Coudotte any tobacco on the 16th day of February?
> A.-I don't know whether it was on the 16th I gave him a piece of tobacco.
> Q.-What did he do with it?
> A.-He had his hand cut here, I put it on his hand.
> Q.-Was that previous to or after the Spicer murder?
> A.-It was before. It was Tuesday.
> Q.-Can you show me where his hand was cut?
> A.-One of these fingers. I don't remember which. [...]
> Question by a juror: Do you remember giving Alec Coudotte and Frank Blackhawk a drink of whiskey about that time?
> A.-No, sir. I never gave them any whiskey.
> Q.-Did you drink with them?
> A.-Yes, sir. They gave me a drink.

[...]

Testimony of Marciana Coudotte

Marciana Coudotte was Alec Coudotte's wife. Her testimony offered support to her husband's and Dr. Ross's claim that on the afternoon of February 17th, Dr. Ross visited her ailing mother-in-law and that her husband was there as well, serving as interpreter. William Coudotte was Alec's brother, Marciana's brother-in-law:

> My name is Marciana Coudotte. The defendant is my husband. We have one girl six years old and a boy three years old. Had one child that died in March. At that time Alec was at the agency guard house. I remember being at William Coudotte's with my husband last winter. I have forgotten who

else was there but I was there on Saturday. I remember Grey Eagle was at William's. Grey Eagle, William and his wife, William's father and mother, and Alec and I were there. We left there on Sunday and went to our home. We went in a sleigh and Alec's mother went with us.

I know Dr. Ross. He came to see Alec's mother Wednesday. I remember when he came. It was about three o'clock. I am not certain about the time of day but I heard it was three o'clock. He came after we had our dinner. He talked with Alec's mother and Alec acted as interpreter. After the doctor left that day Alec stayed at home until dark. [...] Alec and I went to William Coudotte's the same time. When we left Coudotte's, William's house, on Sunday we had in our sled our bedding and the hind wheel of a wagon. That is all. The child that died was one year old.

[...]

Testimony of Alec Coudotte

Alec Coudotte had pled not guilty to the charge that he had murdered Thomas Spicer. When he was placed on the stand his primary strategy, guided by attorney Stevens, was to deny, one after another, the charges against him and the various incriminating statements that had been offered by the witnesses for the prosecution. Chief among these witnesses were Paul Holy Track and Philip Ireland, whose narratives, so far as they involved him, he totally denied. He did admit to stealing and butchering a cow and trading the meat to Red Caldwell for whiskey. As for the wounded left hand, he asserted that he had injured that on February 15th when he was butchering the cow. Of course, he also corroborated Dr. Ross's testimony that he had been with his sick mother on February 17th, acting as translator for the doctor. It is interesting that the jurors were permitted to ask questions directly of the witnesses. To judge from the snide and aggressive questions, the jurors apparently thought Alec Coudotte was telling them a pack of lies:

> (Alec Coudotte [...] testified as follows, after the court cautioned him that he need not be a witness unless he wished:)
> On February 13th, 1897, I was on Oak Creek at my brother William Coudotte's place. I did not see Paul Holy Track or Philip Ireland on the 13th of February. I know I am accused of having killed Thomas Spicer. I had nothing to do with it.
> On February 17th after dinner I was at my house. On that day I acted as interpreter for the agency doctor, that man (indicating Dr. Ross). I did not see Paul Holy Track on Tuesday night [as] he has mentioned. I did not meet him near Bad Horse's place on Monday night. I did not see him anywhere. I went with Paul from the Indian agency recently to Bismarck. The man who drove the team was a mail driver. There was myself, Blackhawk, Philip Ireland and a Santee whose name I don't know. I sat on the back seat with my back towards the horses. Paul sat in the next seat back of the driver [with his] back towards the horses. On that day on the road I did

not have any money and I did not give Paul any. I did not give him any money at any time after that.

Q.-Did you tell Paul Holy Track, Philip Ireland or any one else that you were directly or indirectly connected with or had anything to do with the killing of Thomas Spicer or the Spicer family?

A.-No, I never said it. On the 13th of February we killed a critter at William Coudotte's. I brought two loads of wood in the morning. After the last load we ate dinner, and after dinner Moses and I unloaded the wood and started to split it up.

Then Grey Eagle came there and stopped. William put the team in the barn and as I passed the kitchen when I went [to] the house I saw him eating in the kitchen. After dinner he and William were talking and I heard William ask permission to kill a critter on account of my mother being sick. We sat from half past eleven to twelve o'clock. William, Moses and my father ate first and [then] I. Then after we had finished my wife and William's wife and the children ate last. I think Grey Eagle came there about two or half past two o'clock.

When I came back from the stable I heard William ask my father to give him a steer and he would give him a cow in place of it. He did so and we went out and killed the steer in front of the stable door. William roped it and I took an axe and killed it. After we had finished with the beef, Moses brought the sleigh and we put the beef in. Moses helped put it in. I was arrested and taken to the guard house shortly after Thomas Spicer's murder, the 24th of February, on Wednesday one week after the murder.

I had a talk with Placidus High Eagle, Mr. Armstrong, Mr. Reedy and Mr. Shier in regard to killing the beef at William Coudotte's. I did not at that time say that the beef was killed at William Coudotte's two weeks ago last Friday. I remember I did not say that. Mr. Armstrong asked me about the beef and I told him when we killed it. I told him on the 13th.

The Saturday before I started from William's. I am as positive as that I did not kill Thomas Spicer. The steer we killed at William Coudotte's was red with a little white stripe down his back, a kind of a brownish red. It would have been two years old this spring.

I left William Coudotte's on the 14th on Sunday. I went to my home. I went down to William Coudotte's on Monday when William was in the guard house. On Tuesday February 16th I was at home. I did not say to Placidus High Eagle and Mr. Armstrong and Mr. Shier in the guard house that on the night of the 16th I was near the mission, sixteen and a half miles from there at the house of George Defender. I am sure I never told that.

In the guard house [while] I was cutting wood at Tom Reedy's house, Sam Mackey came up and I told him to tell Moses Martin to burn two pair of pants that was in my stable that had blood on them. They were blue overalls. Frank Blackhawk told me to tell him to do that and that is why I did it. The morning of the 15th I pulled off one pair and Frank Blackhawk pulled off another and threw them in the manger. That was Monday the 15th. Frank Blackhawk and I had killed a critter. Paul Holy Track did not help us. I did not see him. I had killed the critter in my stable. I denied killing that critter when I was in the guard house.

When I found Sam Mackey had told what I had said to him I knew we would be found out so then I told. I think I told Mackey this about a week after I had been in the guard house. I don't remember when I owned up to killing this beef. Some time after I was put in the Emmons County jail.

Q.-And until you owned up to it you denied it as emphatically as you do now the killing of Thomas Spicer, didn't you? (Objected to as improper cross examination, and an improper question to ask. Objection overruled and exception granted the defendant.)

A.-No. We killed the steer and I said we did. We killed the steer Monday the 15th. It was not a steer it was a cow. Blackhawk and I were alone. We put the beef in a sleigh, took it across the river, and sold two quarters of it to Red.

We took the beef and hide south of Andrew Slater's house, that is the rest of it, across from the little bridge three or four hundred yards and threw it in the snow to the left of the road in the woods. On Tuesday the 16th I went back and got one quarter of it and sold it to Red Caldwell. When I went back after the other quarter and the hide, I couldn't find them. When I came there to find the hide and could not find it after I had taken the last quarter and sold it to Red I came back to Andrew's and asked him for some tobacco to put on my hand which I had cut, and he gave it to me.

I was tying up my finger and I had something to eat at his place, and he said to me, Frank Blackhawk told me that some meat was left there, and for him to take it, and I told him that I had gone up there to get the hide and could not find it. One of the quarters I sold on Tuesday had been in the snow all night; put it in in the morning of Monday and sold it after three on Tuesday. I probably put that in the snow in the morning about eight or half past. The snow was deep and we threw it in and it went out of sight. I only sold one quarter on Tuesday. Two quarters sold on Monday. They were the critter that Frank Blackhawk and I sold Monday night. I told those, Armstrong and others, at the guard house that the beef I sold was that I got of William Coudotte. I didn't wish to tell them it was the stolen beef.

Q.-What did you get for the beef you sold to Red Caldwell? (Objected to as incompetent and improper cross examination. Objection overruled and exception granted the defendant.)

A.-Two bottles of whiskey.

Q.-Did you not say in the guard house in your talk with Mr. Armstrong, Mr. Reedy, Mr. Shier, Placidus High Eagle that you got $5.50 for one quarter. (Objected to as improper cross examination. Objection overruled and exception granted the defendant.)

A.-I said I got $5.25. He did not give me any money for it. We were to get $5.25 apiece for each quarter. That would make $10.50. I took two bottles of whiskey and a bottle of beer, Frank the same. The remainder we spent then in there before we left.

Sunday night Frank Blackhawk got a bottle of whiskey there and left his overcoat at Red's. He also paid for that bottle with the beef. For the third quarter I got two bottles of whiskey. Tuesday, February 16th, I was at home all day up to 12 o'clock. After dinner I hitched up my team and went to Paul Holtz's house after a quarter of beef we had received out of the issue. About one o'clock I brought that back to my house. I then went to the agency and from there across the river.

After I had sold Red the last quarter of beef he told me to go in. I went in and saw a young Indian in there by the name of Winter. He asked me what happened to my hand and when I arrived I told him I had just come and that I had cut my hand. I had cut my left hand across the knuckle — you can see the scar there — when I was at the agency guard house. After the Indian left Red's he gave me two bottles of whiskey and I then went to Andrew Slater's house. That is the man I mean (pointing to Andrew Slater). I did not say to those I talked to in the guard house that I had hurt my finger the day before yesterday. I told them I did it on Tuesday the 16th. I did not tell Paul Holy Track or Philip Ireland at the residence of Thomas Spicer that I got my hand hurt there that day. Didn't tell them that the young woman hit me on the left hand and hurt me, and I didn't get hurt anyplace on the 17th day of February.

I left Caldwell's on Tuesday, it was maybe about half past three or four o'clock. I went to Andrew Slater's and tied up my hand there. I had hurt it about half past two. The way I hurt it was by unjointing the forepart of the leg of a forequarter of beef. When I sold the beef that Mr. Chase got, I didn't leave anything there that I know of.

I lost a pocket knife that day. I must have left it in the sleigh and it dropped off there. I did not know I had lost my knife until I got home. I took some apples home and gave them to my little boy and girl. Little boy wanted a knife and when I went to take it out I found I had lost it. When I got to Andrew Slater's he told me he had put the hide and meat away from the place where we had it. Andrew asked me if I wished to take the hide and I said yes. We got the hide and put it in a sleigh. Andrew and I then had a drink, down by the river. Had a wagon wheel in my sleigh that day.

When I got the hide from Andrew's I sold it at Meade's store. There were two hides and I sold them both together. The other one was the one I brought from William's. In my talk to Armstrong, Reedy and them, I told them I had only sold one hide. I bought a half gallon of coal oil, twenty-five cents worth of apples and went home. Got there half-past six or seven o'clock. Put the horses in the stable, took the harness off and gave them hay, and as I came out of the stable I saw Charlie White Bull there.

Frank Blackhawk was not there Tuesday. He came home with me Monday night and stayed all night. Riding home we sat in the same seat. His horse was in my barn. He put it there Monday. He came to my place Monday morning at daylight. There stayed at my house Monday night besides my own family, Frank Blackhawk and Baptiste Cabe. We all stayed there all night and Blackhawk left Tuesday morning about seven o'clock. On Saturday morning before I was home I saw him in the guard house. That was the 20th. I had seen him in the store on ration day.

Didn't see Paul Holy Track or Philip Ireland, either one, that day. Went out with him [Blackhawk] outside and had a long talk. At the time I made the statement to Mr. Wells I told him I was talking about the Spicer murder. Frank and I were not talking about anything of that kind at all but he kept after me and I thought he would quit if I told him that. Mr. Wells asked me about the beef and about the murder April 14th, and I told him that Frank Blackhawk told me that he had shot Thomas Spicer. George Defender was not at my house on the 16th. My mother was there, three children, myself, Charlie White Bull and Baptiste Cabe.

Went to bed about half-past ten. There are two rooms. I slept in the north room in the corner on the floor. I didn't have any whiskey in a jug. I brought a jug of kerosene home with me. Baptiste Cabe got back about two or three o'clock in the morning. I had drank three or four times but was not drunk. I had two bottles of whiskey. Cabe left maybe eight or nine o'clock the next morning and White Bull maybe nine or half past nine. I drove up to the agency and had a wheel in my sled to take to the agency shop, but I forgot it and took it over the river. Before I went to the store I stopped at the doctor's office and told him about my mother's being sick — Dr. Ross. I had a talk in the store that night with Baptiste Cabe and William Burke about half past five or six o'clock.

After Charlie White Bull and Baptiste Cabe left on Wednesday morning I took my horses to water and cleaned out my stable and chopped wood. Stayed home all that day. Didn't see either Holy Track or Ireland anywhere that day.

You say Charles Welch says he saw me and George Defender about six o'clock in the evening near the dump or corrals, close to the mule corrals at Fort Yates. He is mistaken, we were not there. I told Armstrong, when I was in the guard house, that I went home Wednesday, and that Dr. Ross was there. I told him that at the first interview.

Q.-Did you try to commit suicide in the Emmons County jail since being confined there? (Question objected to as incompetent, irrelevant and immaterial and not proper cross examination. The objection overruled and exception granted the defendant.)

A.-Yes, I did that.

Q.-Why? (Question objected to as incompetent, irrelevant and immaterial and not proper cross examination. Objection overruled and exception granted defendant.)

A.-I did it because I did not like to be confined.

Q.-How long had you been confined when you did this?

A.-I don't remember how long it was.

Q.-Had you ever been confined before?

A.-I had not been locked up in a jail.

Q.-Had you ever been in the guard house or in jail before? (Objected to as incompetent, irrelevant, immaterial and not proper cross examination. Objection overruled and exception granted the defendant.)

A.-I have been in the guard house lots of times at the agency.

Q.-Did you try to commit suicide on those occasions? (Question objected to as incompetent, irrelevant and immaterial and not proper cross examination. Objection overruled and granted the defendant an exception.)

A.-No, I did not because it was almost like being at home to me.

Q.-Did you have your family with you in the guard house at the agency? (Objected to as incompetent, irrelevant, immaterial and improper cross examination. Objection was overruled and an exemption granted the defendant.)

A.-No, they were not with me at the time, but I knew the people that were around me, and so in that way it seemed more like home. Besides, we worked out of doors a great deal of the time. (Narrative resumed.)

I never saw Paul Holy Track or Philip Ireland anywhere near Bad Horse's. The last time I saw them they were here in this jail. The last time before that was when we went to Bismarck. The time before that was at the guard house. While I was there they brought them there, took them away and brought them back again. I had not seen either of them until I saw them at the agency guard house. I did not see them on Saturday, February 13th, 1897. I was in Winona Sunday, Monday and Tuesday. I went there Sunday night. I didn't see Paul Holy Track. Frank Blackhawk was with me. Didn't see Paul or Philip during those three days. Didn't tell Wells I did see them on February 17th. Wells asked me that and I had not seen them, but he kept telling me I was there that day so I said, at last, yes, because he said that Paul and Philip said they had seen me there. He asked me three or four times so at last I said yes.

I recollect that I sent for Wells but I don't recollect the date. I didn't tell Wells that the day before the murder I took my wife and mother to Bill's and got back in the evening. I told Wells and others at the Williamsport jail on the 15th of April that Dr. Ross was at my house February 17th. They asked me if he was there and I told him yes.

In going to Bismarck I rode in the same seat with George Defender. Frank Blackhawk rode on the next seat in front of me facing the other way. I rode in the same sleigh with him when we started to Winona, until we got to Pete Shier's and from Pete Shier's place he rode in a different sleigh. When we got to Bismarck they were all in the same sleigh with me, and also Mr. Lyons. I think Ireland was in the other sleigh and Patrick Yellow Lodge in the sleigh with me. I think I may be mistaken about who was in the sleigh. I think the cattle inspector was in the sleigh with us.

I don't quite understand what you mean about the ten dollars. I did not give it to anyone. I don't see where I could get ten dollars to give anybody. I didn't give anybody ten dollars. I don't know Peter Blue Shield. I knew the Santee was in the guard house with us but I didn't know his name. I was in the guard house with him a little over a week. Never talked with Paul Holy Track about the Spicer murder. I didn't know anything about it so I didn't talk to anybody about it. All I know about the murder is what I had heard about it from others.

Q.-When you passed the Spicer house was not your attention called to it as the place where the Spicer murder had occurred? (Question objected to as incompetent, irrelevant, immaterial and improper cross examination, which objection the Court overruled and granted an exception to the defendant.)

A.-There was someone sitting in front as we passed said that is the house, but I don't know which one it was said that. (Narrative resumed.)

I was sitting on the same seat with Defender, and Blackhawk was sitting in front of me. My back was towards the back of the sleigh. Paul Holy Track on that trip to Bismarck didn't say to me, "We are arrested and can't get out and might as well tell it when we get over there." I never had any talk with him about it at all. Neither did I say, "That may be right but let them work a little harder before they find us out." I didn't have any such talk with him anywhere.

I did not give Paul Holy Track ten dollars, and say, "Take it, don't tell it, try to cover it up." Never heard George Defender say anything about "Let them find it out themselves." I did not see George Defender on the evening of the 16th of February. Didn't see him on the 17th. Wasn't in Winona with George Defender on February 18th. Wasn't at Red Caldwell's with George Defender on the day after the Spicer murder. I was not at Red Caldwell's on the 18th. I have not talked over the Spicer murder with George Defender. Since the murder I saw him in the guard house. I was in the guard house when he was brought in. He didn't tell me anything at the time about his being arrested for the Spicer murder. I had no conversation with him.

At the times I have testified to when I was in the guard house, I wasn't accused of any connection with nor did I have any knowledge of the Spicer murder. When I went to Bismarck George Defender had got some whiskey and I had gone up as a witness, before the U.S. court, against Caldwell. What we were trying to cover up was the meat business, and that is why I lied about it. I am telling the truth this time.

When I was in the guard house Mr. Armstrong was there and he was the man that was questioning me. He questioned me about beef and that is all I thought he questioned me about. They had an interpreter there and I understand a little English too, but not very much of it. I cannot understand very much English. A number of times I have started to answer a question before it was interpreted when I heard it good, I started out to answer them. I can understand some of the questions, and understood some of the ones Armstrong asked me in the guard house. Lots of them I did not understand, just a few. Very few of the questions were interpreted to me, I mean most of them were.

Question by a juror: Is it because your conscience hurts you that you correct these lies Mr. Stevens speaks about?

A.-Yes, that is why I tell them straight.

At the time I was at the guard house I didn't know Mr. Armstrong was state's attorney of Emmons County. I heard that he was investigating the Spicer murder at the time he was down there. There may have been other witnesses examined before I was, I don't remember. I know George Defender went to Bismarck to testify for some purpose. I am not now telling any lies to cover up anything. It doesn't make any difference about

5. Trial

my being on oath now, but I am telling the straight truth. I think if I had been under oath I might have covered up these stories. I have told the truth today. I understand that the charge with which I am now confronted is a great deal graver than stealing meat, and I have been instructed by my attorneys to tell the absolute truth about everything I was asked.

Question by a juror: Alec Coudotte, what was Thomas Spicer doing when you saw him last?

A.-I don't know what he was doing as I have never seen the man. I don't know what kind of a looking man he was.

[...]

Further Testimony of Alec Coudotte

The defendant was called to the witness stand again the next day to clarify certain points from the previous day's testimony:

Mr. Stevens had a talk with me last night in my cell in the jail. I told him he was either mistaken or I was. What I meant by saying I knew about the murder at the guard house was that I had just heard about it. It was at the agency guard house where I first heard that Mr. Armstrong was making inquiries about the murder.

When Mr. Armstrong was examining me I did not know anything more about the Spicer murder than what I had heard. I just heard there was a murder. I don't remember being questioned, only about the beef. Mr. Armstrong had never questioned me before that time. I didn't know before that time that he was state's attorney of Emmons County. I thought Armstrong had just questioned me about the beef. When he was questioning me he asked me where I was on the third day and I told him at home. The statements I made to Armstrong about the beef were lies.

[...]

Testimony of Frank Black Hawk

Frank Black Hawk was one of the five Indians accused of murdering the Spicers. He was part African American. In his testimony he indicated that neither he nor Alec Coudotte had anything to do with the Spicer murders. He spoke mostly about killing a cow with Alec and about drinking whiskey with his share of the sale to Red Caldwell and Scar Faced Charley. The most interesting part of his testimony concerns the bloody pants that he said were bloodied by the killing and butchering of the cow. He said Alec Coudotte asked him to destroy the pants:

I reside in the Standing Rock Indian agency. Am acquainted with the defendant Alec Coudotte, and was on the 13th of February last. I have known him for some years. I saw him the night of the 14th at Red Caldwell's. From there he and I went to Andrew Slater's and back, and we went up to Pepper's and came back, and then down to Andrew's, and from there we went across the river over to the agency. There got a heifer and took her back to his stable. We loaded it up about sunrise, came back to Andrew's, then went to Red's and sold two quarters. We stayed around town all day.

Monday morning we came back to Andrew's, went back up town again and went back to Andrew's about noon on Monday. We stayed there until evening and went back to Alec's house. We got to Alec's house a little after dark. Ate supper there and talked awhile and then we went to bed. Alec, his wife and mother and the children, Baptiste Cabe and myself slept there that night. On Tuesday morning I went away.

I first went to Winona on Sunday about noon. I stopped at the outset at Joe Fullers's, then I went into Red's. It was after dark on Sunday night or dusk, when I first saw Alec. I was talking with him. We was drinking. Ate lunch together down at Andrew Slater's. Sunday evening I went to Andrew Slater's, and went to Red's, Jack Flynn's and Jack McCrory's store. I didn't go to bed that night. Sat around Andrew's talking, drinking and smoking. I had a gun with me.

Sunday afternoon we did some shooting at a mark on a post with a Winchester. Sunday night we went to Pepper's for more whiskey, but we didn't get any as he didn't have any. Then we went back to Red Caldwell's. It was not yet morning then. I didn't eat any breakfast Monday morning, but I had a lunch in the back of Caldwell's. Scar Faced Charley was there with me. It must have been almost nine o'clock when we first got to Red's.

After we got there, [we] stayed a part of the time at Red's, sometimes on the road down to Andrew's, and sometimes at Andrew's. I believe I was examined in the guard house by Mr. Armstrong, Reedy, and others on February 24th. At that time I believe I testified to something similar to this: Went to Winona on Sunday; got there at 2 P.M.; stopped at Joe Fuller's; part of the time at Slater's; got breakfast at Red's Monday morning; after we had lunch at Red's Monday morning we was drinking. We went to Andrew's and ate a kind of lunch and was sitting there; along in the afternoon I laid down and went to sleep. Monday evening I got up and went across towards Alec's place. Got there after dark, but I didn't remember just when. Found there Alex's wife, mother and children and Baptiste Cabe.

We left Winona Monday night in a sleigh. I didn't say to Mr. Armstrong that we left on horseback. I am positive of that. My testimony was given in English to Mr. Armstrong, and there was present at the time Mr. Reedy, I think Mr. Shier, the justices at Winona, Matt Chase and a half dozen others. I told them Monday morning [that] when I was going from Winona I was on horseback, and we went back in the sleigh and came back in the sleigh again.

I stayed all night Monday night at Alec's. Left there after sunrise. Left before breakfast. I may have said I got to Alec's about eight o'clock Monday, it was after dark but I did not say I went on horseback. I ate my breakfast Tuesday morning at Andrew Slater's. Stopped at Red's about ten or fifteen minutes but did not drink any whiskey.

I did not see Alec Coudotte at Winona on February 16th. I did see Dr. Muench. I saw him a little before noon. I did not return to Winona that day. Was not at Andrew Slater's Tuesday afternoon. I did not go to the dance that night. I didn't get my gun fixed in Winona on Monday or Tuesday, nor did I so state to Mr. Armstrong. I don't know what time we retired at Alec's on Monday night, but it was pretty late. We drank a good deal of whiskey, I guess I must have had a quart. I might have had pretty close to a quart and a half. I don't know how much Alec had.

I was with Alec Monday morning when he brought the beef in. We sold it to Red Caldwell. I don't know what he done with the beef. Coudotte and I came to town together. The beef was in the sleigh. Stopped first at Andrew's. Took one quarter out at Andrew's and put it in the cellar. We left two quarters in the willows and one quarter we took to Red's. We threw them in the snow and covered them up with snow. We had with us the hide, head, feet and entrails.

We left back at Alec's what was on the inside of the entrails and the blood. Also left at Alec's two pair of pants. I left one pair of overalls that had blood on them. I think I told Alec to destroy the pants. The reason I asked them to be destroyed is there was blood. I told him to dry them and wash them so as to take the blood out of them. He said, just throw them down there and I will take care of them. I told Alec to destroy the pants on Monday morning when we loaded the beef. Mine was an old pair of pants.

When we got to Andrew Slater's we put one quarter in the cellar or root house, two quarters we placed in the snow and took one quarter to Red's and sold it. As far as I know the two quarters are in the willows yet. I got some whiskey for money, the proceeds of the quarters but not of the two quarters left in the willows. The quarter that was left at Andrew Slater's we took and sold to Red Caldwell.

We got to Red Caldwell's with the first quarter about nine o'clock. We got whiskey for that but I don't know how much. I guess we got two quarts. We got five cents a pound. He said it weighed a little over a hundred pounds. I took mine all out in whiskey and beer. I had left my horse in Coudotte's barn and he was there when I went back Monday night.

I know Paul Holy Track and Philip Ireland. I never killed any beef with Paul Holy Track at any time.

[...]

Testimony of Ruby Caldwell

Ruby Caldwell was apparently one of Red Caldwell's prostitutes, but was generally known as his "wife." It is not clear why she was called to the witness stand or what George Defender's tears or Alec Coudotte's grin were supposed to prove about their guilt or innocence. As for the closing sentence in Ruby Caldwell's testimony, I have not been able to discover on what basis Ruby Caldwell was thought to have attempted to murder an Indian. Her trial, it will be recalled, referred to officially as the *State of North Dakota vs. Ruby Caldwell*, had originally been first on the docket of cases to be tried in the Emmons County court in June 1897, but it had been bumped to make way for the more important one of Alec Coudotte. I have found no record that the case was ever tried. It would be interesting to know more about it, and about her. Ruby Caldwell sounds like a colorful figure:

> I reside in Winona. Was at home the 17th and 18th of February. Not away from Winona on the 18th. Was at home on the evening of February 18th. I had heard of the Spicer murder about eleven o'clock of that day. On the evening of February 18th Alec Coudotte came to my place. George Defender was with him. Saw them in the storm shed. I told Alec about the murder. George Defender was with him. George Defender looked at me, cried. Took out his handkerchief and wiped his face, and the defendant he kind of grinned.
> Q.-State what if anything they wanted or asked for at that time.
> A.-I could not understand because they spoke in Indian.
> Q.-Did they come into the house at that time?
> A.-No. They started in but refused to come in. [...] I can't tell how big the storm door is. Don't know how much a yard is. It is about that size (indicating). That was at night. They have got me charged with attempting to kill an Indian.
>
> [...]

Waiting for the Verdict

Not surprisingly, there was a deep interest in what verdict the jury would bring in, but meanwhile the various newspapers had to write something about the trial. Some of the press coverage of the proceedings was nasty. The journalist who wrote the report for the *Winona Times* could not resist criticizing some of the Indian witnesses. The reference below to Charging Eagle is to the witness who said that, while tracking a wandering steer, he had seen George Defender at his home around the time of the murders. Under sharp questioning, however, he found that he could not remember exact dates, times, miles traveled, and so on. The journalist could not resist making jokes about the names of some of the Indians and offering gratuitous comments about the appearance and intelligence of the female Indian witnesses:

Winona Times
Winona, North Dakota
June 10, 1897

Cadotte Trial Still On

[...]
On cross examination the witness [Charging Eagle] said he could not remember any other dates for the past year except February 14th to February 17th inclusive. His testimony was such as to convey the impression that his name should be changed to "The Man Who Can't Remember."

Mrs. George Defender testified next. She is a tall comely young woman, not a full blood Indian, and she appeared on the stand with a well behaved and neatly dressed papoose. She wore a new shawl of bright colors. A blue velvet dress with black ribbon around the bottom. [...]

Leo Smell the Bear [...] was not so much entitled to be called "The Man Without a Name" as Charging Eagle. [...]

Mrs. Alec Cadotte [...] is almost a full-blood Indian, unable to understand English and even with an interpreter it was difficult to get anything from her. Her memory was exceedingly defective, evidently much to the mortification of her husband. She said that on the 17th of February, the day of the murder, the defendant was at home all day. She was the least intelligent witness so far placed on the stand, and was practically dumb so far as the cross-examination was concerned. Simple questions that would be put to her she did not make an effort to answer. [...]

People who are not familiar with the characteristics of Indians have been asking how Leo Smell the Bear got his name. I heard an explanation of it today. The first thing his mother remarked after his birth was, "I smell a bear." Thereupon in accordance with the Indian tradition he was called "Leo Smell the Bear." Now it is in order to find out how another witness, named "Joseph Old White Woman," came by his name.

There was no witness named Joseph Old White Woman. One of the Indian witnesses, a man named Frank Martin, had made passing reference to an Indian named Charlie Old White Woman.

Other journalists had a nastier kind of fun with the trial. One even predicted that a guilty verdict, if it came, would be reversed by the state supreme court. If that happened, he wrote, it would be a good idea for the citizens to provide what he called "a sure and swift punishment" — meaning a lynching. This writer, like the previous one, could not resist making fun of Charging Eagle, but he tossed in an attack on the "eastern citizen who idealizes the Indian":

Mandan Pioneer
Mandan, North Dakota
June 11, 1897

[The Unconscionable Scoundrels]

Let us suppose a case. Suppose one or more of the Indians that are charged with the murder of the Spicer family, and who now plead not guilty, and are found guilty by the jury, and sentenced to death. Such conviction, if obtained, will be obtained partly on the testimony of the two Indian boys, Holy Track and Philip Ireland. Without their testimony no such conviction can be had.

Suppose an appeal is taken to the supreme court. So far every man sentenced to be hung in this state who has taken an appeal to the supreme court, has been granted a new trial. Suppose a new trial is granted in the case of any of these murderers. It will take months — perhaps a year to get around to another trial. If in the meantime Holy Track and Philip Ireland, who will plead guilty, are hung, then how can a conviction be obtained of their accomplices with two important witnesses out of the way? Is it a wonder that communities sometimes take the law into their own hands, and string up murderers when they are caught? It is regrettable that such be the case, but not wonderful.

The unconscionable scoundrels who murdered in cold blood four generations of human beings at the Spicer home, near Winona, on the 17th of February last, must sometimes dream of their crime. Surely at times they must see in their troubled sleep the pale faces of the helpless children, as their frightened eyes plead for mercy. The scarred and mutilated features of the three women they hacked and bruised must at times appear to them by night. These rascals, who at no time this side of the gallows will show a particle of regret for their misdeeds, will never live long enough in an unending eternity to atone for the wrongs they have done. What but a sure and swift punishment can properly satisfy the living, and do a little to insure protection for others who are in the same sort of danger as that which overtook this unfortunate family? [...]

The eastern citizen who idealizes the Indian, if called upon to picture a red man whose name is Charging Eagle, would picture a little creature with clear, piercing eyes, sharp features, a quick alert mind, and legs and arms to match. But, alas! The real Charging Eagle who has been testifying at Williamsport, is a heavy, clumsy creature, with sodden eyes and blunt features. His mind is slow and matches his physical attainments. He is misnamed. He would not charge a cow, to say nothing of an eagle. He has a stock answer to questions put him on cross-examination, and that answer is—"I don't remember"—or the Indian words that mean this.

The Jury Gives Its Verdict

On June 12, 1897, the jury gave its guilty verdict on Alec Coudotte to the judge, Walter Winchester, who is referred to in the transcript as "the court." Along with the guilty verdict the jury recommended the death penalty:

> The court: Gentlemen of the jury, have you agreed upon a verdict?
> Foreman: We have, your honor.
> The court: How do you find the defendant, guilty or not guilty?
> Foreman: Guilty. We have decided that the defendant shall suffer the death penalty. (Written form of verdict prepared and read to the jury and signed by the foreman.)
> The court: Gentlemen of the jury, you have heard the verdict as signed by your foreman. Is this your verdict and do you all agree to it? If you do you may all rise.
> The jury all rise, and say: Yes, sir.
> The court: And you are all agreed to it?
> All: Yes, sir.

Mr. Stevens: The defendant moves an arrest of judgment and enters a motion for a new trial on the ground of insufficiency of evidence and on the further ground of newly discovered evidence, and desires reasonable time in which to prepare his motion, and in which to furnish affidavits required in connection with the newly discovered evidence.

The court: In view of the business that is now before the court, I will set the time for passing sentence in this case on the coming into court next Monday morning, unless for some reason there should be a different time set prior to that time. (Later in the day the time for passing sentence was fixed July 12, 2 P.M., to which time the court stood adjournment.)

Reactions of the Press

Most of the journalists who wrote about the verdict seemed pleased to report that justice had prevailed in Williamsport. At least one reporter, however, seemed to be not quite so sure:

Emmons County Record
Williamsport, North Dakota
June 18, 1897

Guilty!

[...] The court announced that the jury would be allowed to use the courtroom for their deliberations, and the audience filed out of the house.

Downtown there were a number who concluded to sit up and await the verdict. Judge Winchester instructed the bailiff to call him in case a verdict was reached before he arose in the morning.

Hour after hour passed by, and predictions were being made that the jury would disagree. Daylight came, but still no agreement. Judge Winchester had arisen and taken breakfast. Court had been adjourned to 10 o'clock; so he arranged to have the jury taken to the Bussey building, a half mile southwest of town. But a report came that the jury had agreed, and soon a bailiff came downtown and announced that fact.

When the court had been called to order, Judge Winchester asked if the jury had agreed upon a verdict, and was answered in the affirmative by foreman Parker. The judge asked him if the jury had fund the prisoner guilty or not guilty, and the foreman answered "Guilty, your honor." [...]

It is reported that the jury took several ballots, and that, during part of the time they were out, five of the seven were in favor of acquittal.

Mr. Stevens arose and asked a stay of judgment, pending an application for a new trial.

In the meantime how is it with the man whose doom is sealed? He had borne the reputation on the reservation of being a physical coward. But he shows no evidence of it now. The man whom the murderous fiends, Holy

Track and Ireland — after making a statement to the contrary — said was guilty, and whom a reputable young physician said was innocent, sits calm and unmoved. There is nothing about his actions to denote that he is the person most interested in the verdict.

Requested Delay in Sentencing

Alec Coudotte's defense attorneys requested a sixty-day delay of sentencing so they could prepare an appeal. They also presented an affidavit by Alec Coudotte requesting that Emmons County pay to have copies of the transcript of his trial made so that his attorneys could use it to make a case for a new trial:

> Mr. Stevens: The defendant asks for sixty days, or such other shorter time as will be necessary to procure transcript of the testimony from the stenographer, the state's attorney having moved for sentence.
> (Now comes the defendant by George W. Lynn and R. M. Stevens, his attorneys, and moves the court for the postponement of the hearing on the motion on the ground that there is a complete absence of proof which corroborates or tends to corroborate the evidence of Paul Holy Track and Philip Ireland, pretended accomplices in the commission of the crime, without which corroboration there was no evidence before the jury in the above entitled case on which they, the jury, could lawfully find the defendant guilty, for the period of sixty days, and that the court order that the official stenographer of this court furnish a complete transcript in the above entitled case, as provided for in Section 417 of the Political Code of North Dakota, to be paid for by Emmons County and which transcript may be used by the defendant's attorneys in the arguing of said motion for a new trial, and that the sentence be deferred until the settlement of such motion in support of which there is hereto attached the affidavit of Alec Coudotte, the defendant. (Geo. E. Lynn, R. N. Stevens, attorneys for the defendant.)
> [...]

Also on July 12, the defense attorneys brought to the judge an affidavit of newly discovered evidence on behalf of High Eagle, a prison guard at the county jail in Williamsport. The issue was just how isolated from one another the cells of Paul Holy Track and Philip Ireland were. One of the centerpieces of the prosecution was that the two young men had not been permitted to converse with each other. Since their accounts of what happened at the Spicer farm were almost identical, the prosecution argued, they must be true because the two had been given no opportunity to work out a set of shared fabrications. The new testimony seemed to topple that centerpiece:

> At the time of the incarceration of Paul Holy Track and Philip Ireland at Standing Rock Indian agency, charged with the murder of Thomas Spicer

and others, I acted as a guard over the said Paul Holy Track and Philip Ireland, and it was supposed by me and others at that time that there was no communication between the cells. I have since learned that when in their cells they could communicate with each other without the person guarding them knowing it, and I verily believe they did so communicate with each other, and that the hole in the wall through which they communicated was made by Paul Holy Track. I have learned of this since the date of the trial of Alec Coudotte for the murder of Thomas Spicer. (Signed) High Eagle.

Alec Coudotte Sentenced

Judge Winchester was apparently not impressed with the new evidence. He denied the request for a two-month delay and proceeded with the sentencing of Alec Coudotte:

> The court: The application for a continuance of sixty days for the hearing of a motion for a new trial is denied, and an exception granted the defendant. If the defendant wishes to make a motion for a new trial now, I will hear it.
> Mr. Stevens: The defense is unable to make a motion for a new trial as he has no transcript on which to make the same, and has been unable to procure one. The defense desires to correct the record. The defendant now moves the court that the record heretofore made in which the defendant's counsel said he was unable to make a motion now, etc., should be made to read that he is unable to argue a motion now pending because of the absence of the record which he has been unable to procure.
> The court: To what motion do you refer?
> Mr. Stevens: The motion made at the adjournment of this court for the recess to July 12th at the time the defendant was found guilty of the offense charged.
> The court: As the court understands that record it was that the defendant then gave a notice of his intention to make a motion for a new trial. I don't understand that any motion for a new trial is now pending before this court.
> Mr. Stevens: That being the case, and to satisfy the court on that point, I will now make a motion for a new trial in this case on the ground of newly discovered evidence and the further ground that the evidence is not sufficient to warrant conviction.
> The court: The motion is denied. [...]
> The court to the prisoner: You have been informed against by the state's attorney of this county by an information now on file in this court charging you with the crime of murder; that information has been read to you in open court; after having reasonable time to enter a plea on that information you pleaded not guilty; after the plea was entered, a reasonable time was allowed, a jury was impaneled to try the issues of your case; evidence was adduced on part of the state and on part of the defense before a jury

regularly impaneled, the jury being twelve men selected from the body of this judicial subdivision. After hearing the evidence and returning and deliberating upon the evidence the jury came into court and brought in a verdict of guilty as charged. The jury also by their verdict determined that you are to suffer the death penalty. Have you now anything to say or reason to give why the sentence and judgement of the court should not at this time be pronounced against you?

The defendant: I was found guilty, and it was not so. I am not guilty.

The court: In view of the business now before this term of court I shall refrain from making remarks which I usually make on such occasions. The sentence and judgment of the court is, that you, Alec Coudotte, be now remanded to the jail in and for Emmons County, North Dakota, and on Friday the 20th day of October, 1897, that you be taken to an enclosure adjoining or near said jail in said county, and there and then be hanged by the neck until you are dead.

The "Trial" of John W. Cramsie

White settlers had reason to be pleased at the outcome of the trial of Alec Coudotte. After all, the first of the five men to be tried had been found guilty by an all-white, all-male jury, and he had been sentenced to hang. They knew that the case would be appealed, but they saw no reason to doubt that the appellate court and the state supreme court in Bismarck would uphold the conviction and the sentence.

Meanwhile, a different kind of "trial" was taking place, that of John W. Cramsie, the Indian agent at Standing Rock. Because of his role in the investigation of the Spicer murders, some of the settlers felt the need to spread some of the blame for the murders to the white officer in charge of the Indians who had done the actual murdering. Cramsie came under heavy fire for his autocratic ways. The citizens of Emmons County had several major concerns about him. One was that by not preventing the sale of whiskey to Indians, he was at least indirectly responsible for the drunkenness of the Indians who murdered the Spicers and thus for the murders themselves. Another was that he had autocratically prevented non–Indian authorities from having free access to search Standing Rock reservation lands and Indian homes, and so had given the Indians time to destroy important evidence. A third was that he had allowed his wards to wander at will off the reservation. A fourth was that he was nepotistic, giving jobs and housing to his own relatives. A fifth was that he was by nature a bully who punished anyone who challenged his absolute authority at Standing Rock. These concerns were summarized in a scathing editorial by R. M. Tuttle, publisher of the *Mandan Pioneer*. The term "ukase" refers to a proclamation having the force of law issued by a czar or other imperial officer:

5. Trial

Mandan Pioneer
Mandan, North Dakota
June 11, 1897

Regarding Cramsie

There comes a time when abuse of temporary power, and tyrannous conduct must be exposed, to save us from becoming serfs and slaves. The settlers who live south of Mandan, whose location is such that they must have business on the Sioux reservation, have for a long while told of the outrages to which they are subjected by Major Cramsie, the Standing Rock Indian agent. But it is a hard matter to secure from them individual affidavits, complaints that can be used at headquarters, for the reason that they are afraid that if this is done their rights will be still further trampled upon. People who are not personally interested are not aware of the fact, but it is true that today Major Cramsie occupies a position much like that of some petty European monarch, who must be coddled to keep him good tempered, and who visits condign wrath on all those who won't bow down to him. For some time the newspapers in Emmons County, conscious of his tyranny, have published articles setting forth his wrong doings, and people who have read these articles have wondered if there wasn't some personal motive back of them. But the *Pioneer* has made sufficient investigation to ascertain beyond any doubt that one-half has not been told. His conduct is such that he should be removed and that speedily. The interest of the Indians demand it; the interests of the white people who live contiguous to the reservation demand it.

The effects of whiskey

The late developments concerning the horrible murder committed early this year, almost on the borders of the reservation, tend to emphasize the point that Cramsie is wholly unfit for his position. Just how much of the blood of that innocent Spicer family rests upon the head of Cramsie himself, nobody can exactly say, but in the judgment of many people there is no inconsiderable part of it. If the reader will read the confession of Holy Track, who did most of the killing, he will realize that whiskey was the chief incentive to the murder. The murderers, when they felt their courage oozing away — when they felt that they could not kill any more, would retire to the back of the barn, and take another drink of whiskey. So the confession reads from one end to the other.

Any one at all acquainted with the policy of Major Cramsie, and the character of the employees under him, cannot wonder for a moment that the Indians there have a taste for whiskey. Many of the employees of the government are in a chronic state of booziness. They prefer whiskey to bread. The Indians know that they drink whiskey, and the red men see no reason why they themselves should not drink. The result is seen in the Spicer murder. Give a red man whiskey and he at once descends to savagery. All the better instincts that he may have acquired at school or church are gone. He then wants to kill somebody. The whiskey-drinking policy of the present administration at Standing Rock is largely responsible for the horrible crime that was committed a few months ago in Emmons County. After its commission, Major Cramsie placed every obstacle he could in the way of the officers of this state whose business it was to arrest the murderers. He insisted that no Indians were implicated. Instead of rendering assistance to the officers of the state, he obstructed them. There was scarcely an intelligent man in Emmons County, aware of the whiskey-drinking proclivities of the subagents, farmers and other officials on the reservation, but concluded at once that it was Indians under Cramsie that committed the deed. [...]

Acts like a tyrant

Major Cramsie acts as though the Standing Rock Indian reservation were his own private domain, across which no white man may go however legitimate may be his mission, and however much the man wanting to cross, is to be trusted. There is one man living in Winona, who has a ranch southwest of the reservation, and he is obliged to go 100 miles out of his way when he visits his ranch. He must travel north to the Cannonball River, cross it, and go around the reservation. This ranchman has no bad record; he never gave an Indian a drop of liquor; he is a man whose reputation as a good citizen is beyond reproach; but he is not allowed to cross the reservation. If some European monarch were to issue a ukase regarding his domain, the monarch would have a first-class fight on his hands every hour of the day. One is not safe to set his foot on the reservation without a passport. The guardhouse stares him in the face, under the edicts of King Cramsie. The Indians are allowed to prowl at will over the white man's territory. He comes into our towns and villages; he murders the white man's wife and children, and no order is issued to him to stay on the reservation.

In searching for the motive for this conduct on the part of Cramsie, it will not do to say that he is considering the best interests of the wards of the government, in issuing such ukase on crossing the reservation. He is a bully by nature. He is blessed with a little brief authority and he uses it.

Everybody hates the bully

It is interesting to study the Cramsie microbe in Emmons County. It is in that county where his bullying manners are felt as much as anywhere. Emmons County has some very decided factional fights but all factions and all parties are one on this one proposition — their contempt for Cramsie. They hate him with a bitter hatred. They pray for his removal as agent at the reservation. They feel that their rights are trampled upon; that the Indian is lapsing into barbarism under his rule; that rations and goods to be issued are stolen because of his bad management; that he is a contemptible man to have any dealings with; that he should be dismissed as he was dismissed from the service before; that he should be retired to the quiet and peace of the little corner grocery from which he emerged when he came to Standing Rock.

Two weeks later the editor of the *Mandan Pioneer* continued his criticism of Cramsie. The portions of his editorial reproduced below suggest not only the corruption of some Indian agents but also the condescending attitudes of many whites who were convinced that the only solution for Indians was to give up their "barbarous" and "savage" ways and become just like whites. And they suggest, as well, that "the better class of Indians" agree with that solution:

Mandan Pioneer
Mandan, North Dakota
June 26, 1897

Cramsie Hated

The Indians on the reservations, north and south, are tickled to death at the prospect of seeing the last of Cramsie. They dislike to have their rations misappropriated as they are under the present regime. The better class of Indians realize that the residents of the reservation are drifting back into savagery under Cramsie, and this they regret to see. In pursuance of the general policy of the better class of Indians to help along the movement looking to the removal of Cramsie, a few days ago there was a meeting of leaders in the southern part of the agency, and they proceeded to collect a fund to pay the expenses of a delegation to Washington to see the Great Father, urging him to send another agent. The idea spread to the northern agency, known as the Wells sub-station, and in a very short time the sum of $150 was raised out of the meager funds at the disposal of the Indians, with the intention of co-operating with the Indians living in the southern part of the agency. But alas! Cramsie heard of it, and he dispersed the Indians that were there in the movement, and thus forever put a stop to any such movements against the king.

The royal family

The members of the "royal family" as they are called all around the reservation, are getting new buildings galore, built from lumber that should go to the Indians themselves to improve their squalid dwellings. The Indians are getting the worst sort of treatment, so far as buildings are concerned, in which to live and keep their stock, while the bounty of the government is freely distributed among the members of "royalty."

Relapsing into barbarism

We append herewith a letter from a correspondent on the reservation, to whom we have been indebted for much valuable information. It may be added that heretofore the newspapers have been pleased to chronicle improvements that have been made in the condition of the Indians — that under the previous regime, before Cramsie swooped down upon the agency, they were discarding their blankets, and were getting down to industrious habits; that they were cultivating their lands, and only a few years ago they sold thousands of bushels of wheat. These days of improvement have passed. Under the present agent no encouragement is given to this sort of work. Seed potatoes, corn and wheat are sold or used to feed the ponies. The Indians who need an encouraging hand to guide them, are rapidly relapsing back into the barbarism from which the government desires to have them emerge. [...]

The settlers who live contiguous to the reservation are interested in having the Indians as far removed from savagery as possible, and whenever an agent presides over the Indians who is neglectful of their interests — whose employees are appointed not with reference to their fitness, but with reference to their relationship to the agent himself, something must be done in the interest of the Indians and the settlers whose interests are at stake. The *Pioneer* has no hostile feelings whatever towards the Indians, but desires while they live in this section of the country, that they should adopt the better habits and manners of the white people.

It is the policy of the government to encourage in the Indians the industrious habits of white men; to have them take their land in severalty, to farm, raise crops, buy, sell, and trade with themselves and with the white people; to mingle with white people and lose the Indian caste. [...]

What is the result? The Standing Rock Indians today are the poorest, laziest and most shiftless of any tribe of Indians to be found. Of course there are some who have got a fair start in cattle. But take a drive through the camps and witness the ludicrous attempts at farming, the filthy houses and the utterly lazy and pitiably shiftless habits of these unfortunate people, and the reader will agree with us that the sooner a change — and a radical one — is made in officials at Standing Rock, the better for everyone concerned.

It is interesting that the editor of the *Mandan Pioneer*, while claiming to have "no hostile feelings whatever toward the Indians," considered their presence to be temporary. His phrase, "while they live in this section of the country" suggested that he looked forward to a time when they did not. The only hope he saw for them was that they "adopt the better habits and manners of the white people" and gradually "lose the Indian caste." He says that he wants Cramsie gone, but it is clear that he really wants the Indians gone. Not surprisingly, these editorials in the *Mandan Pioneer* came to the attention of Cramsie's supervisors in Washington, D.C. In a letter of June 28, 1897 (not extant), the secretary to the Commissioner of Indian Affairs asked Cramsie to offer his resignation, effective immediately. Cramsie replied on July 8:

Honorable Secretary of the Interior
Washington, D.C.
July 8, 1897
Sir:

I respectfully request to be allowed to defer action upon the honorable secretary's request of June 26, 1897, that I tender my resignation of the office of agent for the Sioux Indians at Standing Rock, until the investigation asked for by me on the date of June 28, 1897, has been made for the reason that in case this resignation were tendered at this time it would be an acknowledgment on my part that the false, malicious, absurd charges published against me were true and would be a gross injustice for me if such charges were allowed to remain unanswered on the records.

The question whether I shall or shall not be retained as agent until the expiration of my term of service is one of utmost importance to me personally, compared with my character as a private citizen and record as an officer of the Indian Department, and I therefore demand in the name of truth and justice a complete and thorough investigation of my administration of affairs at this agency.

I am, Sir, very respectfully, your obedient servant,

John W. Cramsie,
U.S. Indian Agent

Cramsie's letter of July 8 apparently crossed with a second letter from Washington written on July 13, 1897, asking him again to submit his resignation, to be effective at the end of July. That letter is not extant, but Cramsie's handwritten reply is:

Honorable Secretary of the Interior
Washington, D.C.
July 17, 1897

Sir:

I have the honor to acknowledge receipt of your letter of the 13th in which it is stated that on the 26th inst. a letter was addressed to me requesting my resignation at an early day, and not having received any answer the request was now renewed with the advice that my resignation take effect on and after July 31st.

In reply I would invite attention to the enclosed copy of my letter of the 8th instant addressed to the commissioner of Indian Affairs, which was intended to be a reply to the honorable Secretary's letter of June 26.

With regard to the date fixed for my resignation, viz: the 31st instant, I would further state that it would be impracticable and impossible to comply with the request for the reason that one month will be required for my successor to make the rounds of the reservation to see all the property for which he would have to receipt to me and to complete the draft [of the annual report]; and there are many other agency matters now in progress which it is desirable should be completed by me, or put in shape for compilation before leaving the service, which could not be done at a few days notice.

Thus, I most respectfully decline to tender my resignation until the investigation I have asked for be made, and I trust the honorable Secretary's sense of justice to grant my request.

I have served the Indian department for ten years in the capacity of Indian agent, under Republican and Democratic administrations (at Devil's Lake and here) and I have fearlessly endeavored to do my duty to the department and Indians. It is not therefore just to me that credence should be given to the statements of a set of disgruntled "would be" and exemployed, dishonest contractors, whiskey sellers, and others throwing discredit upon my personal character and upon my administration of agency affairs without a hearing in defense and an opportunity of disproving the false testimony against me.

I have the honor to be very respectfully your obedient servant,

John W. Cramsie,
U.S. Indian Agent

If an investigation into the accusations made by Tuttle in the *Mandan Pioneer* was ever conducted, I have not discovered a copy of any report of its contents. Apparently, however, Cramsie's request that he delay offering his resignation was granted. The Standing Rock agency's annual report, dated August 25, 1897, was submitted by Cramsie. His successor, a man named George H. Bingenheimer, did not take over as Indian agent at Standing Rock until March 11, 1898. Bingenheimer, who had been Tuttle's partner in the *Mandan Pioneer* newspaper, served as agent at Standing Rock for the next five years, then, under suspicion of misappropriation of funds, left the Indian service.

We shall probably never know for sure the full truth about John Cramsie's relationship with the people around him. For whatever reasons, he seems to have annoyed almost everyone who had to work with him. It came out in George Defender's trial, which began after Alec Coudotte was sentenced, that Paul Holy Track had attempted to kill Cramsie (see July 22 article below).

The Defender trial was somewhat similar to the Coudotte one, with Henry A. Armstrong being the chief prosecutor and R. N. Stevens being the chief defense attorney. Judge Sauter, however, relieved Judge Winchester. Stevens presented a signed affidavit requesting that George Defender be tried in a different county:

Mandan Pioneer
Mandan, North Dakota
July 15, 1897

[Against the Entire Indian Race]

George Defender [...] has reason to believe, and does believe, that he cannot receive a fair and impartial trial in the County of Emmons [...] which belief is based upon the following reasons, viz: This affiant is an Indian, residing on an Indian reservation adjoining the County of Emmons aforesaid, and great prejudice exists among the inhabitants of Emmons County against all Indians, [...] and for the further reason that certain bad Indians in the past have committed petty depredations against the property of the inhabitants of Emmons County, which has embittered the inhabitants of said county against the entire Indian race, to such an extent that this affiant could not receive a fair and impartial trial in said county. [...] And for further reason that Henry A. Armstrong, the state's attorney of Emmons County [...] has talked with a great number of the citizens of Emmons County conveying to them impressions of affiant's guilt, which he has freely asserted upon all occasions until the people of Emmons County are so prejudiced against this affiant that he cannot receive a fair and impartial trial in said county.

The affidavit was much longer and presented many more reasons, but it was quickly rejected by Judge Sauter. George Defender's trial was held in Williamsport. It covered much of the same ground as the Coudotte trial, but was not nearly so well attended. As a note in the following article put it, "There was very little interest manifested in the trial, and few people in town." There is no need to review the Defender trial here, but newspaper accounts of a couple of incidents in the trial may be of interest:

Winona Times
Winona, North Dakota
July 22, 1897

Defender In Court

The cross examination of Philip Ireland was resumed this morning by Mr. Stevens. The new feature in the examination was as to an alleged hole in the wall in the agency guard house. Witness denied that he knew anything about a piece of cloth which covered a hole in a chinking of the logs. He denied that after the murder and prior to the Coudotte trial he had had any conversation or communication with Paul Holy Track concerning the murder. [...]

At the afternoon session the direct examination of Paul Holy Track was renewed and continued for over half an hour. [...] He said [he] had never asked anybody in jail since the Cadotte trial whether he would be hung, but he had asked if they would all get the same punishment. Witness [Paul Holy Track] was visited in the guard house by Rev. Reed, and they talked about the murders, and witness said he and Philip did it. Never told Mr. Reed how the furniture was located in the house. Witness was not a member of Mr. Reed's church, and yet he was a leading member of the Y.M.C.A. of that church. He did not go and eat meals at Spicer's house on the strength of his being a member of the same church. He admitted that before the Spicer murder he had gone to Major Cramsie's house for the purpose of murdering him, at the instigation of Louis Agaard and Frank Black Hawk's brother. He had written on a wall at the agency that he had killed three people, meaning Mr. and Mrs. Spicer and Mrs. Rouse. The witness denied all knowledge of any hole in the wall between the cells.

George Defender's Hung Jury

George Defender was eventually placed on the stand, but he had little more to say than that he had nothing to do with the Spicer murders. His trial ended not in a hanging jury but a hung jury:

Emmons County Record
Williamsport, North Dakota
July 23, 1897

They Disagreed

George Defender was put upon the stand. He denied that he had anything to do with the death of Thomas Spicer, nor was he at Spicer's house on the 17th of February. His direct examination only took a few minutes. On cross-examination he admitted having written a letter to Joe Packineau, before he was arrested, to the effect that he expected to be arrested in connection with the Spicer murders, and he wanted to be transferred to Fort Berthold agency from Standing Rock. The cross-examination was much shorter than that of Coudotte. [...]

All day Saturday the people who were in town were speculating as to what the jury would do. The jury had been out since the previous night, at 9:15 o'clock. Saturday and Sunday passed, and still there was no verdict. If the jury had asked the court for further instructions, they could have received them; or, if they had asked to be discharged on the ground that they could not agree, the court would in all probability have discharged them. But they did not ask to be discharged. During Saturday the jury came in and asked for all the evidence relating to Defender's alibi, and this was read to them by court stenographer Tuttle. This part of the evidence was the most damaging in the defense, and it was thought that after hearing that they would return with a verdict. But they stayed out all of Sunday. On Monday morning at 9:30 o'clock the jury came in and expressed the unanimous view that it was impossible to agree. They had been out sixty hours, and Judge Sauter decided to dismiss them.

The judge had discussed the matter of the proposed change of venue with the county commissioners. It appeared, after examination of the situation, that, when from the number of voters in the county had been deducted those who could not understand the language, those who are not full citizens, those who live in the vicinity of the murders, those who live in the vicinity of the county seat and have heard the former trials, those who have been examined as jurors for the Coudotte and Defender trials, there would not be enough left in the county to get a jury. This view of the matter seemed to be very general, and the judge therefore decided to remove the case to Burleigh County. An order to that effect was made, and also a similar order concerning Blackhawk. The trials of these two defendants, it is believed, will take place next November or December. [...]

Sheriff Shier and deputy Livermore took Blackhawk and Defender to

Bismarck last Monday, where they will be kept in jail until tried. Holytrack, Ireland and Coudotte are in the Williamsport jail. The force of guards has been reduced, Tom Kelly having been retained as night guard and John Edick as day guard.

The retrial of George Defender and the trials of Frank Black Hawk, Paul Holy Track, and Philip Ireland never took place. Events in Bismarck and then in Williamsport were soon to render these trials either unnecessary or impossible.

6

Reversal

When their request to the appelate court for a new trial for Alec Coudotte was denied, his lawyers, led by attorney R. N. Stevens and John Stowell, appealed the case to the North Dakota supreme court in Bismarck. The justices on the supreme court reviewed the transcripts and overturned the decision of the lower court. The opinion, delivered on November 8, 1897, was written by J. Bartholomew. Reproduced below is the full text of the decision—properly cited as *State v. Coudotte, 72 N.W. 913 (1897)*—leaving out only a half-page of preliminary summary and technical information. The person quoted near the end of the document and described as "a witness in the case, who has spent practically his entire life with the Sioux Indians, speaks their language, and understands every phase of their character" is Harry McLaughlin, son of agent James McLaughlin:

State v. Coudotte

The appellant, Alec Coudotte, was informed against by the state's attorney of Emmons County for the crime of murder in the first degree, in killing one Thomas Spicer, in said county, on the 17th day of February, 1897. He was tried, convicted, and sentenced to be hung, in the district court of said county. A motion for a new trial, made on a statement of the case, was denied, and the appellant brings the entire record to this court by appeal. The errors alleged, and which we shall discuss, relate exclusively to the sufficiency of the evidence to support the conviction. If there was in the case no question as to the proper corroboration of an accomplice, our task, in this instance, would be brief. True, there is strong evidence in the case tending to support the appellant's claim of alibi; but, on the state of this record, no court would be warranted in disturbing the finding of the jury upon that point. But the principal evidence for the state in this case came from two confessed accomplices. Our statute, voicing the almost universal practice in both England and the United States even in the absence of statute, declares, in section 8195, Rev. Codes: "A conviction cannot be had

6. Reversal

The Emmons County Courthouse in Williamsport, North Dakota. Alec Coudotte, Paul Holy Track, and Philip Ireland were incarcerated here when the state supreme court reversed Coudotte's conviction. A week or so later the lynch mob removed the prisoners (State Historical Society of North Dakota 1952-3427).

upon the testimony of an accomplice unless he is corroborated by such other evidence as tends to connect the defendant with the commission of the offense, and the corroboration is not sufficient if it merely shows the commission of the offense, or the circumstances thereof." The specific requirement, under this section, is that the corroborating evidence tends to connect the defendant with the commission of the offense. Whart. Cr. Ev. § 442, declares: "The corroboration requisite to validate the testimony of an alleged accomplice should be to the person of the accused. Any other corroboration would be delusive, since, if corroboration in matters not connecting the accused with the offense were enough, a party who, in the case against him, would have no hope of escape, could, by his mere oath, transfer to another the conviction hanging over himself." And Rosc. Cr. Ev. 130, states the principle thus: "There may be many witnesses, therefore, who give testimony which agrees with that of the accomplice, but which, if it does not serve to identify the accused parties, is no corroboration of the accomplice." Under this principle, which courts were compelled originally to adopt to protect innocent persons, and which, by innumerable decisions, was crystallized into universal law, and which is declared in clear and specific language by our statutes, it will not be necessary or proper for us to discuss any of that portion of the so-called corroborating testimony which simply goes to show that the crime was committed, and the time and manner of its commission. We can profitably discuss only such portions of this testimony as it may be claimed in some degree tend to identify this defendant with the commission of the crime.

The confessed accomplices are Philip Ireland and Paul Holy Track. These parties also accuse the defendant and one George Defender with being present, and aiding and participating in the commission of the crime. All these parties are Indians, or persons of Indian descent. They belong at the Standing Rock Indian agency. This agency is situated on the west bank of the Missouri River, and opposite the town of Winona, in Emmons County. The residence of Thomas Spicer, where the crime was committed, was about 1.75 miles north of Winona, and on the same side of the river, which at that season of the year (February 17th) was frozen over solidly, and could be crossed at any point. The crime that was committed has few parallels in atrocity and wanton cruelty. The sole object for its commission was to plunder the house. To accomplish this purpose, Thomas Spicer and his wife, and his wife's aged mother, Mrs. Waldron, and their married daughter, Mrs. Rouse, were foully murdered; and then, actuated, it would appear, solely by the instincts of a savage, the perpetrators proceeded to murder the twin baby boys of Mrs. Rouse. Six persons in all were killed. It could not be otherwise than that a deed of such depravity should arouse the community where committed almost to frenzy. Every instinct of humanity and of justice demanded the swift and certain punishment of the inhuman miscreants whose minds could conceive and whose hands could execute a deed so dastardly. Standing face to face with such a crime the judgment of a juror, however intelligent and honorable he may be, must inevitably be influenced in some degree by his surroundings. It is to the credit of his nature that it cries out for punishment for such a crime. But under such circumstances it is too plain for argument that the court, if such a thing could be possible, should exercise all the greater care to see to it that the evidence does conform to a well-established and statutory rule, which the experience of ages has shown to be necessary for the protection of innocent persons. It was suggested in argument that as there were two accomplices, and their testimony was substantially the same, a less amount of corroborating evidence than in ordinary cases, and where there was but one accomplice, would suffice. This argument should be addressed to the jury. It can have no weight here, because we are not concerned with the amount of corroborating testimony. If there be any such evidence, coming within the requirements of the statute, its weight was for the jury, and we cannot disturb their verdict. But, if there was no such testimony, then the jury should have been so instructed, or, failing in that, the motion for a new trial based upon that ground should have been granted.

We shall discuss the testimony only so far as may be necessary to an understanding of those portions which the state claims furnish the corroboration required by the statute. It appears that after Coudotte's arrest, and prior to his preliminary hearing, he was confined in jail at Williamsport, the county seat of Emmons County. While thus confined he was visited by several parties who spoke the Sioux language, which was Coudotte's native tongue — and he could speak no other — and they endeavored to procure from him a confession. Prior to this time he had gashed himself in the abdomen with a knife. The state claims, and perhaps correctly, that this was an attempt to commit suicide. He was suffering from the wound at the time of the interview, and stated to the witnesses that he expected to die from its effects. In that interview, if we accept as true what the witnesses state, Coudotte said that he was in Winona on said February 17, 1897; that he left there about 2 o'clock in the afternoon, and crossed over to the agency, where he met one Frank Blackhawk; that Blackhawk was intoxicated, and took another drink of whiskey from a supply that he (Coudotte) had; that Blackhawk then said to Coudotte that he was going over to kill the Spicer family, and asked Coudotte to go with him, which Coudotte refused to do, but immediately proceeded to his home. He gave as his reason for going home — to quote one of the witnesses: "Because people were going to be killed, and he would be home, so there would not be any blame for him." He also stated, according to the witnesses, that on February 20th he again met Blackhawk at one of the agency stores, and Blackhawk told him that he had killed the Spicer family, and wanted to give him money to keep the secret. We notice that the testimony of the accomplices in no manner implicates Blackhawk in the crime. But we assume that he was implicated. The utmost that can be claimed for this statement is that Coudotte was told beforehand that the Spicers were to be killed, and was told afterwards that they had been killed. But how can knowledge alone tend to connect him with the commission of the offense? Clearly, in no manner, and to no extent. The proposition is self-evident. It is proper to add that, through this statement wherein this knowledge is admitted, the appellant emphatically denies any connection with the commission of the crime.

The learned state's attorney claims much in the way of corroboration from the testimony of one Welch, who testifies that he thinks he saw the defendant and George Defender together on horseback at the Fort Yates mule corral at or a little after 6 o'clock in the evening of the day on which the murder was committed. This would, at best, be very dangerous testimony on which to base a conviction for murder. The witness was 200 yards — nearly one-eighth of a mile — distant from the parties. We know that at or soon after 6 o'clock in the evening of February 17th in this latitude, it is nearly or quite dark. Positive identification at that distance would be impossible, and in fact the witness does not pretend to be positive. But assume that his surmise was correct; in what manner does the presence of Coudotte and Defender together at the corral, three miles southwest from the Spicer place, at 6 o'clock in the evening, tend to connect them with the commission of the offense? We doubt not, many other men might have been found together at that hour at points much nearer the Spicer place. Had the accomplices accused such other parties, their presence together would have been no evidence whatever tending to connect them with the commission of the offense. A contrary contention reaches absurdity, and yet the fact, standing alone, would be just as much evidence in one case as in the other. But the state's attorney argues that the accomplices testified that, after the murder had been committed, Coudotte and Defender left the Spicer place, on horseback, going north; that this evidence establishes the parties together on horseback at the scene of the murder; and that, taken with the further fact that they were seen together on horseback, two or three hours later, by another party, tends to connect them with the commission of the crime. We do not concede that the conclusion follows the premises, but in any event, in order that this testimony should show any force whatever as corroborating testimony, it is necessary to include the portion given by the accomplices. In other words, the accomplices must be permitted to corroborate themselves. This is utterly untenable. What we have just said applies with still greater force to the claim made for the testimony tending to show these same parties together at Winona on the night of February 18th. There is much conflict in the testimony as to whether or not they were there. In our judgment, it is immaterial. The fact alone of their presence at Winona thirty hours later would in no manner tend to connect this defendant with the commission of the crime. Nor would such fact, if it were a fact, be any more incriminating because the defendant, on oath, denied it.

The state also claims some corroboration in the evidence relating to some beef which it is admitted was sold by Coudotte in Winona about 4 o'clock on Tuesday, February 16th. We have read and re-read this testimony. We find no element of corroboration of the nature required by statute in it. Paul Holy Track testified that himself, the defendant and Blackhawk killed a steer about daylight in the morning of February 16th in the timber near the Spicer house, and that the beef sold by Coudotte was a part of this animal. Coudotte claims that it was a portion of an animal killed by himself and Blackhawk at an entirely different place, and more than twenty-four hours earlier. But let us concede that the steer was killed as Holy Track testifies, and that Coudotte sold a portion of it in Winona on Tuesday afternoon; how does that tend to connect Coudotte with a crime committed twenty-four hours later? What possible connection could exist between the sale of this beef and the murder of Thomas Spicer? If there be any, it is found in the testimony of Paul Holy Track, and there only.

Persons who examined the body of Thomas Spicer testified that four different weapons had been used, either in committing the murder or mutilating the body, to wit, a gun loaded with a leaden bullet and shot, an axe, a pitchfork, and a spade or shovel. The state claims that this raises a presumption that four persons participated in the crime. This is surmise, merely. The dastard who fired the gun would not hesitate to dispatch a wounded victim with an axe. There is no presumption that a murderer will use but one weapon. But if, from the fact that four weapons were used, a jury would be warranted in saying that four persons participated in the crime, where is the corroborating testimony that declares, or tends to declare, who these four persons were? The use of the weapons points as directly towards any other Indian on the reservation, or any citizen of Winona, as towards this defendant. This evidence is a striking instance of the precise vice against which the rule as to corroborating an accomplice is directed. It fails to tend to identify the party.

There remains but one further fact from which the state claims any corroboration whatever — the only fact that has given us any trouble — and that is the attempted suicide. Upon this question we get no direct aid from the authorities. The question whether or not any presumption of guilt arises from an attempt to commit suicide, made before trial, is one that has never been discussed, or even adverted to, so far as we can ascertain. Counsel seek to assimilate an attempt to commit suicide with flight, and, since the fact of flight is generally allowed to go to the jury as some evidence of guilt, it is urged that, where a party charged with crime attempts to commit suicide, that fact raises a presumption, more or less strong, that such party is guilty of the crime charged. The argument is specious, but we think the parallel deceptive and dangerous. One who flees does so, generally, for the purpose of avoiding the punishment that follows violated law. One who commits or attempts suicide seeks to avoid no punishment. He deliberately accepts the highest punishment that the law could possibly inflict,—death. Hence the very circumstance that raises the presumption of guilt from flight is absolutely wanting in suicide. In this, some impelling motive other than a desire to evade the punishment by law must be the basis for the act, and we think this motive will usually be found along the line of those facts and circumstances which make flight itself innocent. Whart. Cr. Ev., in speaking of flight, concealment, etc., says (section 750): "But it must be remembered that, while these acts are indications of fear, they may spring from causes very different from that of conscious guilt." And the author quotes from Best, Ev. (5th Ed.) 578: "Many men are naturally of weak nerve, and under certain circumstances the most innocent person may deem a trial too great a risk to encounter. He may be aware that a number of suspicious, though inconclusive, facts will be adduced in evidence against him. He may feel his inability to procure legal advice to conduct his defense, or to bring witnesses from a distance to establish it. He may be assured that powerful or wealthy individuals have resolved on his ruin, or that witnesses have been suborned to bear false testimony against him." He who commits or attempts suicide, since he does not seek to avoid punishment, must seek to avoid the disgrace that attaches to being charged with crime — the ignominy that attaches to a public trial for crime. He is deficient in the nerve necessary to face the situation, or it may be that a wild, untamed nature rebels beyond all bounds at being confined. But with what natures would these motives of delicacy be most powerful the innocent or the guilty? That person whose nature was so depraved and hardened that he could commit the crime charged in this information would feel no sensitive shrinking from the disgrace of an arrest or trial. It is a well-known fact that the suicidal tendency frequently manifests itself in insane persons. It has been said that no perfectly sane person ever committed suicide, and there is doubtless an element of truth in the statement;

and, the greater the dementia, the more probable the desire of self-destruction. When we essay the task of accounting for suicide on any general grounds, we undertake a task that, from its very nature, is impossible of performance. The human mind is so wonderfully, yet so delicately, constructed, the human passions are so powerful, yet so varied, that it is idle for any one person to pretend to enter the consciousness of another, and account for the inner workings of that other mind. We only know that, whatever may be the motive, it is not, and cannot be, a desire to avoid punishment. The number of innocent persons who commit suicide within any given time is always many times greater than the number of guilty persons who commit suicide within the same time. Hence suicide can always be accounted for, upon the hypothesis of innocence more readily than upon the hypothesis of guilt. This being true, a jury never could be permitted to treat it as an evidence of guilt. We believe that it would be dangerous to innocence to declare, as a legal proposition, that an attempt to commit suicide before trial raises a presumption of guilt in any case. The danger of such a proposition is well illustrated by this case. This defendant, an Indian, finds himself torn from his tribal surroundings, and incarcerated in a prison of those whom he regards as his hereditary enemies. He is charged with the murder of a white man. He believes himself to be absolutely in the hands of those who hate his race. He is ignorant of our laws and our court proceedings. He knows only too well what would be the result were the conditions reversed, and he cannot understand why he should receive treatment different from that which he would mete out to an enemy. Seeing only the blackness of darkness ahead of him, and that irrespective of his innocence or guilt, would it be strange that his nerve should fail him, and he seek to shut out the hated picture by severing his hold upon life? Moreover, he comes of a race whose untamed natures cannot brook confinement. The defendant was asked on cross-examination why he attempted to commit suicide, and promptly answered that he did it because he did not like to be confined. And a witness in the case, who has spent practically his entire life with the Sioux Indians, speaks their language, and understands every phase of their character, and whose testimony is entirely uncontradicted, says: "I have often known, if an Indian is put in the guard house for any little offense, I have known them to cut themselves, and try to commit suicide in many different ways. That seems to be a predisposition among them, in confinement. I have frequently known of Indians attempting suicide because they were in confinement. I was present at a conversation with Coudotte in the Emmons County jail. He spoke in my presence in relation to his attempt to commit suicide. He said he could not stand to be confined, and he would just as soon be dead as to have to stay in there and stand the confinement." In view of these undisputed facts and the surrounding circumstances, it would shock the sense of justice to say that this attempt at suicide, standing alone, raises a presumption of guilt which so far corroborates the testimony of an accomplice that a conviction could be based upon his testimony.

We have discussed every point in the evidence from which the state claims any corroboration whatever, and we find that in each instance the testimony fails to meet the statutory requirement. It follows that the motion for a new trial should have been granted, and that the judgment based upon the verdict must be set aside, and a new trial ordered. It is proper to add that owing to the enormity of the crime in this instance, and the deep indignation of the public, and the positive statements of the confessed murderers, Paul Holy Track and Philip Ireland, the learned state's attorney of Emmons County could not, in the performance of his official duty, do less than present to the court this information against Coudotte. He has certainly pursued with diligence and intelligence every source of information open to him that promised any corroborating testimony, and he presented the testimony that he could procure to this court in the strongest light that it will bear. But, tested by an inflexible rule of law, that testimony cannot support a conviction. Reversed. All concur.

The abbreviated references included above in the statement of the supreme court decision are to these sources: "Whart. Cr. Ev.," short for *Wharton's Criminal Evidence*, itself a shortened reference to Francis Wharton, *A Treatise on the Law of Evidence in Criminal Issues*, ninth edition (Philadelphia: Kay & Brother, 1884); "Rosc. Cr. Ev.," short for *Roscoe's Criminal Evidence*, itself a shortened reference to [Henry] *Roscoe's Digest of the Law of Evidence in Criminal Cases*, eleventh edition (London: Stevens and Sons, Ltd., 1890); "Best, Ev.," short for William M. Best, *Principles of the Law of Evidence with Elementary Rules for Conducting the Examination and Cross-Examination of Witnesses*, fifth edition (New York: J. Cockcroft and Co., 1878). According to these standard reference tools for those conducting criminal trials, Judge Winchester erred in not instructing the jury to acquit Alec Coudotte. Wharton says, "The practice is uniform for the judge, when the question comes up, to instruct the jury that unless the accomplice be corroborated in such a way as to show the truth of his story, their duty is to acquit" (p. 376). Roscoe puts it this way: "As the law now stands, it is universally agreed by all the authorities that, if the accomplice were uncorroborated, a judge would be wrong who did not advise the jury not to convict" (p. 123). Perhaps as a matter of professional courtesy, Bartholomew chose not to embarrass Winchester by quoting these statements in the decision of the state supreme court. The record, however, is clear: Winchester at no time advised, instructed, or directed the jury to acquit the defendant.

7

Lynching

It is not surprising that there was outrage among the white settlers at the decision of the supreme court of North Dakota. To people who knew the Spicers, the arcane technicalities of the law that were meant to ensure justice had in this case, they were sure, subverted justice. They must have wished they had not bothered with an expensive, time-consuming, and useless trial but had gone straight to a lynching. Had they done so, they would have had before them the recent example of two lynched black women in Alabama. It was widely reported, even in North Dakota:

Grand Forks Daily Herald
Grand Forks, North Dakota
May 13, 1897

Alabama Justice

The corpses of two negroes, Nelly Smith and Mandy White, are dangling from the limb of a live oak just on the outskirts of the village of Jeff. They were hanged last night for poisoning Joshua Kelly, a well-known citizen. They confessed to two attempts on the lives of the Kelly family. The first attempt resulted in the death of Kelly. Sheriff Powell has gone to the scene to cut down the bodies. Nine weeks ago the first attempts on the lives of the Kelly family were made. The family sickened shortly after eating supper and Joshua Kelly died twenty-four hours afterwards. On May 1, the family and tenants of the deceased were poisoned again in some mysterious manner. There were six whites and eight negroes affected. D. E. and Lamson Kelly became critically ill as did Mrs. E. Kelly. Oakley Woodward, a clerk in the store, who came near dying from the other poisoning, and a Tennessee drummer, who spent the night with them, were two of the victims. Incriminating evidence was found Saturday at the Kelly home at Jeff and a clew in the shape of a box of poison led to the detection of the negresses. The premises were searched and underneath the kitchen was found a box of poison. On it was stamped the trade mark D. E. and J. O. Kelly, grocers at

7. Lynching

(Left to right) Alec Coudotte, Philip Ireland, and Paul Holy Track the morning after the lynching. They were hanged from a beef windlass normally used for butchering. In the background is the Emmons County Courthouse in Williamsport, where they had been imprisoned (State Historical Society of North Dakota 0281–0038.)

> Jeff. The poison was placed in the biscuits which all affected ate. The lynching occurred at an early hour this morning and was participated in by a mob of twenty or thirty persons.

That "Alabama justice" was swift, of course, but was it just? Had there been a trial, any defense lawyer would have asked all sorts of questions: What was the motive? Who else might have had a reason to poison the biscuits? Why were so many black people also poisoned? Who had purchased the poison? Was there any evidence that the variety of poison found under the kitchen had been put into the biscuits? Might it have been placed there simply to control the rodent population? Under what circumstances were the "confessions" obtained, and what exactly had the two women confessed to? And so on.

As we have seen, the idea of lynching the five Indians implicated in the Spicer murders had been mentioned many times earlier, but after the reversal by the state supreme court, editorials openly demanded it. The following article suggests that the cost of legal justice was too great for the taxpayers of Emmons County. There had to be a more economical way to do justice. The references to Kent, Swidenski, and Normand in the coming pages are to other North Dakota murderers who, through technicalities and the judgment of a higher court, had escaped the punishment they supposedly deserved:

Mandan Pioneer
Mandan, North Dakota
November 12, 1897

[Too Expensive a Luxury]

As was to be expected, the supreme court gave the Indian Coudot, one of the Spicer murderers, a new trial. No jury was right that ever tried a murderer for the first time in this state, and found him guilty, in the judgment of the supreme court. It was so in the Kent case, but another jury 200 miles away, with a different judge, speedily found the same kind of a verdict. In Emmons County the public feeling was considered so fair by the attorneys for Coudot that they did not even ask for a change of venue. The county went to the expense of a trial, costing thousands of dollars; a jury found Coudot guilty, but the supreme court decides that he must have another trial. It is safe to say that he will not get another trial. Trials of murderers in Emmons County are too expensive a luxury. There are those who claim that the good people of Emmons, who have had more murders than all the other counties in the district put together, in the last seven years, may be expected to take the law in their own hands after this. Of course such conduct will be worthy of blame; every member of a civilized community realizes this. But can they afford to impoverish themselves merely to have their work overturned by a supreme court which sits in calm magnificence at the state capitol?

Coudot will not have another trial. George Defender, who should have his trial the latter part of this month at Bismarck, will in all probability not be tried. These Indians will all be turned loose. It is no use on earth for the taxpayers of Emmons County to impoverish themselves trying murderers who have slaughtered women and children, to have a magnificent supreme court step in and let them go scot free. Turn the murderers loose, and it may be that they will never reach the reservation.

Even less strident editorials often called for the agency of a new judge, named not Judge Winchester or Judge Sauter but Judge Lynch. This one found the supreme court's decision to be "quite as shocking as the crime":

Saint Paul Globe
St. Paul, Minnesota
November 11, 1897

Sentiment Defeating Justice

A few months ago the sensibilities of the whole Northwest were shocked by the brutal murder of the Spicer family. Thomas Spicer, his wife, her mother, Mrs. Rouse and her twin children were found murdered in the Spicer home near Winona in North Dakota, their remains mutilated in a manner that indicated the fiendish nature of those who committed the deed. Following certain clues, five Indians, of full and half blood, were arrested. Two of them made complete confessions, giving in detail the names of the party, the motive of the crime and the manner of its commission. One of the three implicated by the confession was put on trial and convicted on the testimony of the two who confessed. There was no, there could hardly be, corroborative testimony. Coudot was convicted and sentenced by the jury to death. An appeal was taken to the supreme court.

That body hands down a decision that is quite as shocking as the crime. It reverses the verdict because the statute of that state provides that conviction shall not be had in murder cases upon the uncorroborated evidence of accomplices in the crime, and there was no such supporting evidence given. The state's attorney says that, under this holding he will be unable to secure a conviction of any of the brutes and that the cases will have to be dismissed. There is food for very serious reflection in this. It may well be considered whether our laws do not go too far in leniency to and consideration of persons accused of crime. The maxim that a man shall be considered innocent until the state proves him to be guilty came into existence during that long struggle of the commonalty against the privileged classes. It has long survived the reason of its being. It operates now only to cast a burden of proof upon the state so heavy as frequently to cause a miscarriage of justice. French law goes upon the opposite theory. It considers the accused guilty until he establishes his innocence. This goes as much to one extreme as our presumption goes to the other. The sensible position lies between the two with no presumption either way.

Complaint has been justifiably made, less in later years, however, that courts, in trying or reviewing criminal cases, were too technical, reversing verdicts and granting new trials upon grounds that appear to be flimsy to the layman. The natural reaction from this has been the establishment of the summary courts presided over by Judge Lynch. The lay mind does not deal with refinements and distinctions. It reasons directly. It brushes aside as insufficient the excuse that prevents the infliction of deserved punishment because some prosecuting attorney has, for instance, forgotten to prove the venue. Has there been a crime committed, and did this person commit it? These are the only two questions laymen admit as bearing on such cases, and because courts allow other confusing questions to be made material to the, often, defeat of justice, laymen take the law and its execution into their own hands. Where justice permits no trifling with her processes, where trial is fair and punishment sure when conviction is obtained, Judge Lynch holds no courts.

In this case, however, the fault is not with the court, but with the law. It is well, perhaps, that so strong a case as this of Coudot's should arise to reveal the immense possibilities of injustice, of crime successfully evading punishment, that attention may be drawn to the effect of permitting mistaken sentiment to interfere with the work of justice, and to the end that so grievous a legislative mistake as is that provision may be remedied.

Only a few days later Judge Lynch did provide a remedy, of sorts, when a mob of men, some of them masked, stormed the Williamsport jail. That was at around 2 o'clock in the early morning of Sunday, November 14, 1897. They relieved the jailer, Thomas Kelly, of the keys to the cells and summarily hanged the three inmates he was charged with protecting. A deposition from Kelly was taken in the presence of the coroner the next day. Kelly's reference to the "Modern Woodmen's Hall" is to an organization founded in 1890 in Omaha, Nebraska, by a man named Joseph Cullen Root. Modern Woodmen of the World was set up to provide financial protection to pioneers who cleared away the forests to provide farmland for their homesteads. This organization had a chapter that met that Saturday night in Williamsport:

[Testimony of Thomas Kelly]

Testimony Taken Before a Coroner's Jury at an Inquisition Held on the Bodies of Alec Coudotte, Paul Holytrack, and Philip Ireland, Lying Dead. Said Inquisition Being Held in the Office of the County Auditor, in the Emmons County Courthouse, of the 14th Day of November, 1897, Before William M. Derr, Coroner of Said County of Emmons.

Thomas Kelly, being duly sworn by the coroner, testified as follows:
Q.-Where do you reside?
A.-In Williamsport, North Dakota.
Q.-What, if any, position do you hold at the county jail in said county?
A.-I am night guard.
Q.-Were you on duty on the night of the 13th day of November?
A.-Yes.
Q.-State who, if any one, came to the jail during the night of the 13th, after 1 o'clock; and what they did, if anything.

A.-I heard a rap at the door. I thought it was someone from the hall (the Modern Woodmen's Hall, where a meeting was being held that was in session until nearly 1 o'clock). Immediately a second rap came and a voice, not very loud. I walked to the door and opened it; a man shoved a six-shooter up near to my face and said that they wanted the keys — that they had come after those fellows.

I backed in the door and admonished them to be quiet. They told me that they did not want any foolishness — that they meant business — and two of them followed me to the table. Some more of them came inside of the door from the storm-shed and filled the corridor pretty well. I was in my shirt-sleeves and my coat was hanging against the wall on a hook. I went to the door and wanted to argue the case with them. Some one in the storm-shed said, "Take the keys away from him," and one of them spoke up and said, "Don't hurt Mr. Kelly," and I think that he repeated it.

I told them that the Woodmen were having a meeting at the hall, and

7. Lynching

that Mr. Armstrong (the state's attorney) was there, and for them to go down and have Mr. Armstrong come up, and I would turn over the keys to him. They told me that I was the man whom they wanted to deal with, and that they did not want to have anything to do with Mr. Armstrong.

Someone in the crowd said, "Time is up," and I thought I knew what that meant. Then someone said, "Open the doors or give up the keys." All this time there were guns in sight — in plenty. I think that I then got the lantern and went and opened the two outside doors. They were both locked. I handed the keys to somebody, and they told me to hold the light. I told them that there were enough of them to do that, and that I would do nothing of the kind. Someone took the lantern and I came into this room (the auditor's office).

They ordered me to bring a light in there, and I told them they would have to get it themselves. I then went to the door and asked them, "Where is your leader?" They answered that they had none.

I suggested that they take Coudotte and leave the other two fellows there — that they knew that they would be hanged. They said that they did not know anything of the kind — that Coudotte was to be hanged, but he gets a new trial, and the other fellows may get up and say that they are not guilty.

There were three men at the door of the office, and one of them kept suggesting to me that he hoped I would be a gentleman. He kept telling the other two fellows to watch me. About that time they led Coudotte out. They had a rope around his neck. They dragged the other two fellows out. I do not know which one was first, but I think it was Ireland.

I went to the east window and looked out. There was a light in Rush's place, and, I thought, one in the hall. I came back into the office and took a drink of water. I turned around and asked the fellows at the door which route I was going by — the rope or the gun route — and one of the gentlemen again told me that he hoped I would be a gentleman. I asked him to come into the office and we would play a game of seven-up while we were waiting. He thanked me, saying, "We have other business on hand at this time." Then I said I would sit down and play solitaire.

I sat down at the north side of the table that stands east and west. I ran the cards over and beat solitaire. I got up and went to the door and said, "I can beat solitaire, but I can't stand you fellows off." Some one answered, "No." I asked them what they had done with the keys, and one of the men went out. I told them that the sheriff might want the keys some time. In a short time someone came back and threw the keys on that box (pointing to a box in the room). I told him to hand the keys to me, as I had handed the keys to them. He did so, and the one who had frequently told me to be a gentleman again said, "I hope you will be a gentleman." In a short time they bade me "Goodnight!" and walked out.

I then went upstairs and pounded on the door, and Jimmy (James McCormick, of the *Record*) came and opened the door. I told him that there had been a hanging-bee. That they had taken the Indians out and that they were gone. I asked them (McCormick and D. R. Streeter, who, with young Frank Streeter, slept in the second story) where they had been, and they said they had been asleep and had just waked up.

I started to go downstairs, and McCormick said he would go down with me. We walked downtown, and I saw some men or moving objects at Mike Rush's beef windlass. A little further down I saw someone by some wagons near the log buildings west of the windlass. There were two persons, I think. There were four people in front of Rush's west door—Baxter, McGinness, Rush and Dennis Casey, I think. I went down to Mr. Yeater's. I thought that Mr. Armstrong might be there. They told me that Armstrong had gone home about an hour before. I asked for Braddock (the auditor) or Macdonald (chairman of board of county commissioners), and was told that they had gone to bed.

I went upstairs and knocked on what I supposed to be their door, and got into someone else's room and found Jaszkowiak there. I then went into the room where Messrs. Macdonald and Braddock were and as briefly as possible related to them what had occurred. I asked Braddock what I had better do, and he said that I had better notify the state's attorney and the coroner, and that they would know best what was to be done.

I came back to the jail and picked up a pair of pants and threw them into the corridor and locked the lattice door of the jail. I went back to Yeater's place and then down to Armstrong's place, and then back to the jail and went upstairs to bed.

Before locking the cell door I went over near the beef swing and saw three bodies hanging there, which I took to be Coudotte, Holy Track and Ireland. The one on the west side I was satisfied was Coudotte, but I was not entirely satisfied as to who the other two were.

In a taped interview in 2012, Archie D. Fool Bear, a relative of Philip Ireland, told me that, according to a family story, there was an Indian who saw the lynching:

Interview with Archie D. Fool Bear
Fort Yates, North Dakota
August 20, 2012

Basically Tortured

The three young men, Paul Holy Track, Alex Coudotte, and Philip Ireland, were basically tortured, according to the stories that came back to the Indian people. The lynch mob had ropes tied around their necks, and you had horseback riders running up and down the street with them, dragging them behind their horses. And when they got done terrorizing them and doing what they did to them, they took them over by a butcher shop and hung them up for display.

One of the tribal elders from Cannon Ball happened to be in that town that day. Supposedly, these guys all had hoods on when they broke into the jail. And a friend of this Indian elder from Cannon Ball—I can't remember what his name is — was told by his friend who was in the mob, "You stay out of sight. This is our business. You don't want to know what's going on. Stay out of sight." So he did, but he watched. And these guys on horses put the ropes around the boys' necks, saddle horned them up and made them run at first until they couldn't run any more, and then started dragging them.

This elder saw it happen. He went back and told the old people in Cannon Ball what he had seen. Now, of course, if you look for documentary proof that this torturing happened, you won't find it. But that's the way it happened according to the stories that my family heard.

The three bodies were left hanging on the windlass until about Sunday noon, when the coroner, William M. Derr, with assistance, lowered them so that he could examine the bodies and determine the cause of death. The bodies of the three men were placed in wooden coffins assembled for them that Sunday. The state's attorney, Armstrong, wrote to Standing Rock agent John Cramsie inquiring whether he wanted the bodies returned to the reservation for burial. Cramsie replied by a letter to Armstrong on November 15, 1897:

Dear Sir:

In reply to your letter just handed to me, I have to request on behalf of the friends of Holytrack, Ireland, and Cadotte that the remains be buried by the authorities of Emmons County. [...] Please have the graves marked so that when the excitement shall have died out, and the friends desire to remove the bodies, the graves can be identified.

Very Respectfully
John W. Cramsie
U.S. Indian Agent

The bodies were buried on Tuesday, November 16, in the prairie north of Williamsport, but the relatives of the dead men asked to have them brought back to the reservation. They were disinterred and brought back the next day. The priest refused to let them be buried in the church cemetery. They were finally buried, on Wednesday, November 17, just nine months after the murder of the Spicer family, on reservation lands but outside the Catholic cemetery.

In his statement, Thomas Kelly had referred to a couple of men sleeping in guest quarters above the jail in the courthouse. The room had a small trap door through which a jailer might look down upon the prisoners. One of the upstairs guests, D. R. Streeter, editor of the *Bismarck Daily Tribune*, later gave this account of the incident:

Bismarck Daily Tribune
Bismarck, North Dakota
November 20, 1897

Coroner's Verdict

The bodies of the three Indians who were lynched at Williamsport Sunday morning last were buried on the reservation at Fort Yates yesterday. They were buried twice, first at Williamsport, it being thought best not to take them to the reservation until the excitement of the lynching had died away, and their graves there were opened and the bodies removed to the reservation yesterday, where they were buried.

The coroners jury, F. D. Smyth, S. E. Kurtz and Charles Bouillier, returned a verdict of death by strangulation at the hands of some persons unknown.

[...]

Editor Streeter, who sleeps in the jail, has the following account of his observance of events:

There was a confused sound of voices while the prisoners were being taken from the cells and the ropes tied about their necks. Not a word or a sound from either of the prisoners was heard at any time by the guard or by those in the second story. Those above saw Coudot standing under the hole with the rope around his neck. As Coudot was jerked out of his cell some one said, "Your are the villain I want." The lynchers had their hats on, which precluded identification from above. And it may be stated that those above weren't trying particularly hard to recognize anybody, contenting themselves by listening to the sounds.

Presently the crowd started from the cell corridor to the front of the building, and the "audience" upstairs went to the front, or south window. As the crowd came out Coudot was seen standing in the dim moonlight with a rope around his neck. The crowd stopped about a minute in front of the building. Then with two forms dragging on the ground, with several men ahold of each rope and Coudot walking, the crowd, which seemed to be composed of some fifteen or twenty men, started rapidly to the southeast. Those in the auditor's room with the guard had hankerchiefs over their faces. The men with the three prisoners passed out of vision at about forty yards, and nothing more was heard for a minute or two, save an occasional subdued voice. Then came the creaking of Rush's windlass, about 130 yards south of the jail.

As the crowd left the front of the building and went out of sight, the writer struck a match and looked at his watch, hanging on the wall. It was twenty-four minutes past 1 o'clock. The voices and other noises were heard at the windlass for about ten minutes, and then all was still. At the beginning of the proceedings at the jail, after he awoke, the writer locked the up stairs hall door, as he thought some anxious chap might come "snooping around" up stairs, wanting to know if anything had been seen by anybody. And guard Kelly says one of the first things the crowd did was to barricade the bottom hall door. And this double-headed arrangement seemed perfectly satisfactory to everybody — to the two men up stairs who didn't want to see anything in particular, and to the folks in the lower story who didn't seem disposed to issue formal invitations to the spectacle.

After the job was done the crowd filed down the main street by twos in regular marching order. They said not a word, except to give a "Yip! Yip!" as they got about a hundred yards around the corner, from the post office. The party had made the deserted Bussey house, half a mile southeast of town, their rendezvous, and their rigs were seen by state's attorney Armstrong on his way home, after midnight, from the Woodmen's meeting. He saw no men and thought the rigs belonged to Emmons County settlers returning from harvesting and threshing further east. The lynchers had probably at that time started down town by a round-about route. Two or three persons who were on the street say that the lynchers came up to the jail from the southeast, passing north of Mr. Farrel's blacksmith shop. The affair had been so well planned and so quietly and cooly carried out that not a soul in town had any idea as to the identity of a single one of the party. And it is doubtful if any man, woman or child in the county would have cared to know their identity, unless — to thank them for what they had done.

A more complete version of these events appeared in the Bismarck newspaper, which focused on the local people involved and on the fate of the two remaining suspects.

Bismarck Daily Tribune
Bismarck, North Dakota
November 15, 1897

A Terrible Vengeance

Paul Holy Track, Philip Ireland, and Alec Coudot, the first two the confessed murderers of the Spicer family, and the latter the first of the men to be tried and convicted and to whom a new trial had just been granted by the supreme court, were lynched by a mob of twenty-five or thirty men at Williamsport at 2 o'clock Sunday morning.

News of the lynching was brought to the city yesterday afternoon at about 3 o'clock by Harry Procunier, who came up from Williamsport to notify sheriff Shier, who was in this city at the time the lynching occurred.

According to the reports received in this city, the lynching was done by a party of men who rode into Williamsport on horseback late at night and left their horses just outside the town where they could be readily secured. [...]

The three prisoners had been awakened from sleep by the noise of the entrance of the men, and cowered back in their cells, realizing that their time was short. Holy Track and Ireland were confined in the same cell and Coudot in another. As soon as the doors had been opened, ropes were fastened about their necks by the mob and they were dragged forth from their cells. Holy Track and Ireland came in for less consideration than Coudot, as they were dragged to the place of hanging. Coudot was allowed to walk.

When they had dragged the men outside the jail, the members of the lynching party cast about for a place to lynch them. An attempt was first made to suspend them from the frame of a well curbing, but that proved impossible. The victims were then hurried to an adjacent log-house, and an attempt made to hang them from the projecting logs but that proved also futile. A huge derrick that served to raise and suspend the bodies of slaughtered beeves stood near the house of Mike Rush and that offered the means for which the men were looking. The prisoners were hurried to that and ropes thrown over a cross beam.

It was reported in the city that before any of them were swung up, Coudot was asked whether Frank Black Hawk and George Defender were also guilty of the murder of the Spicer family, and an affirmative answer received. The rope was then tightened, and the body of Coudot raised from the ground and suspended in air.

Holy Track and Ireland were nearly if not quite unconscious when the scaffold was reached, and their limp bodies were raised from the ground and dangled in air.

The three bodies were then left swinging in the air from the windlass, and the members of the party dispersed as they had come, mounted their horses and rode away.

A few of the residents of Williamsport were aroused from their rest by the unusual proceedings, and gazed in awe from windows and the shadow of buildings upon the actions of the lynching party. There was no possibility of offering any resistance, and none was offered. The party was in force sufficient to overcome whatever opposition there might have been.

It is stated that there was not much resistance on the part of the men who were hanged. They were dazed by the sudden appearance of the mob, as they were roused from sleep, and before they had realized what had happened, the ropes were about their necks and they were being dragged to the place of execution.

When daylight broke and the startled people of Williamsport had recovered from the shock of the affair, three bodies were swaying in the breeze from the windlass, attesting the vengeance of the mob.

Coroner Derr was not at Williamsport, and a messenger was at once sent to apprise him of the affair. He did not arrive until noon, until which time the bodies remained suspended in midair. They were cut down upon his arrival. A coroner's inquest will probably be begun today.

There was a rumor that an attempt would also be made to take Frank Black Hawk and George Defender from the jail in this city, where they are confined, and treat them in the same fashion. Not much credence was given to the rumor, but sheriff Taylor placed an extra guard about the jail as a precautionary measure.

When Coudot was tried last July, and the term of court at Williamsport was adjourned, Black Hawk and Defender were ordered confined in the jail in Burleigh County, since the jail in Emmons County was too small to accommodate all of the men. To this fact alone, in all probability, is due the escape of these two men from the fate that was dealt to the three victims of the lynching.

7. Lynching

Reports of the affair say there was no noise and no disturbance on the part of the lynchers, and the affair had been apparently carefully planned and was carried out without a hitch in the proceedings. The party was characterized by an air of grim determination to secure the three men and hang them.

It is stated that there has been fear of lynching especially since the granting of a new trial to the Indian Coudot, but of course, as with all such affairs, no one not concerned in the lynching could bring himself to believe that the men would meet with violence, although the feeling against the prisoners had been intense ever since the murder, and especially since the news that Coudot had been granted a new trial. No doubt, the fear that the men would escape punishment for their awful crime led to the tragedy of Sunday morning.

Sheriff Shier received word of the affair from Harry Procunier yesterday afternoon. He was shocked to learn of the lynching, and yet he has had to exercise considerable strategy at different times to keep the men out of the hands of those who would have used them roughly had they secured them, and realized that such an outcome of the affair, from the beginning, was possible. [...]

Black Hawk and Defender were informed yesterday afternoon of the fate that had befallen their comrades. It is reported that Black Hawk was considerably nervous and agitated over the fate of the other men. Defender is such a man as nothing makes much impression upon and he did not appear to be much concerned. Defender has consumption and it is stated that he cannot live over a year in the natural course of events.

An interesting legal aspect of the case is that there is now no evidence against the two men confined in jail here. Holy Track and Ireland were the witnesses for the state, upon which the state relied mainly for a conviction of the several murderers, and now that they have been hanged, there is no evidence to be presented against Black Hawk and Defender.

No action had been taken by the authorities in the matter so far as heard from today. Inquiry at the executive office revealed the fact that there was nothing to be done by that department, so far as could be seen. Governor Briggs has been informed of the lynching, but no word had been received from him.

Prisoners removed

Black Hawk and Defender have been removed from the jail here, and while sheriff Taylor will not state where they are, it is presumed they are occupying cells in the state penitentiary, where they will be safe from any efforts to secure them.

A remarkable telegram

Attorney R. N. Stevens, who conducted the defense of the prisoner Coudot, this afternoon received the following rather remarkable telegram from J. D. Flynn, dated at Mandan: "Please accept my congratulations for your success in saving Coudot."

The account in the *Winona Times* was much the same, but differed slightly in a couple of particulars. It hints that Paul Holy Track and Philip

Ireland may have been dead — dragged to death, or strangled by the ropes, or paralyzed by broken necks — before the actual hanging. It makes Coudotte's reply about the involvement of Frank Black Hawk and George Defender more ambiguous. And it gives a direct quotation from the coroner's report:

Winona Times
Winona, North Dakota
November 18, 1897

Their Crime Expiated

[...] As soon as the doors had been opened, ropes were fastened about their necks and they were dragged forth from their cells. Holy Track and Ireland came in for less consideration than Cadotte, as they were dragged to the place of hanging. Cadotte was allowed to walk. [...] Holy Track and Ireland were nearly if not quite unconscious when the scaffold was reached and their limp bodies were raised and left dangling in the air.

It is reported that Cadotte was asked if Frank Black Hawk and George Defender were implicated in the Spicer murder, and he answered yes, I don't know. [...]

The following verdict was reached [by the coroner's jury]: "Death was caused by strangulation by a rope being placed around the neck, by unknown parties."

There was, of course, some nervousness about the flat-out illegality of the lynching by the supposedly "unknown parties." The editor of the *Bismarck Daily Tribune* phrased his views carefully, condemning lynching in general but hinting that he fully understood why in this particular case it seemed justified:

Bismarck Daily Tribune
Bismarck, North Dakota
November 16, 1897

The Lynchings

Swift and summary vengeance was demanded by a party of men Sunday morning for the atrocious murders of the members of the Spicer family last February. Three men under arrest, and of whose guilt, doubtless, the lynchers were satisfied, were taken from the jail in the night and executed. The lives of the three men were taken, in vengeance for the lives of six members of an innocent family, who were heartlessly murdered, and brutally and fearfully mutilated.

The principle involved in the mob vengeance is never to be sanctioned, for the reason that it is opposed to the basic principles of law and order, which demand that punishment shall never be inflicted except by a proper authority, under the approved finding of a court and jury. The stability and maintenance of the law depend upon the respect of all persons for law, and when the execution of the law is taken into the hands of a mob, the sanctity of the law is attacked, and its safe continuance threatened.

Lynching is to be deplored for many reasons — not alone for the reason that there is a grave possibility of punishing the innocent in the heat of frenzy and passion — not alone for the reason that the example of defiance and contempt for the law is dangerous — but for the additional reason that it gives rein to the worst passions of men, and sets an example opposed to the calm and dispassionate workings of legal machinery.

There is of course another side to the question. In the case in point, the crime for which the men were executed was peculiarly horrible. Its details were enough to sicken the most hardened. Men, women and children were ruthlessly slaughtered and mutilated. Those who were not given the opportunity to see the results of the fiendish deed of the murderers, in the hacked and mutilated bodies of the innocent persons, suddenly and brutally stricken down by the hands of fiends, cannot appreciate the passionate indignation of those who lived near the murdered family, and listened to the recital of the details of the crime from two of the men who were executed Sunday morning. If the punishment of the men was summary and its manner deplorable, the crime was horrible and revolting. There was the fear that the men would escape punishment altogether to further madden those who took the law into their own hands and meted out to the prisoners what in their opinion the demands of justice and vengeance called for.

Then, too, there is the additional fact that, in this state and many other states, many murderers have escaped what public opinion has set as a righteous punishment for their crimes. The law has become so careful of the lives of defendants in murder cases that it has become a difficult matter to mete out the extreme punishment provided by the law. Legal questions are often raised successfully to defer, if not to prevent, executions, which public opinion has declared to be called for. Normand, the murderer, escaped a death sentence. Kent likewise escaped, Swidenski escaped. It is not to be said that the escape of these men is due to any man or body of men, nor is it to be claimed that it is due to any single influence, other than the tendency which has come upon the civilization of the nineteenth century to pass every law with the idea of protecting the defendant, and none with the idea of aiding in the prosecution of an offense. We deplore the methods adopted in olden times, to force confessions and extract the guilty secrets of criminals under pressure, and deplore them rightly. But there is an opposite extreme in the too careful protection of the criminal, and in many cases that extreme has been reached.

Lynchings are deplorable, but they point one moral — to speedier trials, fewer legal objections and technicalities and sterner and swifter punishments.

The lynching of the three Indians received widespread news coverage, if only in just a sentence or two in columns summarizing the news. These almost all left out the qualifiers "accused" and "alleged" and to refer the three men as simply "the murderers," even though only one had actually stood trial for murder, and his conviction had been reversed by a higher court:

The Herald
Los Angeles, California
November 15, 1897
The North Dakota murderers of the Spicer family will not need a new trial. A quiet mob took them from the jail and hanged all three.

The Warren Sheaf
Warren, Minnesota
November 18, 1897
Paul Holy Track, Philip Ireland, and Alec Coudot, the three Indians who murdered the Spicer family on February 21 [sic] last, were taken from the jail in Williamsport, N.D., by a mob and hanged.

Local and national newspapers, of course, were eager to report more fully the news about the lynchings. Most of the reports were approving — or at least not critical — of the actions of the unnamed lynchers. The editors of the *Bismarck Daily Tribune* apparently enjoyed the attention — and usually the approval — that other newspapers gave to the white settlers in Emmons County for the action they took in lynching the three Indians. On November 16 and 17 they published a medley of excerpts from other newspapers. Some of these, not surprisingly, got some of the facts wrong:

Bismarck Daily Tribune
Bismarck, North Dakota
November 16 & 17, 1897

Press On the Lynchings

St. Paul Dispatch: It was not a healthy public sentiment that promoted and justified the lynching of three murderers in North Dakota yesterday. What must be said of it is that it was a human sentiment; that under the attendant circumstances and in view of all the aggravating delays and costly legal blunders, it is but little to be wondered at that the citizens so far forgot their duty to the state, so far lost control of their passions, that they took the law into their own hands and executed summary justice on the foul murderers. No one will pretend to deny that the death penalty was wholly deserved by the self-confessed assassins, and the only wrong is in the manner of its execution.

Pioneer Press: The cause of their exasperation was the recent decision of the supreme court of North Dakota, that the unsupported testimony of an accomplice of a murderer was not sufficient to convict him, and thus Coudot, the half-breed, who had been convicted and sentenced to be hung upon the testimony of the Indians who were parties to the murder, was relieved of his sentence and remanded for a new trial. As at that time there was no other testimony against him except that of his Indian accomplices, the people of the neighborhood came to the conclusion that under this decision the murderers would escape scot free, and they therefore determined to cut the Gordian knot of the law and hang the murderers without judge or jury. Although there appears to have been no doubt of the guilt of the three victims, it is a relief to know that on his way to his irregular execution Coudot confessed his guilt; and one of the Indians had already testified to his own part in the murder and that of his two accomplices. If ever a lynching was justified by the circumstances, it was in this case. For although their guilt was apparent, the decision of the court made it practically impossible to comply with the legal requirement of sufficient proof to warrant conviction. But exasperating as was this prospect that the murderers would escape punishment to a community inflamed with such indignation at the horrible atrocity of the unprovoked crime committed in their midst, it forms no adequate justification for thus taking the law into their own hands.

St. Paul Globe: It was only when the law broke down and admitted its inability to visit merited punishment upon the whiskey-maddened demons that the community rose and said that if the law could not secure the ends of manifest justice, they would take the responsibility. We do not justify this act of theirs, but the conditions leading to it should be considered in passing judgment upon it. We will not even assert that their act was excusable, but, if ever such act was excusable, the facts in the case supply the excuse.

Grand Forks Herald: Entirely aside from the considerations that constrain civilized communities to observe the forms of law and order and leave to the legally constituted courts of justice the construing of law and the trial of criminals, which considerations inexorably forbid resort to lynch law even where guilt is clearly proven and circumstances do not admit of a shadow of doubt, there is this fact to be always recognized, that self-constituted vigilantes, or if you please, a mob of lynchers, do not constitute a fair tribunal; a mob of lynchers is not guided by reason nor by a spirit of discrimination between guilt and innocence. No evidence is considered and no effort made to ascertain facts. And so it often happens that innocent men suffer death together with guilty men. And the fact in the lynching of the Indians in Emmons County undoubtedly show this case to be exactly of this nature.

Jamestown Alert: It is not often that people of North Dakota are roused to take the law in their own hands but when they do there is sure to be some good reason for it. The cold blooded murder of an entire white family by a band of savages in Emmons County had gone unpunished by the law for nearly a year, and the residents of the county, fearing that justice would not be given, hung three of the self-convicted murderers without the aid of the sheriff.

News of the lynching was of special interest to readers in the west and midwest, but the story was so compelling that it made the headlines even in eastern newspapers like the *New York Times*. The following story is almost identical to ones published elsewhere on the same day (for example, in the Sacramento, California, *Record-Union*):

New York Times
New York, New York
November 15, 1897

Mob Law In North Dakota

Alexander Coudot, an Indian half breed, and Paul Holytrack and Philip Ireland, the first of whom was sentenced to death for the murder of six members of the Spicer family last February, and had just obtained a new trial from the supreme court, and the latter two self-confessed accessories in the murders, were taken from the county jail in Emmons County last night and lynched by a mob. The lynching apparently had been planned carefully, and was carried out without a break in the programme.

Williamsport, where the hanging took place, is about forty miles from [Bismarck] and off the railroad. The news of the hanging was brought [to Bismarck] this afternoon by a mounted messenger. The sheriff of the county, Peter Shier, was in [Bismarck] at the time the hanging occurred, and it was to him that the messenger brought word. The men had been in the custody of Thomas Kelly, and they were taken from his control by the mob and hanged to a beef windlass several hundred yards from the jail, where their bodies remained today, the coroner not having arrived, and no one else having volunteered to take them down.

The mob came on horseback

There were about forty men concerned in the lynching. They rode into Williamsport on horseback last night, and tethered their horses a short distance from the city in order that they might remount as speedily as possible after their purpose was accomplished. The jail in which the prisoners were confined is a substantial stone structure, and was in charge of deputy sheriff Kelly. Since the confinement of the prisoners there, so great has been the fear that one of them might escape, one man has watched all night within the jail, and last night Kelly was on the watch. There was a meeting of the Lodge of Woodmen in a building near the jail, and Kelly expected to meet some of the members of the lodge after the meeting had adjourned.

To while away the time during the night he was playing solitaire in front of the cells in which the murderers were confined. About 2 o'clock in the morning there was a rap at the outer door of the jail, and Kelly arose quickly and turned the key to the lock, thinking that the persons he expected to meet had arrived. No sooner had he opened the door than the mob crowded into the corridors. All of them were masked, and the leaders carried ropes.

The jailer surrenders

Kelly at once realized that the mob had come after his prisoners. The lynchers were quiet but determined. The leaders presented revolvers at the head of the deputy sheriff and told him that they wanted his prisoners and demanded that he open the cells in which they were confined. Kelly demurred, but saw that resistance was useless and unlocked the cells. Two of the prisoners were confined together, and the other in a separate cell. They had been aroused from sleep by the entrance of the men and sat up half awake and trembling with terror.

The Indians were taken from their beds, ropes were fastened about their necks, and they were led out of the building, after being told to prepare for death. The men were dragged to a huge beef windlass which had been erected to suspend the carcases of slaughtered beeves, and strung up on a cross beam. Coudot was the first man to be hanged. It is reported that he was asked before he was hanged whether Holytrack and Ireland had also been concerned in the murder for which he was about to be hanged. He answered that they had been.

The rope, which had been fastened about his neck, was then thrown over the crossbeam, and he was raised off the ground and suspended in the air. Holytrack and Ireland were so nearly unconscious from the effects of being dragged to the spot that they did not realize what was about to happen when the ropes about their necks were tossed over the same beam. They were unable to stand and were slowly raised from the ground and their bodies swung in the air and dangled from the windlass with that of Coudot. The mob then dispersed, mounted their horses, and rode away.

The public were, of course, eager to hear whether there was to be any further violence by white citizens wanting to lynch the remaining two prisoners, Frank Black Hawk and George Defender, who were incarcerated in the prison at Bismarck. This next article is particularly interesting in that it describes some of the photographs taken of the murdered white people and the lynched Indians:

Bismarck Daily Tribune
Bismarck, North Dakota
November 16, 1897

No Developments

The Kodak fiend is omnipresent, even in Williamsport, and he got a snap shot at the three bodies of the Indians who were lynched at Williamsport Sunday morning, as they swayed from the windlass that had been made to serve as a scaffold. The picture was a clear one, though small, and the three men could be easily recognized from the photographs. The windlass is located in an open space, about forty feet from the house of Mike Rush, and perhaps a hundred yards from the jail. It stands about nine feet high and six feet wide, and is constructed of cottonwood logs, two of them set upright, and one at the top crosswise. The windlass was used to raise the carcasses of beeves, and at the right side of the frame, are two or three poles joined together, and serving to act as a sort of pulley, by which the heavy carcasses are raised.

The bodies of the men are close together — necessary because of the fact that the cross beam to which they were hanged is narrow. Coudot is at the left, Ireland in the center, and Holy Track on the right. The men were clothed, with the exception of their coats, and it is doubtful if they possessed these garments. The heads of the victims are dropped upon their breasts, and their bodies appear limp. Their hands are tied behind their backs, and the bodies of the men are in different positions. The face of Coudot is turned to one side, that of Ireland a little more so, but Holy Track's countenance almost faces the spectator.

Frank Black Hawk, since his confinement in jail here, has had an unalterable opposition to the leg shackles that are used to ensure the prisoners from escape. Some time ago Judge Winchester, being informed that the Indian prisoners were suffering from the effects of their confinement, directed the sheriff to give them daily exercise out of doors. Black Hawk has refused on many occasions to wear the leg irons, and as a consequence has not been benefitted by the exercise that he might have obtained had he been less scrupulous, as the sheriff did not feel like allowing him the liberty out of doors, unless he was so shackled as to prevent his getting away. When the sheriff decided Sunday morning to remove the men, it became necessary to explain to Black Hawk the reason for his removal, in order that he might submit to the shackling process. The sheriff accordingly told him the fate that had befallen the three men at Williamsport, and Black Hawk could not get his feet into the shackles fast enough, so willing was he to be removed.

State's attorney Allen, who was concerned with the prosecution of the case against the prisoners, has a rather gruesome collection of photographs, which, taken in sequence, make a thrilling story without words. There is a picture of the Spicer house — a common log building, where the murders were committed. Then follow pictures of the scenes inside the house after the murders were committed, showing the victims as they lay in different rooms — a horrible sight. Following this is a photograph of five men arrested under suspicion of the murder with the two officers who had charge of them, Sheriff Shier and Deputy Livermore. Next is a picture of the Emmons county jail, a solid and substantial structure of stone, and following this is a trial scene, showing the court, the prisoners, the jury and the spectators. Last scene of all — is the photograph of the three men swinging from the crude framework of an improvised windlass, taken last Sunday morning.

There was a report last night that there was a party on the way to attempt to secure Black Hawk and Defender from the jail here and administer to them the same fate as was meted out to their companions. The officials were notified of the reported coming of the men, but the statement that the men had been removed from the jail, was circulated, and if there was any attempt on foot, it was given up.

Adjutant General Miller today received a telegram from Governor Briggs authorizing him to take whatever steps he may deem necessary should occasion arise for action. But General Miller has been ready to act all along if there was any necessity for it, but as when the first news of the affair was received in the city, the three men were dead, there was not much that could be done.

The bodies of the men will probably be turned over to their relatives should they be claimed by the latter. It is said the faces of the victims are not badly disfigured, and the usual discoloration and suffusion were missing. Their necks were gashed from the ropes cutting into the flesh, but other than this there was no disfiguration.

Men here must be protected.

There have been rumors that an attempt might be made, if the prisoners here were brought back to jail and it was thought possible to secure them, to take them from the jail and treat them as the other men. Sheriff Taylor and officials of this county have determined that the men will not be removed from their custody in an unlawful manner, and all preparations have been made and steps taken to protect them to the fullest extent. Adjutant General Miller has been authorized to respond with troops if called for, so that no lynching will ensue here without serious trouble. Indeed, with the precautions that have been taken to guard the men, it will be impossible for any lynching party to get them.

Not surprisingly, the prosecutors of Alec Coudotte were annoyed that state supreme court chief justice Corliss was openly critical of both the work of the prosecutors and of the mob. Before the lynchings Corliss had ruled that the jury had on insufficient evidence condemned Alec Coudotte. After the lynchings he proclaimed that the mob had killed an innocent man. He insisted that Alec Coudotte had a strong alibi and was not at the scene of the murders. Corliss's statement was reported in slightly different ways in different newspapers (for example, the *Princeton Union* in Princeton, Minnesota, and the St. Paul, Wisconsin, *Globe*), but the effect was the same:

Salt Lake Herald
Salt Lake City, Utah
November 16, 1897

One Indian Innocent

"An innocent man was hung by desperadoes at Williamsport," was the startling statement made today by chief justice Corliss of the state supreme court. "I have ample documentary evidence to [prove] the statement," continued the judge. "The supreme court ordered a new trial in Coudet's case because it appeared that he was convicted on the uncorroborated evidence of Holy Track and Ireland, both of whom confessed to taking part in the murder of the Spicer family and whose statements were refuted by the strong alibi testimony given by Dr. Ross, the resident agency physician at Standing Rock. Dr. Ross's veracity is unquestioned and his testimony is supported by notes from his memorandum book.

"Another fact is that Holy Track and Ireland made two other previous confessions in neither of which did they implicate Coudet. Holy Track and Ireland were sure to have expiated their crime on the gallows as there is no doubt of their guilt, but the mob made no distinction and hung the innocent with the guilty. The lynching of Coudet is a foul crime, and a blot on the fair name of the state, and his murderers should not go unpunished."

Black Hawk and Defender were removed by sheriff Layton tonight from the jail to the state penitentiary to protect them from possible mob violence. Black Hawk and Defender are visibly frightened by the fate of their three comrades and their change of quarters is a source of relief to them. Reports from Standing Rock reservation where friends and relatives of the men reside are to the effect that there is no great excitement.

Not everyone, of course, agreed with Corliss's reported assessment of the reliability of Dr. Ross's testimony. One who wrote to try to clarify the facts of the case was Edward Allen, a member of the prosecuting team. Another was J. Bartholomew, who wrote the judgment of the state supreme court that reversed the jury's verdict and called for a new trial. Both letters appeared in the same edition of the Bismarck newspaper:

Bismarck Daily Tribune
Bismarck, North Dakota
November 18, 1897

The Coudot Case

EDITOR *TRIBUNE*: In an interview published in the St. Paul *Globe* of the 16th instant, Chief Justice Corliss is quoted as saying that "the mob who lynched the Indians at Williamsport hung an innocent man, and I have ample documentary evidence of that fact." As assistant state's attorney of Emmons County in the prosecution of the Indians, I know that every effort was made, both by the prosecution and the defense, to obtain the true facts, and the jury, under the evidence, held that Cadotte was guilty, and although Mr. R. N. Stevens, the attorney for the defendant worked unceasingly in preparing his case he was not able to produce before the court the ample documentary evidence referred to by Judge Corliss. After word came to this city that the Indians had been hung, one member of the supreme court stated that he expected that they would be lynched. Were the other members of the supreme court of the same opinion? If so then the ample documentary evidence in the possession of Judge Corliss should have been made public and thus avoided the awful calamity of an innocent man being hung. Perhaps the interviewer of Judge Corliss misquotes him. But if Mr. Corliss is not misquoted I now challenge him to produce ample or any documentary evidence showing that Alec Cadotte was an innocent man.

It is true (according to the decision of the supreme court) that Cadotte was convicted on the unsupported evidence of two accomplices. The supreme court has so decided the law of the case. But when Judge Corliss says that the conviction was in the face of "the strongest kind of an alibi," the judge is giving his opinion as to facts, and not the law, and in our humble way we beg to differ with him. I do not believe that any unprejudiced man will call the defense of Cadotte "the strongest kind of an alibi." Judge Corliss refers to the testimony of Dr. Ross and states that the "doctor's veracity is unquestioned." The record shows that his veracity was questioned and further that he was thoroughly impeached, and that he had stated many times, immediately after the murder, that he was at Cadotte's house on the day of the homicide and that Cadotte was not at home. The memorandum book of Dr. Ross did not show that Cadotte was home on the day of the murder but simply that Dr. Ross was at Cadotte's, a fact that Dr. Ross stated a day or two after the murder at which time he said that Cadotte was not home, but a few days before the trial of Cadotte (months after the murder) he remembered that Cadotte was home. The record shows that the veracity of Dr. Ross was questioned and I believe that every juror that tried the case will say that his testimony was so thoroughly impeached that it was unworthy of belief and that the jury considered it unworthy of belief.

In the *Globe* interview Judge Corliss is quoted as saying, "Philip Ireland and Paul Holy Track had made two previous confessions, in neither of which did they implicate Cadotte." The record does not so show. Cadotte was implicated in every confession except in the one wherein Ireland and Holy Track stated they did it themselves without any help from anyone.

As to whether or not the lynching of Alec Cadotte, for his part in one of the most atrocious murders in the history of the world, where four generations, from the great grandmother to the babes, were foully murdered and mutilated, after having been once convicted by an unprejudiced jury, but liberated on a question of law, was, as Judge Corliss states, "as foul a murder, as unjustifiable and as hideous as the murder of the Spicer family," is a matter of opinion, and I am pleased, on that point, to differ with Judge Corliss.—Edward S. Allen

Judge Bartholomew's Statement

EDITOR *TRIBUNE:* In your issue of yesterday there appeared a kindly worded criticism of Chief Justice Corliss in connection with certain language that he is reported to have used in an interview at Grand Forks. It is evident that the criticism, while kindly meant, proceeds upon a wrong theory and leaves a wrong impression. There is absolutely no inconsistency between the quotation given from the opinion in the Coudot case and the language attributed to Judge Corliss. As the case was being sent back for a new trial it would have been highly improper for the court to have expressed an opinion as to the weight of the evidence on the question of an alibi. That was exclusively for the jury. It is the province of a court to decide whether or not there is any evidence on any given point. But once admit there is any evidence and its weight is entirely with the jury, and a jury once having passed upon it their finding is conclusive on a court, although the court may think the finding entirely wrong. To illustrate, let us suppose that an accomplice needs no corroboration, and let us suppose further in this case that Holy Track testified, as he did, that Coudot was present at the Spicer place at or about a certain hour on that fateful afternoon of February 17th. Now let us suppose further that Dr. Ross, Major Cramsie and Major McLaughlin had each and all sworn that they were at Coudot's house many miles distant on that same afternoon and at that same hour and that Coudot was at home. Now, if under these circumstances a jury had found Coudot guilty no court could have disturbed the finding, and yet every member of the court would have been morally certain that the man was innocent, and had the court reversed the verdict upon another ground it would have been entirely proper to say that the court could not disturb the finding of the jury on the question of the alibi. I have put an extreme case to illustrate the conditions that actually existed in a modified form in the Coudot case.

It must be remembered that the Coudot case was not reversed on the ground that Coudot had established an alibi. It was reversed simply because the state had failed to produce any such corroborating evidence as the statute says must be produced before a conviction can be had on the evidence of an accomplice.

I wish to correct another error that seems to prevail. It seems to be thought that the decision in the Coudot case rendered it impossible to convict Holy Track and Ireland. Nothing could be further from the fact. There was abundant evidence to show that Thomas Spicer was murdered. That fact being established, the voluntary confession of Holy Track and Ireland was all the evidence that the law required to sustain the death sentence. — J. M. Bartholomew

A more visceral rejection of Corliss's opinion appeared in the same newspaper a week later. It is all well and good, the writer said, for Corliss to turn dangerous criminals loose to kill again, since he would not be personally endangered, but it was different for white people who lived in dangerous proximity to those foul murderers:

Bismarck Daily Tribune
Bismarck, North Dakota
November 26, 1897

[Imagine My Wife's Feelings]

A correspondent of the *Minneapolis Tribune*, writing from Cannon Ball, takes Judge Corliss to task for his interview in the Coudot matter and incidentally justifies the lynchings in his own mind as follows:

"Chief justice Corliss of the supreme court, this state, is quoted as saying that in his opinion the murder of Coudot is as foul and hideous a crime as the murder of the whole Spicer family. This extraordinary statement, emanating as it does from one who is supposed to be one of the foremost jurists of our state, calls for an answer from some one familiar with the facts in the case. Let me for one minute show the other side of the picture. I will take my own case, which is similar to dozens of others. I live within a stone's throw of the Indian camp with my wife and child. In the day time my business keeps me away from home nearly all day; sometimes far into the night. Imagine if you can my feelings or my wife's feelings by day and by night, if we knew that murderous gang had been turned loose; as they must have been according to the supreme court's decision. This winter [there] would surely have been another, maybe a dozen horrible murders. It was just as likely to have been us as anybody else. The tension on a woman's nerves is bad enough at any time to live close to an Indian camp with the knowledge that foul murderers have been found in their midst; but if those fiends had been freed it would simply have been unendurable. We would have had no option but to leave the neighborhood, and dozens of other lonely settlers who have toiled and earned a cozy home, just as dear to them as Judge Corliss's city mansion, would have had to pull up stakes."

Meanwhile, the authorities had a related matter to attend to. If, as Corliss had stated, the white settlers had indeed murdered an innocent Indian, then what was to prevent the Indians from seeking their own revenge for that criminal act? The editor of the *Mandan Pioneer* felt that he could describe more accurately the mood on the reservation:

Mandan Pioneer
Mandan, North Dakota
November 19, 1897

[A Worthless Indian]

On the reservation, the wonder has been for some time that the murderers of the Spicer family have not been hung before. "They killed the white people, and why don't the white people kill them?" is the question that has been frequently asked. The white people have killed three of them now, and while some of the administration at Standing Rock have been talking about "Poor Coudot" for months, the rank and file of the Indians feel that it is a good thing he is gone. He was a worthless Indian, happiest when drinking whiskey and making trouble, and his death is not regretted.

Several of the settlers had earlier petitioned, through their senators in Washington, to have the Standing Rock Indians forcibly confined to the reservation. This petition resulted in a letter written by Thomas P. Smith, acting commissioner for Indian Affairs, to the Secretary of the Interior, dated July 16, 1897. Although dated the summer before, it was not published in the *Emmons County Record* until the fall, when the issue took on increased importance. When it was published, it was prefaced by an editorial warning — can it be called a threat?—to the Indians across the river: stay where you belong! Smith refers to the fifth Indian as "Pierre" rather than Frank Black Hawk, because Frank Pierre was another name he went by:

Emmons County Record
Williamsport, North Dakota
November 26, 1897

[Promiscuous Crossings]

The opinion seems to prevail among settlers that the Indian and the military authorities at Fort Yates will do their utmost to prevent any crossing of the river by Indians when the river freezes over. But the following shows that they have no power to do much. The letter was written by acting Indian commissioner Smith to the secretary of the interior. A copy of it was furnished to Senator Hansbrough and to Senator Roach, who presented to the secretary the request made by the board of county commissioners of Emmons County that no Indians be allowed to come to this side of the river. But, with the present state of feeling, it is certain that no Indians from the reservation ought to cross the river from the other side, unless they are Indian police or other persons with proper permits from the agent. As it appears that there is no legal authority to prevent any Indian from crossing, it will not be strange if the settlers insist that their families shall not be frightened or their lives endangered by promiscuous crossing by Indians. There are a good many more able-bodied men in the counties of the Missouri Slope than there are on the reservation. And serious trouble is certain to occur if the Indians are allowed to cross at will.

"Department of the Interior, Office of Indian Affairs, Washington, D.C., July 16, 1897. The Honorable, The Secretary of the Interior.

"Sir:

"I am in receipt, by your reference for report, of communications dated July 2 from Senators Hansbrough and Roach, enclosing copies of resolution adopted by the board of county commissioners, Emmons County, North Dakota, declaring that the Indians of the Standing Rock reservation have destroyed life and property in that county; and asking that the department issue an order to the U.S. Indian agent, Standing Rock agency, to effectually and perpetually keep all and any Indians belonging to said reservation from coming within the limits of Emmons County, and that the said agent be forbidden from issuing any permit to any Indian or half-breed to come within the limits of Emmons County.

"I have the honor to report that however desirable it may be that these as well as other Indians be confined to the reservation set aside for them, and however willing this office may be to issue the necessary orders to that end, experience has fully shown the futility of attempting to confine Indians to a reservation. The Indians doubtless claim the legal right as persons under the constitution to travel the public roads and highways, enter stores and public places and transact such business as is not prohibited by law. And, further, it is expressly held, in *United States vs. Crook*, that in time of peace no authority, civil or military, exists for transporting Indians from one section of the country to another, without the consent of the Indians, nor to confine them to any particular reservation against their will; and where officers of the government attempt to do this, and arrest and hold Indians who are at peace with the government, for the purpose of removing them to and confining them upon a reservation in the Indian territory, they will be released on habeas corpus (5 Dillon, 453). It is a reasonable presumption on legitimate business errands, that their dealings with their white neighbors are at least of some benefit to the latter, and that the number of Indians who improperly conduct themselves and violate the law is so small as to render their punishment an easy matter. It would be a wrong and work hardship to both Indians and whites if the ninety-nine well-behaved Indians should be denied the privilege, even if the power existed, to leave their reservation on legitimate business because the one Indian goes wrong.

"Destroying life and property either within or without the reservation are crimes punishable by law, and when committed beyond the limits of the reserve, the jurisdiction of the state to try and punish the criminal is unquestioned. That this jurisdiction has been exercised by the state of North Dakota is shown by letter of May 12, 1897, from the U.S. Indian agent, Standing Rock agency, in which he stated that five Indians—Holy Track, Ireland, Defender, Pierre and Coudotte—belonging upon the Standing Rock reservation, were in jail awaiting trial in the Emmons County Court, June 1st, for a murder committed in that county. This letter also showed that the agent had assisted the county authorities in affecting the arrest of the accused.

"It is advised, therefore, that it is impracticable, if not impossible, to keep the Indians of the Standing Rock reservation within the limits of their reserve at all times, as requested, and that, if they leave their reservation and commit any unlawful act within the limits of the state of North Dakota, they may be dealt with in the manner provided by the laws of the state.

"Copies of this letter are enclosed for Senators Hansbrough and Roach, and their communications are returned herewith.

Very respectfully, your obedient servant,

Thomas P. Smith,
Acting Commissioner."

It is not surprising that when a mishap did happen, the settlers would first-off blame it on the local Indians, whom they assumed to be murderous. The juxtaposition of the final paragraph in the next article with the cases of mysteriously dead or missing white settlers is subtly suggestive of the assumed link:

Bismarck Daily Tribune
Bismarck, North Dakota
December 13, 1897

Probably Fatal

Lee Featherston, a private soldier at Fort Yates, was the victim of an assault at Winona Friday night, that will probably result in his death if it has not before this time. Featherston will be remembered as a young man who got into some trouble in this city through the burglary of Eppinger's store a year or so ago. The matter was fixed up, and afterwards Featherston went to Fort Yates and enlisted. He was well liked around the fort, and Friday night last came across to Winona, where he got on a little spree. How he was injured no one seems to know positively, but a short time after coming over he was discovered lying in the middle of the road with a gash in his head and a fractured skull. From appearances some one had struck him with an axe, and there was a deep wound in the right side of his head, four or five inches long and over an inch wide, where the weapon had penetrated. He was taken to an adjacent house and medical attention summoned, and the doctors who examined the wound pronounced it mortal, stating that he could live but a few hours.

A soldier named Bowers belonging to Company D is missing from the post and it is believed he walked into an air hole in the river and was drowned. He went over to Winona and started back, and nothing was heard from him afterwards. A searching detail was sent to look for him but no trace of him was found, and it is presumed he was drowned.

A night watchman has been employed by the residents of Winona to keep watch over the place during the night, and give an alarm if there are any signs of danger from across the river. Since the lynching of the Indians there have been threats that vengeance would be taken by the Indians, and to guard against being taken unawares the residents of Winona have subscribed to engage a watchman.

There was, then, general concern about any Indians coming across the river from the reservation. But as the next article shows, there was also a growing concern that local Winona businessmen would suffer if the Indians and their money were kept on the reservation for too long. The white settlers were especially interested in the travel plans of two specific Indians if and when they were released from prison — the two who had escaped the lynchers' nooses because they had been in jail in Bismarck. If Frank Black Hawk and George Defender had been guilty of complicity in the Spicer murders, there was virtually no chance that they could be brought to trial for that complicity now. The lynch mob, after all, had dispatched the only living eyewitnesses to what had happened to the Spicers back in November. There were apparently fairly elaborate plans to bring these last two to "justice" if they ever dared to return to the reservation or to lands surrounding the reservation:

Emmons County Record
Williamsport, North Dakota
November 24, 1897

Planning a Lynching

A sensational report has gained currency here that after the Indian prisoners, Black Hawk and Defender, who are now in jail here, are released at the next term of court, as has been settled, will be done, and after they have returned to the reservation at Standing Rock, if they succeed in reaching there safely, they will be rearrested for the murder of Mrs. Thomas Spicer, they now being held on the charge of having murdered Thomas Spicer. This arrest would lead to their confinement in the Emmons County jail, from which place the other three Indians were taken out and lynched. If they are ever placed again in confinement in the Emmons County jail it is not likely that the cases against them will ever come to trial. It is doubted if any such action as this will be taken, however, as it could be but for one purpose, and the authorities would hardly be party to such a scheme.

Indian traders who live on the Emmons County side of the river and have dealt for many years with the reservation Indians, have material cause to regret the lynching. Since this occurrence none of the Indians from the reservation have shown up on the east side of the river, opposite the reservation, and as a result many dollars' worth of trade is lost to the traders.

The businessmen were opposed to the proposed lynching, then, not because lynching was bad morally or legally, but because it was bad for them financially.

Frank Black Hawk and George Defender were eventually released:

Bismarck Daily Tribune
Bismarck, North Dakota
November 29, 1897

Will Be Dismissed

In the district court this morning state's attorney H. A. Armstrong of Emmons County made a formal motion for the dismissal of the cases against Frank Black Hawk and George Defender, the two survivors of the five men charged with the murder of the Spicer family, and filed with the court his reasons for moving the dismissal of the cases. Briefly, they were that after due consideration of all the facts in the case, considering the decision of the supreme court in the Coudot case, involving the same alleged facts, and the absence of material witnesses, who had passed from the jurisdiction of the court, the state being satisfied that they would never return, or become at any time amenable to the jurisdiction of the court having been unjudicially executed, he was satisfied that no conviction could be had upon the charge of murder. Prior to the reading of the reasons attorney Stevens, for the defendants, waived objection to the sitting of Judge Winchester in the case, this being done because of the fact that at the last term of court in Emmons County Judge Sauter was called in to try the cases. Attorney Stevens also excepted to the language of the reasons for dismissal, and the case was taken under advisement by the court. The prisoners, it was generally understood, would be discharged from custody in the course of the day.

Black Hawk and Defender were brought into court during the proceedings that were had in the case, and heard the reading of the motions for dismissal. If they were moved by any part of the proceedings they did not show any evidences of emotion. Black Hawk does not show any particular ill effects of his confinement, but Defender looks bad. His cheeks are sunken, his eyes hollowed, his hair long, reaching almost to his shoulders, and his face and appearance betray all the evidences of consumption.

After the matter had been submitted to the court, the prisoners were remanded to the custody of the sheriff to await the decision of the court in the matter. It is stated that agent Cramsie will arrive in the city this evening to take the men back to the reservation after they are discharged. Whether any attempt will be made to hinder their safe return to the reservation is difficult to say.

The safe return of the two remaining suspects was on the minds of lots of people, including Frank Black Hawk and George Defender. While they did not like being in prison, they realized that at least there they were relatively safe from the vengeful wrath of the white settlers of Emmons County. They were kept in prison for several more days until safe escort could be arranged for them. The sheriff at Bismarck was happy to see them on their way, since their return to the reservation relieved him of the responsibility of keeping them safe.

Bismarck Daily Tribune
Bismarck, North Dakota
December 1, 1897

Good Bye, Indians

Black Hawk and Defender, the surviving two of the five men arrested for the murder of the Spicer family, are free men, having been discharged from custody this morning by Judge Winchester. The motion for their discharge was made by state's attorney Armstrong Monday morning, but their discharge was delayed until the arrival of Indian agent Cramsie, who arrived from Mandan last night and was in the court room when the men were released this morning.

Even after the men had formally been discharged by the judge, they were not anxious to taste immediately of the sweets of freedom, preferring to wait until arrangements had been made for their safe escort to Mandan, from which place they are to be taken to the reservation. It was feared that some attempt might be made to seize and punish the men if an attempt was made to take them to Mandan unassisted, and there were reports that the militia might be applied for to conduct the prisoners safely across the river. After a discussion of the matter between agent Cramsie and attorney Stevens, who has represented the prisoners, the idea of securing the militia was given up at the suggestion of the latter, who assured the agent that there was no probability of any difficulty so long as the men were in the city, and that any display of military authority in the removal of the men might have the opposite effect to that intended.

At Mandan there is a party of forty Indians who were brought up from the agency for freight, and they will act as an escort for the two men back to the reservation. Agent Cramsie states that there are thirty Winchester rifles in the party, and that any attempt to waylay the party to secure the recently discharged prisoners will meet with sanguinary results. It is improbable that any attempt will be made at this time and under the existing circumstances to secure the prisoners.

Sheriff Taylor is not sorry to see the men go. In fact it is doubtful, in the course of his career as sheriff, whether he has had two prisoners with him whom he would parted more gladly and who have been as difficult to get rid of. Since the lynching of the three Indians at Williamsport, the sheriff has been on constant watch, lest an attempt be made to break into the jail here and get the men, and two weeks of that kind of possibility, when it is impossible to get guards to protect the men, is wearing to say the least.

What are the feelings of the two prisoners, it is difficult to say. Black Hawk's principal sentiment during the past two weeks has been one of fear lest he meet the fate meted out to his alleged comrades. He is not as brave as he was when he was first confined. The two weeks of constant expectancy has worn upon him. But he is no less a desperate man, and as he is armed, he will take care of himself, and the party that gets him without trouble will have to be alert indeed.

It was intended to take the men to Mandan on a freight train but even the train did not seem to want them and pulled through without stopping. Accordingly they were taken across in a hack, the party consisting of agent Cramsie, editor Tuttle and the two prisoners.

What became of the two released prisoners? George Defender died of tuberculosis (sometimes known as consumption) in December of 1898, a year after he was released. As for Frank Black Hawk, he apparently had few friends even among the Indians:

Mandan Pioneer
Mandan, North Dakota
December 3, 1897

[A Bad Man]

Here is the neat way the Indians put it: "The Black Man (meaning Black

Hawk) made the road and the others followed in it; he should have had the rope about his neck first."

It is not generally known among white people that some years ago Black Hawk murdered a man on Porcupine Creek—at least the Indians say so. He has a "bad man" reputation and the Indians are afraid of him.

A note in the *Bismarck Daily Tribune* a little more than a year later, on January 15, 1899, reported that "the half-breed Indian Frank Blackhawk, the only survivor of the five men arrested for the Spicer murders, is a regular attendant at the Episcopal church at Cannon Ball." According to LaDonna Brave Bull Allard, Frank Black Hawk died in 1926, but as we will see in Win Tracy's recollection in the next section, some people thought he had been poisoned not long after he was released from prison.

What ever happened to the reward money that Governor Briggs and the people of Emmons County had offered to the person delivering the murderer or murderers to justice, the money to be paid "upon conviction of such murderer or murderers"? So far as I have been able to determine, it was never paid to anyone. To be sure, one of the five men arrested was convicted, but his conviction was quickly overturned. The lynch mob would not, of course, step forward to claim the reward, even though they no doubt felt they had earned it. I did, however, find this editorial in the Bismarck newspaper, a year after the mob had done its dark work.

Bismarck Daily Tribune
Bismarck, North Dakota
December 17, 1898

[The State Should Keep Its Faith]

It is an old saying that "republics are ungrateful." Whether this be so or not, it is certain that states are sometimes unjust. On the 20th of February, 1897, Governor Briggs made public the following:

A reward of $500 will be paid to the person delivering into the custody of the sheriff of Emmons County, North Dakota, the murderer or murderers of Thomas Spicer, Mrs. Thomas Spicer, Mrs. Ellen Waldron, Mrs. William Rouse and her twin infant children, who were killed near Winona, in said county, on or about Wednesday, February 17, 1897. Said reward will be paid upon the conviction of such murderer or murderers.

The sheriff of this county spent much time and money in rounding up the murderers. He has not received from the state or from any other source a cent of the money he expended. The governor's offer was for the conviction of such murderer or murderers. One of the murderers was duly convicted by a jury and sentenced by the court. When the conviction took place, was not the reward, as a matter of justice and equity, earned and due? If the members of the legislature believe that, when the governor of the state offers a reward for the doing of a certain thing, and the thing for which the reward was offered is done, the state should keep its faith, they will pass a bill appropriating money to pay the man or men who earned the reward offered by Governor Briggs for the conviction of a murderer.

So far as I know, the legislature never passed such a bill. Perhaps, they reasoned, since the sheriff, Peter Shier, was doing his official, paid duty in conducting the investigation and making the arrests, he was not eligible for the reward, especially since the reward was to be paid to "the person delivering into the custody of the sheriff of Emmons County, North Dakota, the murderer or murderers." How could the sheriff deliver the murderers into his own custody? Perhaps, they reasoned, since the conviction was reversed by a higher court, no murderer was actually convicted. As for Paul Holy Track and Philip Ireland, they were themselves murdered before the state had a chance to convict them. Officially, then, none of the five men whom sheriff Peter Shier arrested was legally guilty of anything, unless one takes the contradictory confessions of the two youngest as legal proof of guilt. Certainly, they were not convicted of the murders, unless we take the actions of the lynch mob as constituting a de facto conviction. Perhaps, the state officials reasoned, it was the lynch mob that delivered the three Indians, quite dead, into the custody of the county authorities. The legislature, of course, was not likely to offer those men a reward, though it is possible that some legislators would have liked to.

Surely it occurred to no one in the legislature that the reward money should be paid to the mother of Paul Holy Track. It was her son, after all, more than anyone else, who gave to the sheriff and the prosecutor the information that brought about Alec Coudotte's temporary conviction.

By and large, of course, the Indian point of view has been missing from the documentary record. History is written by the winners, and the winners were the white men. The white men owned the newspapers, the stories were written by white reporters, and they were written for white readers.

A story appeared in the *Mandan Pioneer* just at the end of the tumultuous year 1897. It concerns vague reports of a plan by Standing Rock Indians to attack not the white settlers but the town of Winona:

Mandan Pioneer
Mandan, North Dakota
December 10, 1897

[No Winona]

A story is in circulation that Indians have declared that "some morning the white man will wake up and find no Winona." Several Indians have been interrogated regarding the authenticity of this threat with the usual result—"Me don't know; may be so." Whether the Indians have any such blood-thirsty intentions, or the statement is without foundation, your correspondent is unable to determine. It is quite evident, however, that Indians have been purchasing firearms.

The knowledge that three of their number had just been lynched, of course, would have been ample reason for the Indians to purchase guns to protect themselves and their families from attacks from across the Missouri, but a statement made much later by Dr. Aaron M. Beede, an Episcopal missionary to the Standing Rock Lakotas, suggests that the threat to Winona may indeed have been a real one. Dr. Beede knew the Indians, spoke their language, and was sympathetic to their needs and concerns. He reported that a number of the Standing Rock Indians had spoken with him about their dreams of eliminating from Winona the whiskey and prostitutes that were corrupting both the white men and the Indians. He reports that, indeed, they had hoped to eliminate Winona altogether. The two-page typescript entitled "The Spicer Murder at Winona: The Indian View of the Matter," is in the archives of the State Historical Society of North Dakota in Bismarck (SHSND Libby #10085, Box 37, Folder 15):

The Indian View of the Matter

I had often heard old Indians conversing together on this matter and by intently listening came to realize that there was something here worth knowing. Finally I got their story in full. And the story was confirmed to me by twelve old Indians, maybe at least fourteen or fifteen Indians, who I met at Fort Yates at the time of the 1913 Fair. Their story briefly is as follows.

At Winona there was much whiskey and numerous harlots (witko wiyan — an abnormal woman). They say there were thirty harlots. And countless jugs and barrels of whiskey. The Indians wished this practice stopped for two reasons: First because it made the soldiers brutal and abusive towards Indians, as they said. And second because they feared its influence upon their own people.

There had been many Indian councils regarding this matter. They had asked the agent to stop the bad practices in this town, but he replied that it was on the wrong side of the river. They asked him to have the President stop this practice, and he made many excuses and pretended to write the President letters but the Indians did not think he wrote him any for if the President knew of it the Indians knew he would have stopped it. At last the Indians formed the plan to clean out the town themselves. There was to be an uprising of all men able to bear arms the next time the moon would be right for a night attack. (The moon being right for an attack means that the moon must rise in the morning before dawn.) The five men who committed the murder — Ireland, Holy Track, Cadotte, Black Hawk and Defender — went over to Winona and became partly drunk. In their confused state of mind they imagined that the set time for the uprising had come and so these five of them made the uprising and committed the murder. It was Black Hawk, the part-blood Negro (ha sapa), who raped the old woman in the stable, and it was Cadotte, the part-blood Chippewa (wasi cu ta cinca haba towan), who raped the young woman in the house. This was bad. And all of the Dakotas felt their heart bad on account of it. The Dakotas, the good people, never do such things as that. And if the white men say the Dakota ever raped a white woman they lie.

Had it not been for this murder all the Dakotas would have gone over the river when the moon became right and would have cleaned up the town. They did not intend to kill the women or to take them as captives for they did not want such women as these. They intended to drive the women off to their own people, the white man who want such women as these in their cities. The Dakotas did not want to kill the men in the town. The Dakotas did not want to kill anybody, but they had decided to clean up this town even if they had to kill everybody and fight the soldiers and kill them and kill everybody at the agency and burn it up.

Dr. Beede asked them, "Would you have burned up the town of Winona if you had gone there?" And they answered, "Certainly we would have burned up everything so they would not come back again" (toksha taku oyasin ide un yanpi yelo; hechen di pi kte shni). They had some other conversation here. Then they said that when the three men who were lynched were brought back the Indians were so full of bitterness that they would have then crossed the river and cleaned up the town if they could have gotten across the river. But the ice in the river was broken up so they could not cross. They considered that the white man's whiskey and harlots were responsible for the whole matter. And that the white man's bad customs were the cause of it.

When I asked them why they did not attack the soldiers and destroy the agency on this side they answered, "It was not what was on this side that caused the trouble, it was what was on the other side." When I told them that I ought to make these things known so the white men who were good would know the truth of the matter they said, "You have promised not to make our matters known and you must not do so. It might get us into trouble now. We simply wanted good examples (waonspekiye waste) for our people and not bad ones."

If there is any truth to the story recorded by Dr. Beede, it is interesting to speculate about how successful the Indian destruction of the little Gomorrah across the river from Fort Yates would have been if five Indian men had not, by tasting too much of its liquid pleasures, thought the moon was right.

What happened to the mob of lynchers, the white men who illegally murdered three Indians? Agent Cramsie, in a letter to the commisioner of Indian affars in Washington, D.C., recommended that they be punished for their crime:

Letter to the Commisioner of Indian Affairs
from James W. Cramsie
November 19, 1897

[This Outrage Against Law and Order and Civilization]

I have the honor to report that three of the alleged murderers, Indians belonging to this agency, who had been awaiting trial for the killing of he Spicer family on the east side of the Missouri River in February last, were taken from the jail at Williamsport in Emmons Country, North Dakota, on Sunday morning last, by a mob and hanged. At the request of the relatives and friends of the dead men on this reservation I have had the bodies brought to the agency and they will be buried today.

I respectfuilly recommend that the matter be presented by higher authority to the governor of the state in order to secure and prosecute a full and compete investigation of this outrage upon law and order and civilization and also in order to secure proper precautions by the state authorities to prevent a similar outrage, which is threatened, upon the other two Indian prisoners, alleged accomplices in the murder, who are now in jail at Bismarck, when they are brougth to trial.

So far as I know, no such investigation was ever carried out, and none of the thirty-odd lynchers was ever punished, except perhaps by his own troubled conscience as he recollected the part he had played on that cold, dark November night in 1897.

8

Recollections

In 1934, thirty-seven years after the Spicer murders, Henry A. Armstrong, the Emmons County prosecuting attorney who led the investigation and then represented the state in the trials of Alec Coudotte and George Defender, wrote a long essay in which he told his recollection of the events of 1897. In doing so he was apparently responding to a request by the editors of the *Emmons County Record*. By 1934 the Emmons County seat had shifted from Williamsport to Linton. Both Winona and Williamsport had by then ceased to exist as political entities, and neither can be found on recent maps of Emmons County. Armstrong's retrospective is a useful reminder of the main sequence of events and of the racial biases at work in the world in which the Spicer murders and the subsequent lynchings took place:

Emmons County Record
Linton, North Dakota
September 23, 1934

[That Horrible Homicide-Massacre]

Editors, *Emmons County Record*:

Pursuant to your request, and being one of the actors in that terrible drama, though not in the tragedy part of it, I will undertake to give you a close-up of at least the highlights of that horrible homicide-massacre that occurred at the home of Thomas Spicer about one and one half miles north of the old town of Winona, on February 17, 1897, in which six people — four generations — were brutally murdered.

As more than thirty-seven years have come and gone since that fateful day, it will hardly be expected that I will be able to give the minor details of human history made during those exciting times. The facts and incidents connected with that sad event are drawn from memory, except the names of the jurors who sat in the trials of those accused of the crime. The treachery of human memory has oft been remarked, and if I overlook some incidents that remain in the memories of others who were familiar

198 Murdering Indians

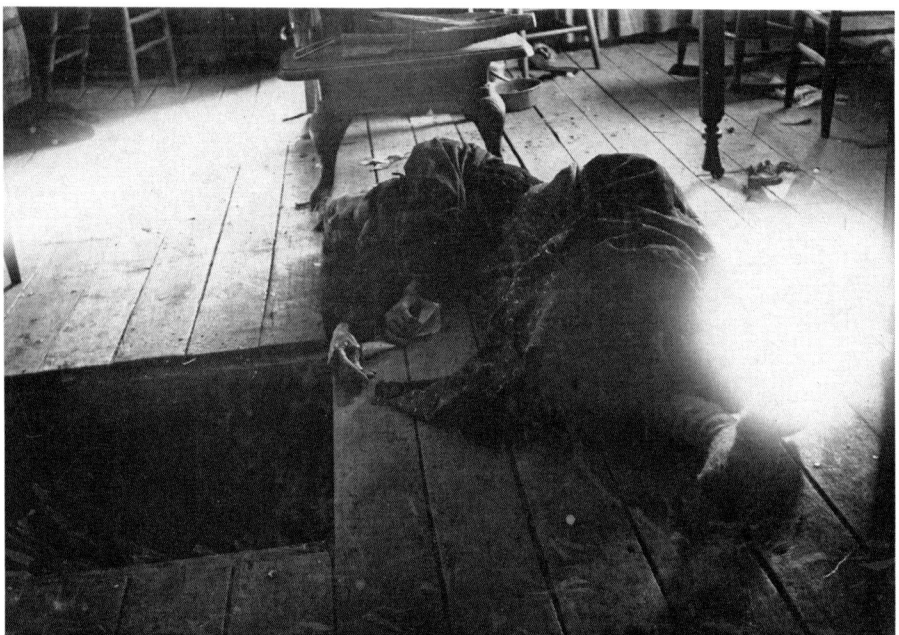

The body of Ellen Waldron on the floor of the Spicer home near Winona. She was found next to the stairway leading to the basement. She was the mother-in-law of Thomas Spicer, the mother of Mary Waldron Spicer, the grandmother of Lillie Spicer Rouse, and the great-grandmother of Alvin and Alfred Rouse — all also dead (State Historical Society of North Dakota 1952–3537).

with the homicide and the incidents following it, I will not be at all surprised.

There are many minor details, such as where the persons arrested were taken after their apprehension, etc., which have faded from my memory; but, as I view it, that is a matter of little importance and will not interest future generations should they read this account. What I here write are the facts to me personally known, almost entirely. Some portions of this narrative, of course, are hearsay, and they will be so stated.

Thanksgiving blizzard

As a prelude to this narrative, I will state that the winter of 1896–97 was, in my opinion, the worst winter I have ever experienced since coming to Dakota more than fifty-one years ago. The blizzard beginning on Thanksgiving Day, 1896, known to old timers as the "Thanksgiving Blizzard," was a scorcher. It began in the forenoon of Thursday and ended sometime during the following Saturday night. At times the mercury descended to the zero mark. The snow that was already on the ground and what fell during the storm was piled into huge drifts, which made traveling, in places, impossible without shoveling a track. I drove a team to Bismarck the forenoon of Thanksgiving day and was marooned there until the following Monday afternoon, when I left for home. I arrived home the third day following. If I had been using an automobile I might not have reached home until the spring.

Nine saloons in Winona

During Territorial days there were, at times, no fewer than nine saloons operating in the small town of Winona. The patronage for these saloons was drawn largely, but not entirely, from the Fort Yates military post, located within the Standing Rock Indian reservation and directly across the Missouri River from the town of Winona.

While I have no proof of the fact, it has often been stated some of the patronage came from the Indians. It is a quite well established fact that a small minority of the regular army soldiers stationed at the post, if any of them, were prohibitionists. It is a historical fact that when this state joined the sisterhood of states it came in as a prohibition state. The adoption of the state constitution with its prohibition schedule made it such. After statehood the saloon, as such, was outlawed; but the thirst of the erstwhile patrons of the saloon had to be quenched and the once-legitimate saloon became a "blind pig," and continued to do business at the old stand. How many of the former operators of saloons continued to dispense the "stuff" they had formerly dispensed I am not prepared to state; but certainly some of them did, which flew in the face of the state laws.

"Red water" made braves more brave

The federal government has always been very solicitous of its wards, the Indians. While it furnished them rations — something to eat, and clothing to keep them warm — it made it a serious crime to introduce intoxicating liquors onto the reservations, or to the Indians. The government entertained the conviction that the imbibing of "red water" made the "brave" more brave and more difficult to control. While rations and clothing were furnished its wards, little or no money was distributed to them, and as the "piggers" had established the system of "cash and carry" in their illegitimate business, it meant that the Indians were forced to resort to some method whereby they could provide the necessary cash, or its equivalent, to pay for the "red water." The scheme resorted to was to steal cattle, butcher them, and sell the meat to secure the cash with which to quench their thirsts. [...]

Indians sought liquor

A few days prior to the awful tragedy that shocked the entire community, the whole state, and the states adjacent to it, two of the suspects, Frank Black Hawk and Alec Coudotte, entered one of the "blind pigs" and asked for liquor, but were informed by the proprietor that they had none on hand. This answer of the proprietor was based upon the fact that a few days prior thereto a prohibition scare had frightened him and he had his stock removed and cached elsewhere.

While the "piggers" were without serious fear of state authorities on the prohibition question, they did not care to get mixed up with Uncle Sam, which they feared a raid upon their places of business and the discovery of "goods" therein might result.

In order to appease his would-be customers he informed them that one

Mr. Pepper, the drayman and water hauler in the town, had hauled his "goods" away and cached them and he did not know where it was stored. This was in the nighttime. The two Indians then made their way to the home of Mr. Pepper and pounded on the door of his home until he was aroused and came forth.

Just what Mr. Pepper told them will never be known, but there was, at the time, a strong suspicion that he told them that the liquor was stored in Mr. Thomas Spicer's cellar. Why? It was a fact, and well known to Mr. Pepper, that Mr. Spicer was of a religious turn of mind, sometimes preached, or exhorted, he not being an ordained minister, however, but most bitterly opposed to the use of intoxicating liquors. No one ever accused Mr. Pepper of intentionally saying, or doing, anything that might cause Mr. Spicer any trouble, or harm, but that it would be a huge joke for the Indians to visit Mr. Spicer and ask him for liquors. There is no proof, as far as I know, that Mr. Pepper told them anything of the kind, but it is a fact that Mr. Pepper, soon afterwards, betook himself to the far west and has never returned, to my knowledge. It is all conjecture, of course, but subsequent happenings might be a straw pointing in that direction.

The last incident related occurred on Sunday night, February 14th, 1897. Three days later, February 17th, 1897, according to sworn testimony of Paul Holy Track and Philip Ireland, Alec Coudotte, George Defender, Paul Holy Track and Philip Ireland approached the barn, or stable, of Mr. Thomas Spicer. At the time Mr. Spicer was engaged in cleaning out his stable, using a wheel barrow with no rear legs supporting it. The "visitors" all went into the stable and stood around while Mr. Spicer wheeled out a few loads of manure. The visitors carried with them a muzzle loaded shotgun and a jug of "booze."

Spicer shot in back

When Mr. Spicer had wheeled the next load out onto the manure dump, a short distance from the stable, one of the number, with the shot gun, fired a load of shot and slugs into his back and he fell. They then proceeded to finish the job by mutilating his face and body with an axe, spade and pitchfork.

After life was extinct they dragged his dead body into a partially open shed adjoining the stable and deposited it beside one of the feed mangers and covered it over with straw and manure. A discussion then arose as to who should notify Mrs. Spicer. At last Paul Holy Track, who had often been a visitor at the home, consented to be the messenger, and he went to the house, a few rods north and on a little higher ground than the stable.

He notified Mrs. Spicer that her husband desired to see her at the barn and returned to the stable.

Wife their next victim

Mrs. Spicer, who had been over the wash tub and with her sleeves rolled up, followed Paul to the barn. Just as she arrived at the stable door one of the party, Paul, as I remember it, fired a load of shot and slugs, the gun having been reloaded, into her face, her mouth, and she fell. The job of murdering her was accomplished in about the same manner as was that of her husband, finishing the job of brutal murder by the use of the axe, spade and pitchfork. Her face and body were mutilated as was that of Mr. Spicer.

After completing the second fiendish murder the party went to the house, picking up a club enroute. The house was a log building with the kitchen part of it on the west, and the only opening to the outside was through the kitchen door, facing the south.

Arriving at the house the murder party entered the kitchen. The only person in the kitchen was the old lady Waldron, the mother of Mrs. Spicer. Owing to her advanced age she put up no resistance, and they killed her with the club.

Mother fought vainly to protect twin babes

This being accomplished they started to enter the other portion of the house through a doorway. Alec Coudotte, as the leader, started to go through the doorway to the room where Mrs. William Rouse with her twin babes, two boys about eighteen months old, had taken refuge, but was met by an infuriated mother who, willing to fight to the last ditch to save her offspring, was standing with a shot gun in her hands which she used as a club-musket and landed a blow across the breast of the intruder which staggered him back and cooled his Indian bravery.

It was then that Paul Holy Track entered the breach and attempted to enter the room, but he was met by the same infuriated mother with a broken bladed hoe in her hands and with this she landed a blow on his head which cut a hole through his hat brim and into his forehead which made a wound, the scar from which, he carried to his untimely grave. This staggered him somewhat but he still pressed on.

The mother, fighting like a tigress to protect her cubs, made the second swing of the hoe, but, unfortunately, the hoe caught in a wire stretched across the room, upon which curtains were hung to separate the living apartment from the bed room apartment, and the intended blow failed to be delivered. She was then overpowered and was beaten to death with the leg of an extension table that had never been used in the table. There may have been other weapons used in effecting her death, the axe and club being found in the room, but there was unmistakable evidence that the table leg was one of the weapons used. These fiends incarnate, having destroyed the adult members of the family who might have identified and given evidence against them, now turned their attention to those innocent and helpless twin babes and snuffed out their young lives. What weapons were used in effecting their deaths is not exactly known, but the axe was found on the lounge, or settee, upon which their dead bodies were found. [...]

Slayers ransacked house

Completing the sextuple murder, the party then ransacked the house, even to the cellar. Just what articles of loot that they stole and carried away with them can never be definitely known. It is known that it consisted of a suit of clothes belonging to Mr. Spicer, some neckties, a leather cigar case, used by one of the daughters as a jewel case. Just what money they found is also not known, but it is known that they overlooked a tin can under one of the beds containing about eighty dollars. Having finished one of the boldest, most cruel and wanton, and unprovoked murders ever recorded, the party returned to their reservation, across the river. [...]

A very unfortunate circumstance entered into this case. Mrs. Rouse was a real frontier woman and could handle and use fire arms, but she had no ammunition for the shot gun, else there would, undoubtedly, have been some good Indians, dead ones.

Brother makes discovery

The discovery of the crime was not made until the following morning while Mr. John Spicer, a brother, enroute to the river for a load of wood called at the house and made the gruesome find. Finding the slain bodies of those who had been murdered in the house, he rushed to the barn and discovered the body of Mrs. Spicer therein. The body of Mr. Spicer having been covered up, he did not discover it.

This aroused in his mind the thought that his brother might have become mentally deranged and murdered the family and disappeared. Mr. John Spicer then rushed to the town of Winona and gave the alarm. Many of the residents of the town then rushed to the scene of the massacre, and the greatest excitement prevailed. A messenger, a Mr. Jack Flynn, was dispatched to the agency, across the river, and soon the Indian agent, Mr. J. W. Cramsie, appeared in Winona.

Prior to leaving the agency the agent had instructed some of the Indian policemen, among them one Standing Soldier, a bright and intelligent Indian policeman, to proceed to the scene of the homicide and investigate, which he did, but, on account of the earlier visitors thereto, most of the footprints and other evidences, had been obliterated, and little material evidence was revealed to him.

While in Winona, the agent, whose wife was an Indian woman, and whose sympathy leaned toward the wards of the government, expressed the opinion that it was not the work of Indians. This, momentarily, caused suspicions to be aroused as to whether it might not have been some other than Indians that had perpetrated this diabolical deed, but such suspicions were soon allayed and gained little headway. The consensus of opinion was that it had been the work of Indians.

News reached Williamsport the following Saturday

On account of the deep snow which made traveling difficult, and the further fact that we had no telephones in those days, the news of the massacre did not reach the then county seat, Williamsport, until the following Saturday afternoon.

The excitement produced by the sad news which was relayed by the "grape vine" telegraph, knew no bounds and the feeling ran high. To hear that a whole family of God-fearing, peace-loving people should have been wantonly and cruelly murdered, in cold blood, aroused a spirit of sympathy hitherto unknown in these parts.

The bodies of the victims of the homicide had been buried before the people in the northern part of the county knew of the sad occurrence.

8. Recollections

Investigation started

The following day, Sunday, the writer, who was then the state's attorney of the county, made his way to the town of Winona on horse back to investigate, but little could be done along that line as the Indian agent had issued an order preventing the civil authorities from entering upon the reservation to investigate the case, but this order was soon revoked by the Indian department at Washington, which had been communicated with, and we were permitted to enter the reservation and press our investigation. Soon thereafter, in company with the sheriff of the county, Peter Shier, we proceeded to the Standing Rock Indian agency, the headquarters of the Sioux Indian reservation, and undertook to unravel the mystery and ascertain, if possible, the perpetrators of the crime. [...]

While we had the cooperation of the Indian authorities, a part of the instructions from Washington, we were able to uncover little evidence germane to the main issue — who the perpetrators were — but we did discover evidence of cattle stealing, etc., which gave us a slight "lead." We left the agency not overjoyed with the results of our detective work, but we felt that we were on the right track.

Two arrested in Bismarck

A few days later Frank Black Hawk and Alec Coudotte went to Bismarck and the sheriff followed them thither and filed complaint against them and had them arrested, as suspects, and placed in the Burleigh County jail. In passing, let it be noted, that Black Hawk was a half-breed (Indian and Negro) and Coudotte a half-breed (Indian and French), and the others that afterwards came into the picture were all full-blooded Indians. Black Hawk was a semi-educated Indian, it being reported that he lacked only one term from graduation at the U.S. Indian school at Carlisle, Pennsylvania.

A little later, at their insistence, we prepared to give the two suspects a preliminary examination, some witnesses having been subpoenaed to support the charge made against them, and they were transported to Williamsport, then the county seat of this county, but upon carefully analyzing the testimony of our witnesses we were doubtful if we had sufficient evidence. [...]

Aaron Wells aids in unraveling mystery

Mr. Aaron C. Wells, the "boss farmer" at the Cannon Ball sub-agency, was present for the hearing. Mr. Wells was a man through whose veins coursed some Mohawk Indian blood, and who was nick-named by the Indians "The Fox." He was intelligent and shrewd and to him was due the greatest credit for the unraveling of the mysteries of the case. [...]

Acting on the facts gleaned by Mr. Wells, a few days later I went to the Cannon Ball sub-agency and through the hearty cooperation of Mr. Wells, a vast number of Indians were called in and interrogated as to what they knew concerning the matter.

Other arrests follow

As a result of this semi-judicial proceeding, Philip Ireland, in custody of Indian police, was sent to the agency and placed in the guard house, Mr. Wells and I following him to the agency. The facts disclosed at the hearing at the sub-agency involved Paul Holy Track as a suspect. So the following morning an Indian policeman was dispatched to the Porcupine, where Paul was at the time, and he was brought to the agency and locked up in the guard house, but was not permitted to communicate with Philip Ireland.

Securing a typist to reduce their statements to writing, we proceeded to find out what they had to say, examining each separately. After taking their statements, in writing, we adjourned the hearing in order to analyze and consider the same. The next day we again called them out, separately, and took a second statement from each of them in writing, and again adjourned to analyze and consider the statements. As the first and second statements differed in many particulars we became fully convinced that they were lying and not telling us the truth. The next day we again called them out, separately, as before, and proceeded for the third time to extract from them the truth.

By this time we were entirely convinced that they were two, at least, of the guilty parties involved in the massacre. As a part of the loot taken from the Spicer home at the time of the murder was a leather tobacco case, used as a jewel case, but with clasp broken, and we had in our possession its counterpart, in perfect condition. We "flashed" this cigar case and inquired if they had ever seen it before, and they replied in the affirmative, but with the further statement that we had had it repaired.

As was usual, Paul was the first to be examined in our investigation at each hearing. He was led to believe that we had discovered some of the loot taken and he began to weaken. Mr. Wells, thoroughly conversant with the Indian language, acted as the interpreter during the investigation. Paul, a boy in his late teens, had acquired some education and could read quite well in the English language. At last Paul expressed his belief that the white man could read his mind, broke down and consented to tell the whole truth of the horrible affair.

He then proceeded to give us a closeup of the whole transaction, and which later, upon the witness stand, both he and Philip Ireland delineated to the juries in the district court, and at the preliminary hearings.

As soon as he had confessed and made a clean breast of the whole matter, and Philip Ireland was informed of it, he, too, made a complete confession, corroborating the statement of Paul Holy Track in every material matter. These confessions of the "boys" (Philip Ireland was also a boy in his late teens) involved George Defender, besides the two already in custody. All three of them were then arrested and taken into custody. [...]

In the interim between the preliminary examination of Black Hawk and Coudotte, and the next term of the district court, feeling ran high and was attended by fears that possible trouble might be encountered when the trials were entered into. Some feared that the prisoners might be lynched while being transported from the jail to the court room, which was the Williamsport school house located in the southern part of town, others feared a conflict with the Indians that were expected to attend the trials. The fears were so intense that many insisted upon securing the attendance of a company of militia to quell any possible trouble that might arise. [...]

Coudotte trial first

The first case moved for trial by the state's attorney was the case of the state of North Dakota vs. Alec Coudotte, charged with murder in the first degree, the murder of Thomas Spicer. No grand jury having been called and the accused having had a preliminary examination before a magistrate, under the law, it became the duty of the state's attorney to file an information against the accused. Owing to so many different weapons having been used in committing the murder, the information filed contained five counts, to correspond with the five different weapons that were used to wit: shot gun, spade, axe, pitch fork and club. The defendant, when arraigned, pleaded "Not Guilty." [...]

The main evidence produced by the prosecution was the testimony of the two "boys," Paul Holy Track and Philip Ireland, with such corroborative evidence as the state was able to furnish. As much of the testimony was given by Indians, it was necessary to use an interpreter and Harry McLaughlin, a son of Major McLaughlin, a former agent at Standing Rock was selected.

Taking testimony slow process

Taking testimony through an interpreter is a slow process and considerable time was consumed in presenting and submitting the evidence to the jury. The fact that the defendant, Alec Coudotte, had attempted to commit suicide while confined in the jail, and which the prosecution contended was an evidence of guilt, may have been a strong factor in the determination of the jury.

The trial lasted several days even though the judge made every effort to hurry it along by holding night sessions of court. At the conclusion, when the attorneys from each side had submitted all the testimony that they considered material in the case, both sides "rested." [...]

Jury verdict "guilty"

The deliberations of the jury was not long-drawn-out, and when they returned into court the following day the foreman announced that the jury had arrived at a verdict, "guilty, as charged," and giving the punishment as death upon the scaffold, by hanging.

The usual motion in arrest of judgment and for a new trial was made by defense counsel, but the motion was denied. In due time thereafter an appeal to the state supreme court of the state was perfected by the attorneys for the defendant, and the execution of the sentence of the jury was postponed.

This ended the first chapter, in the district court of the accused perpetrators of the greatest and most heart-rending incident that had occurred in Emmons County up to the time, in its whole history.

Defender tried next

After the conclusion of the Coudotte case, the state's attorney moved the case of the state vs. George Defender, who had been given a preliminary examination and had been bound over to the district court. The information filed by the state's attorney against Defender was similar in all respects to the one filed against Alec Coudotte.

At this juncture, the attorneys for the defendant made, and filed with the court, an affidavit of prejudice against the presiding judge and moved for a change of judges and also for a change of the place of trial. The judge granted the motion for a change of judges, but denied the motion for a change of venue. This caused a delay and a recess of court was taken. In the meantime Judge Winchester selected Honorable O. E. Sauter, judge of the district court of the seventh judicial district of this state, to preside at the trial of George Defender. [...]

After instructing the jury as to the law of the case, a bailiff was sworn and the jury retired. It stayed retired for more than sixty hours without arriving at a verdict. At last the court called the jury in and satisfied himself from questioning the jurymen that longer consideration by the jury would be fruitless of a verdict, he discharged the jury. It was a "hung" jury. It was afterwards learned that on the last ballot the jury stood eleven for conviction and one refused to join to make it unanimous. The "stubborn" man was said to be Gus Frederickson. [...]

At the close of the Defender trial, in which the jury failed to agree upon a verdict, a mis-trial, George Defender and Frank Black Hawk were returned to the Bismarck jail to await trials. The other three, Alec Coudotte, under a sentence of death imposed by the verdict of a jury, and Paul Holy Track and Philip Ireland, neither of which had been placed on trial, were placed in the county jail at Williamsport to await the outcome of the appeal to the supreme court in the Coudotte case.

Some weeks later the appeal was argued in the supreme court by Mr. Stevens on behalf of the defendant Coudotte, and by the writer on behalf of the state. During the argument to the court the writer, as far as professional ethics permitted, informed the court as to the effect of an adverse decision, a decision granting the defendant a new trial, might have on the minds of the people of Emmons County, and particularly on those residing in the vicinity of the scene of the homicide — friends and neighbors of the Spicer family.

The wounds in the feelings of the people were, apparently, healing, but the scars of those wounds still remained, vivid reminders of that horrible and most cruel massacre.

Coudotte granted new trial

The supreme court, after carefully and judiciously analyzing the record, the testimony introduced in the district court and the rulings of the judge thereof, arrived at the conclusion that the corroborative evidence in support of the testimony of Paul Holy Track and Philip Ireland, two of the participants in the homicide, was insufficient to support a conviction and that the judge of the district court presiding at the trial should have granted the motion for a new trial. The decision of the district court was reversed and the defendant, Alec Coudotte, was granted a new trial.

The decision of the supreme court rendered, and announced it, in the early days of November, 1897. The counsel for the state, at the time of the trial were well aware of the fact that the corroborative evidence was none too strong, but we had combed every possible source to add thereto without being able to furnish more. This meant, in common parlance that upon a second trial we would be unable to convict the defendant, and he would go "Scot-free."

Lynchers move on Williamsport

This knowledge had the effect of opening up the old wounds to their feelings; and on Saturday evening November 13th, 1897, a number, about forty, it was reported, of the sympathetic friends of the Spicer family, who they were or where they came from was not known to the writer, nor was it ever revealed to him, appeared at the jail in Williamsport, where Alec Coudotte, Paul Holy Track and Philip Ireland were confined, and demanded from the night watchman, Mr. Thomas Kelly, the keys to the doors of the cells in which the prisoners were confined.

Three hung from beef windlass

The watchman remonstrated, but his remonstrance was overcome by force of numbers and the keys were taken from his possession and the doors of the corridor and cells were duly opened and their occupants were bodily removed from the jail and taken to a beef windlass about one hundred yards distant, and suspended thereon by means of ropes around the necks of each of them. Reports were that the party, of whomsoever it may have been composed, acted very deliberately, but quietly and orderly, and departed, leaving three dead Indians hanging on the beef windlass.

This unjudicial execution took place a little after midnight, in the early hours of Sunday morning, November 14th, 1897. Shortly thereafter, at about 2 o'clock A.M., the night watchman appeared at the residence of the writer and informed him that there were three "good" Indians, dead ones, hanging on Mike Rush's beef windlass.

The next day after the suspended bodies of the dead Indians had been viewed by a host of people who had been informed through the "grape vine" telegraph of what had occurred the previous night, the bodies were taken down, a coroner's inquest held and were buried a short distance northeast of the town of Williamsport, and were later removed to the reservation and buried among the dead of their people.

The above is a bold statement, without embellishment, of what happened at Williamsport as a sequence of the cruel and inhuman butchery of the Spicer family on February 17th, preceding.

There was a report current at the time that another party of sympathetic friends of the Spicer family had planned to give similar treatment to George Defender and Frank Black Hawk, then confined in the Burleigh County jail, but that it was abandoned after one of the number, Mr. Charles McIntyre, had unwittingly swallowed a draught of aqua-ammonia in a blind pig in Mandan, which caused his death the following day.

Claimed lynchers were known

It was later reported to the writer by Mr. Stevens, one of the defense counsel, that he had unearthed the names of each and all of the party who had visited the jail in Williamsport and who had been participants in sending the three Indians therein confined to their "Happy Hunting Grounds."

There was some talk, some threats, of prosecuting the parties engaged in that "midnight ride," but it never materialized. Mr. Stevens informed the writer that he had that list of names tucked away in the bottom of his trunk.

In closing this account of that massacre and the incidents related thereto, the feelings of the writer were, at the time, and have ever since remained, that exact justice had been dealt out to the three Indians who paid their penalty for their crimes at the hands of an infuriated party of friends and sympathizers of the murdered family, and that before I would be a party to such threatened prosecution of them I would resign the office of state's attorney.

Sheriff sought safety in Bismarck

The treatment accorded the three Indians at Williamsport had the effect of arousing considerable feeling among the Indians on the reservation against the officers of this county who had been instrumental in securing the apprehension and arrest of the suspects. The knowledge of this antagonistic feeling was such as to arouse in the mind of the sheriff, Peter Shier, a fear for his safety, and he removed to Bismarck, temporarily. Others of us gave the reservation a wide berth for some time afterwards, until the troubled waters had become more calm.

Sidelights

After spending some time on the reservation and learning more of the sterling qualities of the policeman, Standing Soldier, I was convinced that if the Indian agent had so instructed this policeman, inside of twenty-four hours after the homicide, he would have rounded up the perpetrators of the crime and had them locked up, for it was revealed to us that they, one and all, were renegades on the reservation and inherently "bad Indians."

In my younger days I had read of "Indian uprisings" of "Indians going on the war path" and murdering and scalping, in cold blood, of white people, but I had reasoned that it was in revenge for some real or fancied wrong that had been done them, but in the Spicer massacre no evidence was adduced that this family had ever mistreated or wronged any member of the Indian tribe. In "Indian uprisings," "mob psychology" might have been a factor, but in this case that spirit was certainly absent.

After knowing and studying the Indians, and especially Paul Holy Track, to whom I loaned books to be read by him, while in confinement, I could not imagine that he, in his sober mind could have done the cruel and heartless acts that he had admitted that he did; that his mind must have been clouded from the effects of imbibing strong, intoxicating, liquors; that the precautions taken by the federal government, and the heavy penalties provided therefor, to prevent the introduction of intoxicating liquors onto the Indian reservation, and to Indians, was and is a wise one.

Showing the contrast between that period, thirty-seven years ago, and the present time, I desire to state that the salary of the state's attorney was then four hundred dollars per annum. Considering the responsibility and labor loaded upon the shoulders of the state's attorney during that exciting and trying period, the emoluments of the office were small remuneration and compensation for the labor performed.

Respectfully yours,
H. A. Armstrong

It is interesting that Armstrong's parting comment had to do not with the injustice done to the Indians lynched without proper trials, but with the injustice of the fee he received for prosecuting the Indians — and failing to prove any of them guilty. It had to do not with his presumption of the guilt of five Indians or his refusal to prosecute any of the white men who illegally lynched three of the Indians, but with polysyllabic financial terms like emoluments, remuneration, and compensation.

Another mid-thirties recollection focused on the fate of the town of Winona. The town no longer exists and does not appear on any modern maps. In the 1940s, long after the town of Winona had disappeared, an earthen dam was built just north of Pierre. It created an enormous lake, known as Lake Oahe, that stretches some 230 miles north to Bismarck. Usable land was lost on both sides of the Missouri (including more that 55 thousand acres on the Standing Rock reservation on the west side of the river).

Route 1804 is a two-lane road that runs north-south just east of the Missouri River between Bismarck, North Dakota, and Pierre, South Dakota. On the east side of the lake in some places the road goes right along the lake, but most places it is several miles to the east. Opposite Fort Yates, still the headquarters of the Standing Rock reservation, motorists driving along route 1804 will see a green sign with an arrow pointing west and the words "WINONA ISLAND 4 MILES."

The town of Winona was built on a small hill. When the waters of Lake Oahe rose to their full height in the early 1960s that small hill became a small island. It is accessible now only by boat, though when Lake Oahe is low, someone with tall waders could probably make it out to the site. A local farmer told me in the summer of 2012 that he sometimes takes a boat out to the island to hunt. The only traces of what he called "the old wild-west town of Winona — you know, saloons and brothels — are crumbling stone foundations of some of the buildings."

The following article was written by Frank Bennet Fiske (1883–1952), who took several of the photographs published in this book. Fiske was a historian and writer as well as a photographer. Among his published work is this article about old Winona. The centerpiece of the article about the town is his description of the Spicer murders and his recollection of certain conversations about the guilt and innocence of the three men who were lynched. Fiske himself was only about fifteen at the time of the murders, but he reconstructed a conversation he had overheard about Alec Coudotte's attempted suicide. Jack

Carignan erred when he says that Alec Coudotte had cut his wrists and stabbed himself in the chest; in fact, he had stabbed himself in the abdomen. Particularly insightful is Carignan's speculation that Paul Holy Track and Philip Ireland "did the whole thing because they wanted to be warriors like their fathers." The ferry that Fiske mentions was probably the one that agent John Cramsie had at one point shut down in a futile effort to keep his wards away from the saloons of Winona:

Fargo Forum
Fargo, North Dakota
May 3, 1935

Old Winona, Now "Ghost" Town, Won Doubtful Fame

Winona [was] started in 1884 on a high level tableland in a wide valley on the east side of the Missouri River, directly opposite the new military post of Fort Yates that had been constructed to protect the Standing Rock Indian agency and preserve treaties against violation by young warriors of the Sioux. Like all early western towns Winona boasted of at least ten business places designed to satisfy the cravings of men for the cup that cheers and the society of woman along with the wine and inevitable song. "Let's go to Winona," was the slogan when life grew tiresome at Fort Yates, and be it summer or winter, rain or blizzard, nothing could stop men from following the lure of the lights that shone from the row of establishments that faced the west on the "main street" of Winona.

There was but one building on the west side of this street — a respectable store owned by Jack McCrory. This was the last building to mark the spot where the town once flourished and it was removed in January, this year [1935]. At the height of its career Winona had ten saloons or places of amusement, where glasses and poker chips clinked while fiddlers played and soldiers, cowboys and wild women danced. The old time quadrille was the favorite and the caller was duty-bound to wind up each change with "all promenade to the bar."

Hilarious revelry was order of Winona nights

Thus business boomed and everything was more or less orderly until some cowboy yelled, "Smoke 'em out!" Then every gun-toter took a shot at the lights after which darkness reigned until candles were fetched and broken chimneys replaced. The round of pleasure continued until the light of dawn flooded the eastern sky. Then soldiers called it a night and made for the river, which in summer was crossed by a ferryman piloting a large skiff. This was in the days before the gasoline engine began its puffing career and boats of the smaller kind were propelled by the mighty muscles of hardy, old river men.

As a boy the writer heard many times the call, "Jake, bring over the boat!" And Jake was a patient man. Usually there were more men than could be safely accommodated in the boat on a morning after a Winona night. When Jake loaded, only a couple of inches of the gunwales were above water. With a dozen more or less inebriated men in the boat, all anxious to get back to Fort Yates to report for reveille, Jake's job was no sinecure. However, he was an expert, but could not always avoid a ducking in the swirling waters of the mighty Missouri. [...]

Of all the exciting events that transpired at Winona none equaled the slaying of the Spicer family on February 17, 1897. This story, with some new observations, may best be told in the vernacular of the old time friends of the writer.

Killing of Spicers is retold by old timers

We are grouped about the big stove in the Indian trading store owned by the late J. M. (Jack) Carignan. Sam Bruguire, old time scout and freighter, has come in that day from a long trip and is enjoying the comfortable heat while indulging in feats of memory in his usual entertaining manner.

"Twenty-three years ago last night I was drunk," says he.

"Sure you was," says Jack Carignan. "You were drunk twenty-three years ago night before last and the night before that, as well. You were always drunk so why bring that up?"

"Well, I tell you how I come to know that," Sam goes on, not at all ruffled by friendly joshing. "I slept on a pool table in Slippery Dick's place over in Winona. The next morning I walked out on the porch to look at the weather and here come Jack Flynn — you fellers knew Jack, he and his brother, Paddy, run the saloon at the north end of the front street — and Jack was yelling, "The Spicer family has been killed!" I didn't believe it until Slippery Dick come running over from McCrory's store and said the same thing. It was cold that morning and lots of snow   the hard winter of 1897."

"I reckon they got the right Indians when all was done," says Tom Short. "The way they was killed was enough to prove that. It was two miles out of town and the Indians got Spicer in the barn and killed him. Then they called his wife from the house and killed her. Next they done for Mrs. Spicer's mother, old lady Waldron, and then finished Spicer's daughter, Mrs. William Rouse, and her twin babies. She put up a fight with a hoe, but when it caught in a stove pipe wire they closed in on her. Alec Cadotte, Ireland, Holy Track, Defender and Blackhawk was sure the guilty ones and they got what was coming to 'em."

Carignan doubts guilt of certain Indians

"I always had my doubts about that," says Jack Carignan. "You see, I happened to be called to Williamsport, Emmons County seat, at the time, as an interpreter for the state. They had the accused Indians locked up there after they had been run down on the reservation, but the trial wasn't going to suit the people. Cadotte had been found guilty, but the jury had disagreed on hanging Defender, and it was beginning to look like the rest would go free. R. N. Stevens, famous Bismarck lawyer, was defending Holy Track, Blackhawk (the Negro-Indian), and Ireland. He came to me one night and said that Cadotte had tried to kill himself by cutting his wrists and stabbing himself in the chest. Stevens said, 'Jack, I wish you'd go to Cadotte and tell him he had better make a clean confession to you. I will be where I can hear what he says and will have A. C. Wells as interpreter and a stenographer to take it down!'

"So I went to Cadotte's cell. He was feeling pretty bad, and I told him the doctor said there was no hope and he was sure to die in a couple of hours.

"'Cousin,' he says — he called me cousin — 'I'm going to die. I am glad of it as I don't want to live with such a thing against me. I'll tell you the truth as sure as God is looking at me. I never had anything to do with the killing of the Spicer family. Blackhawk and I killed a beef in the woods below Fort Yates that day and after we were through butchering we went to your store and was talking in the shed at the back door. While we were talking there you came through and says, "What's up, plotting against the whites?" After that we went across the river and traded the beef for whiskey at Red Caldwell's place in Winona. Then we went back and divided the whiskey between us in the woods and Blackhawk struck north for home and I went south. I never knew of the murder until afterwards.'"

Blackhawk's story said identical with Cadotte's

"Those were practically Cadotte's words," says Carignan. "After I left him I went to Blackhawk's cell while Stevens and the others placed themselves where they could hear what was going on. I told Blackhawk Cadotte had stabbed himself and confessed the two of them helped to do the murder.

"'He is a liar!' Blackhawk declared. 'I'll tell you about it. You remember the time you come through the shed of your store and said to me and Cadotte, "What's up, plotting against the whites?" ' Then Blackhawk told me the same story Cadotte did almost word for word. From that time on I never thought those two, at least, had anything to do with it. And I don't believe Defender was in it, either. I think Holy Track and Ireland — his real name was Standing Bear — did the whole thing because they wanted to be warriors like their fathers. They got started by killing Spicer in the barn and then finished the whole family."

For a few moments there is silence in the store as the fire purrs. I know it means something portentous. Sam opens with:

"Well, I think they were all in it. They acted mighty suspicious. I was in Red Caldwell's one night, not long after the murder, and Blackhawk and Cadotte were standing at the bar. Their whiskey was poured out and Caldwell says, 'I want to tell you fellers something. The white people think you had something to do with this killing and I give you a pointer. You better pull your freight out of the country if you know what is good for your hides.'

"And those two fellers stood there and never said a word. They just fingered their glasses and turned them around and looked down, then drank their whiskey and walked out."

Ammonia saved two from being lynched

"Jack Flynn was the cause of that murder," Sam said. "He and his brother Paddy were expecting the U.S. marshal to come and close up the saloons. I guess they hadn't paid their license, or something, and they hid all the whiskey and other drinks when Blackhawk and the rest of them came in and wanted something. Jack told them they were too late, everything was sold out. 'You better go up to the Spicers if you want a drink. They got plenty.' He said that just for fun because Spicer was a sort of a preacher and his family was strictly temperance and law-abiding."

"Yes, and old Blackhawk died of fright," says Tom Short. "Yes sir, he could see the young woman (Mrs. Rouse) and her children all the time he was raving before he died. Some say he was poisoned and maybe he was. You can't tell me he and Cadotte and Defender wasn't in it. Blackhawk and Defender would have been lynched too if it hadn't been for a bottle of ammonia. Cadotte, Holy Track, and Ireland were lynched at Williamsport. In November a bunch of fellers, mostly from around Winona, when they see that Stevens was going to free the Indians, rode up to Williamsport and took Cadotte, Holy Track, and Ireland out of their cells and strung 'em up on a beef windlass just across the road from the stone court house.

"A few days before that the sheriff, Pete Shier, took Blackhawk and Defender to Bismarck for safekeeping as he had wind something was in the air. And I guess you won't find the equal of this where a lynching was pulled almost a year after the crime was committed.

"But, as I was saying, a bottle of ammonia saved Blackhawk and Defender, and it was all because John McSorley had taken a notion to have his windows cleaned that day. It was planned to string up the three at Williamsport on the same night that another crowd was to ride to Bismarck and do the job before too many'd get interested. The fellers met at Mandan and was all ready to ride across the river to Bismarck when it was suggested that they better have another drink. McIntyre, the leader and another feller went into McSorley's and called for whiskey. The feller on duty reached under the bar and fetched up a bottle.

"McIntyre poured his and downed it. The other one just got a sip. Mac died that night from the affects. That busted up the party and Blackhawk and Defender were set free. The Indians that were hung took the evidence with them and there was nothing on the other two. As I said, Blackhawk died a hard death, not long after, and Defender passed out by the tuberculosis route."

[...]

Winona declines as military quits Yates

With abandonment of Fort Yates as a military post, on September 13, 1903, Winona saw a steady decline. Saloons closed and buildings were torn down. One store survived for several years but finally gave up the ghost. [...] Today no building remains of the once hustling frontier town. Few old timers are left to recall its gay days.

As late as 1935, then, there was still speculation about whether Paul Holy Track and Philip Ireland had worked alone in murdering the Spicer family, or had been assisted by Alec Coudotte, Frank Black Hawk, and George Defender. The members of the lynch mob had no such doubts that they were all five "guilty as hell." George "Win" Tracy (1862–1956) was one of the members of the original, November 14, 1897, lynch mob. Just before his own death more than a half-century later, he distributed a brief memoir entitled "The Win Tracy Story." I am grateful to his granddaughter, Jean Marilyn Tracy Hanson, for permission to quote from her grandfather's account of his experience, as a man of 35, in the lynching party. "The Win Tracy Story" is only a dozen single-spaced typed pages long. Win Tracy moved to Winona in 1883. He worked as a farmer, but to supplement his income he began hauling goods from Eureka to the merchants of Winona. Quoted here are only the few pages that deal directly with Winona, the Spicer murders, and the lynching. It is interesting that Tracy and others attended Alec Coudotte's trial with a gun hidden in a blanket in his wagon so that, if the defendant was found not guilty, they could shoot him on the spot.

The Win Tracy Story

There was [in Winona] a restaurant, also a blacksmith shop, barber shop, two large dance halls, and about five or six saloons. The inhabitants were a floating population — especially the female population. They came and went. Even the saloons were all the time changing hands. [...]

After that job of freighting, other jobs came my way, occasionally. Most of the beer and whiskey sold in Winona came from Eureka, and I made a deal with Beecher to deliver it every week, as it was needed.

There was a lot of tragedy in those early days. [...] That evening [February 18, 1897] Joe Clark and his wife and girl, Rosie, were at our house at about 11 P.M. Joe and myself were at a cribbage game and the men had all gone to bed. I heard a wagon stop at our back door and holler, "Tracy!" By the sound of his voice I knew something bad was coming and I stepped to the door. It was Frank McConville. He said, "Tracy, the whole Spicer family have been found dead. We don't know why or by whom." I said, "Joe Clark is in the house." He said, "Tell Joe and get the word around," and drove right back.

We didn't sleep much that night. My wife got me some breakfast and I jumped on a horse and was soon at Winona. I guess there were most of them up all night. [...] Jack McCrory was standing there. I think he had been watchman there all the night. He says, "Tracy, this is awful, and we can't imagine who would kill these people who haven't an enemy in the world." So I found out nothing. They were buried as soon as Rouse got home. We didn't even go to the funeral as we were afraid to leave our children.

Our men and I talked and talked about it and all agreed it must have been some crazy man. My men, for a month, didn't dare go out after dark alone, even to the barn. As for myself, I didn't dare go out at all. I just kept as close to the gun rack as possible. [...] The tension was still on for thirty days, and then a story broke and people began to feel more secure.

8. Recollections

> The theory was broken by a man, Aaron Wells. He was boss farmer at Fort Yates and lived on the Cannonball River. His wife was an Indian girl. I knew Aaron very well and he told me all about it. His wife told him one day, "Aaron, I have found out who killed the Spicers." It seems these two Indian boys had bragged about it to some of their relations and Aaron's wife got on to it. Aaron got word at once to our sheriff, Pete Shier, as the murder was committed in Emmons County. He had the right to arrest them wherever found. The boys both admitted the killing and said that Black Hawk, Cadotte, and Defender were along, also. There would have been no trial, but the three indicated that they were not there.
>
> They were tried at the June term of court. Hal, myself, and two of our men went to the trial. All of us had guns rolled in blankets in our wagons. I don't know how many others did that from Winona, but the idea was that if for any reason they were acquitted, we would get them right there. [...]

Well before the state supreme court reversed the lower court's guilty verdict and Judge Winchester's execution date, Tracy says, a prominent man in Winona came to him and asked whether he could be counted on to provide men for a lynching if Alec Coudotte was declared innocent or was granted a new trial. Tracy assured him that he could promise ten or twelve men. The unnamed prominent man said that was fine, since he himself could bring another twenty from Winona. They were ready, then, when the word came that the conviction had been reversed. Presumably "the husband of this woman" who placed the ropes around the necks of the three "culprits" was William Rouse, the husband of Lillie Rouse and the father of their twin infant sons:

> That settled it, and we weren't surprised one afternoon about five or six o'clock when Frank McConville drove up, called me out and said, "Be at the old Brindle barn one mile west of the jail at eleven this evening." That was short notice, as it was forty miles to go. My wife started supper at once and I sent Pete Knudsen at once to notify our gang. [...] There were ten of us that went — Hal and I went with two of our men in the platform wagon and two men on horses, Tom Sleasing, both Keiffer boys, and Joe Safton. There were eighteen in the Winona bunch.
>
> We met at the time appointed at the Brindle barn. After a forty mile drive horses do have to rest and feed. Christ Naaden and Tom Keiffer volunteered to stay with the teams. That left twenty-six to go on foot about one mile. We got in at midnight. The town was dark and not a person in sight. In fact, we were in town an hour and not a light showed. The sheriff, Shier, was himself an old timer and I am sure he was let in on this affair for he took a vacation and left his deputy, Tom Kelly, on the job. Kelly sure didn't know of it for you never saw a more surprised man. We went up quietly to the jail front door and knocked. Tom came and unlocked the door with a lamp in his hand and we were all inside before he realized it. He, of course, knew us all and we didn't care. He tried to argue but finally threw

us the keys. We tied handkerchiefs over the faces of two men, Jess Keiffer and Joe Safton, as they had never seen Tom Kelly before and they went in to guard him while the other twenty-four men did the job, which I must say was a good one.

Of course, the culprits put up a fight, but they were all in separate cells and were taken one by one, thrown, and their hands tied behind their backs. When we were at the barn someone spoke about ropes to hang them with. None had been provided, but most of the riders had cattle ropes tied on their saddle. Someone said, "Well, a rope that will hold a steer should do for a murderer." So that was that. Pete Knudson furnished one rope. After they were all tied up it was voted that the husband of this woman be allowed to tie the ropes around their necks. What a satisfaction that must have been. I can still see him in my mind's eye as he stood at their shoulders and slipped the noose over their heads. To the first one he said, "Now you son-of-a-b—, I have you right where I want you."

There was a high beef-hoist just back of Mike Rush's hotel. The two Indians wouldn't walk, and so they were hauled down about one block. One, Cadotte, walked but none of them would talk. After they were pulled up and the ropes tied down, the crowd still stayed about thirty minutes. We took beats on the streets to see that no one let them down, but we got out of town and not a light showed. Later, I found out that Frank Wallace and Oliver Bales were on their way home from a threshing trip up north and slept that night at Bill Yeater's Hotel. They never did get over the fact that they were there and didn't take it in. Well, that was that.

What a trip that was for our horses. Eighty miles between, sun to sun. Not so easy on the men either. Of course, there was a big holler about it. The Indians figured that their man, Stevens, would take it up, but he said nothing doing. Besides, you know they were all guilty as hell. Not an attorney in Bismarck would help prosecute and our state's attorney told me that if anything was started he would resign.

And so it finally blew over. The other two, Black Hawk and Defender, were turned loose. Defender was in the last stages of tuberculosis and soon died, but a trap was set for Black Hawk. We all knew that the first thing he would do would be to visit Winona and the idea was to get him. A deal was made by someone. I couldn't swear just who it was, but anyhow, one of the girls at the dance hall slipped him a pint of whiskey when he left and he was found the next day about one-half mile from town — dead.

9

Healing

In the late summer of 2012 I wrote to the Standing Rock Sioux tribal headquarters in Fort Yates to introduce myself, to explain my project, and to ask whether my wife and I might pay a visit to the reservation to chat with the descendants of the five men accused of involvement in the Spicer murders. My letter eventually found its way to LaDonna Brave Bull Allard, director of tourism for the Standing Rock Sioux reservation. She is a tribal historian. Part of her job is to keep track of family genealogies and tribal rolls. She arranges tours and tells visitors about the tribe and its stories and traditions. She replied that she was related to Philip Ireland and would be happy to chat with us.

Anne and I arranged to meet LaDonna on Monday, August 20, at the agency building in Fort Yates overlooking the wide Missouri River. What follows is an edited version of the question-and-answer interview.

Interview with LaDonna Brave Bull Allard
Fort Yates, North Dakota
August 20, 2012

Stories That Heal

My name is LaDonna Brave Bull Allard. My real name is Ta Maka Waste Win, which means Good Earth Woman. My nation is Ihunktonwana (upper Yanktonais [Nakota]), Pabaska (Cut Head [Nakota]), Sisseton (Dakota), Hunkpapa (Lakota), Sihasapa (Blackfeet [Lakota]), and Oglala (Lakota).

What's is the difference between your "name" and your "real name," and how does that help us understand a name like Paul Holy Track?

I will try and explain. We don't have a system like non–Natives do when it comes to names. We are each given a name at birth. Holy Tracks was his own name, not his father's name. So even though his father was Wandbi Wanapeya and his mother remarried Siyaka, Paul would still go by Holy Tracks. When he started school he was assigned an English name, Paul,

The burial of Philip Ireland, one of the lynch victims. The grieving woman in the background is his mother. Originally buried near Williamsport, his coffin was removed to the reservation for reburial at the request of the family (State Historical Society of North Dakota 1952-2025).

because the United States insisted that we have first and last names. The government just added an English name and turned his real name into a last name, and in the process dropped the "s" from "Tracks."

As for me, my "real" name is Ta Maka Waste Win, which means "Her Good Earth Woman"—"Ta" means "Her," "Maka" means "Earth," "Waste" means " Good," and "Win" means "Woman." But the government said I have to have an English name so I became LaDonna. Then the government said I had to take a last name as well. My great-grandfather was Tatanka Ohikita which means Brave Buffalo, but because of a problem with translation we became Brave Bulls. Then they said that married women had to have their husband's last name so now I am an Allard. Here at the tribe I am just Ta Maka Waste Win, pronounced *ta ma ka wash-tay ween*.

I am related to Philip Ireland, who was my great-grandma's brother. We have a lot of stories in our family of this Spicer incident that happened a long time ago.

To get right to it, do you think Philip, Paul, and the others murdered the Spicer family in November 1897?

I cannot tell you because I was not there. I do know that a very nice family was killed. Children were killed. Women were killed. As to who exactly did it, we have a lot of mixed stories here on the reservation. I know that both Philip Ireland and Paul Holy Track were very young boys, so young that I do not think that they were the masterminds behind the incident. But that's a personal opinion.

Who do you think was the mastermind?
When the original stories were told to us by our families, it was Frank Black Hawk and Alec Coudotte, the two older men who first went to Winona to get alcohol. They were told that the Spicers kept the alcohol in their basement. It was not the other three men. According to what was told to us, that they went across the river — Winona was across the river from us — so they had to come back across the river, and that's when they met George Defender, Paul Holy Track and Philip Ireland. They said, "Hey, you want to come with us? We're going to get some alcohol, go party and stuff." That's how they got the younger boys to come with them.

One of the things that I see in the transcripts of the trial is the Indians were asked very detailed questions about times and dates. What time was this, what day was that? Indian people don't think like that. So it got very confusing for the people giving the testimonies as to times and dates of things. I see that as one of the problems of the testimony. You see, when a non-Indian comes and asks about time, it's like, "What did you do at 8:45 A.M. on February 16?" An Indian person is more likely to ask, "Where were you in the mornings that week?" In other words, we don't have the concept of those precise times. It happened in the morning, or it happened in the afternoon. When we set a time for a meeting, a white person says, "Let's meet at 8:00 A.M." The Indian says, "We'll meet sometime in the morning." Precise time is not really in our world view. When we're being questioned by the legal authorities and we get questions like, "On June 23rd at 8:15 P.M., where were you?" we don't know.

When I read a confession or a trial where an Indian gives really precise dates and times, I wonder how true can they be. Precise times and dates are a foreign concept to us, so I wonder where those times and dates came from.

So you think that Paul Holy Track's and Philip Ireland's confessions were not genuine?
I suspect that parts probably were "doctored." When someone says, "Goodness, what a good writer Paul Holy Track was," I can't help wondering who exactly did that writing. Paul was just a confused Indian boy, not a fully assimilated man. In order to fully assimilate a child, you take them from birth to adulthood, and then from there, you change their family structure. So it takes fifty years.

What do you know about Paul Holy Track's family?
Not very much. He came here from Montana when he was three or four. He was probably the person who appears on our tribal rolls as Paul Siyaka, born in 1878. He was the youngest in his family, possibly his parents' only child. I cannot find any descendants of him or his family on our rolls. He testified that he went to the Farmers School. That was a reservation boarding school just across the state border in Kenel, South Dakota, where Indians learned the basics of farming.

I assume that when he and Philip Ireland were young they were brought up in traditional Indian homes with their language, their culture, and their ways of thinking about things. But they were taken off to a boarding school or other school for X number of years. What do you have then? Just a child with a confused culture. You don't have enough time for full assimilation. None of these boys have been assimilated. So then you take them and you say, "What time did you do this, and what time did you talk to so and so, and when did you meet so and so, and what time did you come across the river?" All of those things would be foreign matter to those boys. That's one of the concerns I have with the testimony.

What other problems do you have with the testimony?

There were no peers there. I guess there were some translators and lawyers for part of the testimony, but I don't think there were people from the reservation who were allowed to help with anything. These boys were removed from their own cultural support system. They were interrogated by people from another culture. So what do you get, you get three or four different confessions or testimonies from one individual. "Did you really do this?" "Are you sure?" "Didn't you do this, really?" I think that's how they were interrogated. You see it today in court, where lawyers kind of take charge of your story. Pretty soon it's his story, not yours. And it's in English, not your own language.

Of course, everybody on the jury was white. So the defendants were in hostile territory already. The trials were conducted by white lawyers and judges interpreting white laws and legal traditions. If the five accused men had been dealt with by the tribal authorities, what might the procedure have been? Who would have made the decision about guilt and innocence? What might the decision have been?

When a crime like this happened within the Lakota-Dakota-Nakota nation, the accused would come before the people who had lost their relatives. A council of elders would get together. They would bring the young men forward, and they would say, "Okay, tell us exactly what happened." And then the elders would go over the information. If they decided that the accused was guilty, they would ask, "Okay, is there a reparation for this crime?" So if they could, they would give the family gifts to alleviate the loss. If a child was left orphaned, they would take that child and raise it as their own. But if they committed a crime involving the killing women and children — well, that is just not allowed. They would have issued a death sentence.

How would the execution have been accomplished?

We have police societies, and they would be responsible for that. An honorable man would take his own life.

Who would have been on that council of elders? Would it be men, women, both?

Men. In our society, they would have been the men. We had a group called the Shirt Wearers. The Shirt Wearers were somewhat like your policemen. They were responsible for keeping the camp safe, making sure everybody obeyed the rules and regulations. They made sure that nobody hurt the neighbors. If there was a dispute, they came in to solve it.

Why do you suppose the two younger ones, Paul Holy Track and Philip Ireland, would have confessed so willingly to their parts in the murders?

As I read the confessions and transcripts, those boys were trying to say, "Okay, bad things happened. We're at fault." They wanted to tell the truth. As for changing their stories, I think it got awful confusing for them. Even though Holy Track was very well-versed in English, I don't think he wrote his testimony. Actually, I don't think any of them wrote their own confessions. Even for me, there is still this conflict of languages that we have, even to this day between Lakota (the Dakota language) and English. And all of these boys were fluent speakers of Lakota. And so when you start going through this back-and-forth, back-and-forth over questions and answers, it gets really confusing to know what exactly you're saying. English is a strangely precise language. Something vague or general in Lakota can come out more precise and specific in English. Incidentally, there are now only about 6,000 of us who are fluent in Lakota, and the average age of these is sixty. We are working to get Lakota taught regularly in our schools.

Can you describe what it might have been like to be a young man in the 1890s on the Standing Rock reservation? What would it have been like growing up here?

It was a time of huge sorrow. There was a lot of starvation because there was not enough food anywhere. The ones who agreed with the agent were the only ones receiving food. It was during this period that we had what the Indians called the "starve or sell" bill. The United States government was trying to starve us into selling the Black Hills. It was also the time of the great influenza that went through most of the families. Lots of children got it. In my own family, my mother was one of nine children. Only two of them lived to adulthood. Death was everywhere in those days.

Life was changing fast. You woke up one day, and who you are is no longer a good or safe thing to be. You have the school officials who dump flour and sugar on your head and tell you that you have to be white. You have to speak white, you have to dress white, you have to walk white. You cannot pray as you've always prayed. You've got to believe in a new god. Everything around you is changing. All of a sudden, the language you speak is bad. All of a sudden, the clothes you wear are bad. It would be a very confusing time. It would be a time of extreme sorrow, a time of trying to figure out who you are, where you belong. These young men had a hard life because everywhere around them there was change, hunger, confusion, death.

You try to remember that free-spirit life where you made your own decisions. You try to remember that, but it is hard to do that in a time where you can't make your own decisions any more. You suffer and watch your family suffer. It was a hard time for those boys. It was a really hard time. And then going to schools where, all of a sudden, you're forbidden to speak your language, you're forbidden to be who you are. If you resist, you're beaten. It's a hard life. Those boys grew up in a time of massive change. They were born into one kind of life but it all changed, and the transition changed them, sometimes in bad ways.

What were they expected to do, these young men?

They were expected by the whites to assimilate and become Americans, even though we did not officially become U.S. citizens until 1924. They wanted to be hunters and warriors, but they were expected to become farmers.

What kinds of jobs could a young man find?

There were no jobs here. Most of the people at this time were still sustaining themselves by hunting, fishing, gardening, gathering. We still do a lot of gathering — roots, berries, et cetera. The buffalo were no longer around. They had been our main source of food. So a lot of these young men, starting from the age of ten, eleven, twelve, spent a lot of their time out hunting all the time to keep their families from starving. But for these boys, Paul and Philip, there was little for them to hunt.

Some of these young men would have been children when Wounded Knee happened.

In 1890, yes. Paul and Philip would have just entered their early teens.

Was there a connection between Wounded Knee and the Spicer murders? The white soldiers killed lots of your people at Wounded Knee. Could the Spicer murders have been retaliation for that massacre?

I don't think so. There were some Standing Rock Indians killed at the massacre at Wounded Knee, but they were Hunkpapas and other Lakota bands. For the young men accused of the Spicer murders, the massacre at Whitestone Hill on September 3, 1863, was far more important, because they had all had members of their own families murdered at that place. Philip Ireland, Paul Holy Track, George Defender — they all had family members in the Whitestone massacre. The soldiers killed almost 400 of our people, and then they forgot they killed us. They took 600 of our people to a prisoner-of-war camp down at Crow Creek, and the remnants of our people scattered. Half of our people went to Sioux Valley, another portion went to Fort Peck, and a few went to Devil's Lake.

And when our people were released from their prison camps, many came to this northern side of Standing Rock, this part in North Dakota. Three of the accused young men, then, were already remnants of a large massacre where we lost the majority of our people. The United States forgot they killed us. We did not forget.

Wounded Knee did not really play into any of this. The Whitestone Hill massacre was something that each of us remembers. Philip Ireland's mother was nine years old at that massacre. She was shot, and because she lived, we're still here. Her name was Grey Hand Woman. She took the English name of Mary, and she was married to Philip's father. Her last husband was named Moccasin, so she became known as Mary Moccasin.

Almost every day we heard about this Whitestone massacre because every day it has been passed down to us. Remember, we're talking about different groups of people. The Lakota were involved at Wounded Knee. The Dakota and Nakota were involved at Whitestone Hill. So Wounded Knee would not have been much in the minds of these two boys. They were the remnants and survivors of the first massacre, the one that most Americans know nothing about. If the massacre at Whitestone Hill is remembered at all, it is remembered as one of the Civil War battles, not as a massacre of Indians.

Dakota, Nakota, and Lakota — is there any easy way for us outsiders to understand the difference?

Not easy, no. The Dakota, Lakota, and Nakota nations are three different nations, and under those different nations we're separated into different bands. The Dakota, which is the mother tribe, are separated into the Sisseton, Wahpeton, Wahpekute, and Mdewakanton bands. The Lakota are separated into the Oglala, Sicangu, Hunkpapa, Miniconjou, Oohenonpa, Itazipco, and Sihasapa bands. And the Nakota are separated into the Yankton, the Yanktonai, the Yanktonai-Ihunktonwana, Hunkpatina, Pagaska, and Assiniboine bands.

The Dakotas move two times a year, plant gardens, and fish. They have a more sedentary village. The Nakota have even more sedentary villages. Lakota don't eat fish. Dakota eat fish. We have different bead designs, different clothing designs, different home designs. So there are important difference among the various branches. We originally were all under one nation, the Dakotas, but now we've tended to go our own separate ways.

The three lynched men, and Frank Black Hawk, too, were all Dakota. Coudotte is French, Chippewa, and Blackfeet Lakota. I know that outside people don't understand the distinctions among our bands and the different locations people come from, but for us, our band affiliation gives us the orientation for how we are raised, what our backgrounds are, what our families are, and what our relationships are to different historic events. Wounded Knee was not a direct or meaningful part of the lives of Holy Track, Ireland, Defender, and Black Hawk. Their people did not go to Wounded Knee.

That is not to say that here on the reservation we don't think Wounded Knee is important. Every year we recreate the journey some of our people took there in 1890. We used to call it the Bigfoot Ride. Now it's now called the Future Generation Ride. They've been doing it for thirty, maybe forty years. They meet at Sitting Bull's cabin site in mid-December because he was killed December 15th. They start with prayers. Children, old people, young people go. They make their trek on horseback. It takes them two weeks to ride from Sitting Bull's cabin site to Wounded Knee. Each night they camp and they tell stories. They try to pass down traditions and culture to all the young people. The young people are excused from school at that time. Each young person who goes to Wounded Knee gives up Christmas, and every kid that rides on that ride comes back a changed person. It's an amazing, amazing thing.

How many people might go on that journey?

I think they start off with like thirty or forty people, and they pick up people all the way down.

Do they ride the horses back home?

No, they all have horse trailers. They'll bring their horses back. Two years ago we had a really bad winter with the blizzards and everything. It's really cold here that time of year. And so one of the horse trailers couldn't make it up the hill and just rolled down the hill and crashed. They were able to get down there and get the horses out of that trailer. They were pretty spooked, but they were okay. The man lost his trailer and pickup, but everything else was okay. They continued on. Every year it is an amazing event. A lot of Sitting Bull's descendants go on that ride, and we have children from each one of the schools that go.

I take it that you are not a descendant of Sitting Bull?

No, I am Dakota. He was Lakota. Although I do have some Lakota blood, I come from Red Thunder's brother, Rain in the Face. I come from Iron Horn, Shaved Head, Little Bear, Bear Face. Everybody around here should know who they're related to seven generations back. And at any time an elder can ask you who you are related to, because it is important to know your families.

Do the people on the reservation still pay much attention to the Spicer murders and the lynchings resulting from them?

Do they learn about these events in school?

Until recently we didn't learn any of our tribal history in schools. We finally got control over our schools in the last few years here, but before that there was no Indian history taught in the schools. Right now, teachers are starting to teach Indian history and Indian languages. Information about the Spicer murders is something that's handed down through the families that were involved. Agatha Ireland has passed away now, but I remember when she came to my house and said, "Do you remember the Spicer business?" and I was like, "No." And she said, "Well, Philip Ireland was my uncle. And I remember ..." So that's how I know. She would come and tell us.

What kinds of things would she say about Philip Ireland?

She said her uncle was innocent. She said he was just a young boy. She said her mother gave testimony, but when I asked people to look in the legal files, they could find nothing. No one wrote down Mary Moccasin's testimony. There are some photographs up at the state historical society in Bismarck. There is a photo of the three men hanging. And there is another photo of a funeral. In the background of that photograph, all alone, is an Indian woman standing with her head covered, watching. That woman is Philip's mother, my great-grandmother, Mary Moccasin.

Was there a stigma connected with the families of those five people after all this? Were they embarrassed by it? Were they made to feel inferior by other members of the tribe?

No. I don't think so. George Defender died of tuberculosis, but his son George Defender, Jr., went on to lead a good life. He was a rodeo rider and is in the Cowboy Hall of Fame. I never heard that he or his children were ostracized because of George Senior's possible involvement in the Spicer murders.

Would you like to say anything about the role of alcohol in the murders?

At the time when the reservation first started, the soldiers here at Fort

Yates would use alcohol to get favors. They created alcohol out of almost anything. Indeed, one of the biggest causes of death here at the military fort was alcohol poisoning. That's what most of the soldiers died of here. The town of Winona was created specifically for the soldiers. They had lots of saloons. They had a ferry that went across the river every day, back and forth, to take the soldiers over to the saloons because there was no alcohol allowed within the reservation.

Many young men, including Indian men, became addicted to alcohol. If you don't know who you are or where you belong, you tend to have problems, and most of these men had problems. Alcohol can have good effects and bad effects. Anything you can have in life can be abused. When the alcohol was outlawed here, it was still available over there, and a lot of white people made big profits selling whiskey to Indians. Lots of white men got money from alcohol. Indians just got poorer and sicker.

I doubt that the Spicers would have been murdered at all if whiskey had not been available to Indians at Winona.

Do you think justice was served by the lynchings?

A vigilante group never serves justice. The white people wanted to kill someone. Anyone. It had nothing to do with logic. It had nothing to do with justice. They wanted revenge. They wanted to even the score. None of the five was convicted of anything. That lynch mob murdered innocent men to get their revenge. Revenge is something that damages you. Revenge eats you alive. Revenge eats you up from the inside. We Indians try not to seek revenge. We try not to think, "I am mad at you because you did this thing, and I will get even with you." That is not right. That is not keeping in balance with your body, your mind, your soul, your energy. It will make you sick.

Native culture is about forgiveness and healing, not revenge. We call this the seventh generation that's inside us. Everything we do is an effort to support this innermost part of us. I think the non-natives call it a soul. We're not quite sure what to call the innermost, the seventh generation that God gave you. You must do everything in your lifetime to heal that, to keep that in balance.

Do you think any good came out of this whole murder/lynching sequence of events?

I don't see any good, not for the families, not for the people who died, not for the whites, not for the Indians. We all lost.

The Spicer family was a very good family. They did not do anything wrong. Some crazy saloon keeper told a story about their having whiskey in their basement. The Spicers were innocent people. From everything that I can find out about them, they were hard-working, honest people. They came here to this land, to our land, to try to find a life. So I don't really believe that the Spicers did anything to deserve the treatment that they got.

On the other hand, our people who went over there and killed the Spicers had been treated badly by whites and were treated badly by whites. What good came out of it? Three young, confused men were lynched. George Defender later died a terrible death by tuberculosis. There is a story that Frank Black Hawk died soon after the lynchings of poisoned whiskey, but our tribal records show him still alive a quarter-century after he supposedly died. We keep pretty accurate enrollment records, and our records show that he died years later after the alleged poisoning. But no, no good came of the murders or the lynchings.

What do you know about Frank Black Hawk's ancestry?

We've been doing a lot of background research on Frank Black Hawk. Frank Black Hawk's grandfather was a black soldier named Isaac Dorman. His Indian name was Black Hawk. He was a black man who was an interpreter for Abraham Lincoln and Custer's seventh cavalry. He went to the Little Bighorn where he was killed by Mary Crawler, Moves Robe Woman, who was the daughter of Chief Crawler. But that is another whole story. Issac Dorman was married to an Indian woman from another camp. He was a leader of the Minnesota uprising in 1862, and they were here on Standing Rock where his children were all raised. His sons, Peter and Frank, were two of the individuals that were with the group of Indian children that were taken from here to Hampton Institute in Virginia, where they were educated.

You can go to the Hampton Institute and pull up their school records. Peter returned and I believe died of tuberculosis. And Frank returned, and I believe that he married three times and has many desendants. He was the first African American-Native American to attend at Hampton Institute. Hampton Institute was first created for African American students, and later they brought in the Indian students. So he was unique there because he was both native and African.

Where does my family fit into Frank Black Hawk's? Frank Black Hawk's wife divorced Frank and married my great grandfather and had my grandmother, Sarah Brave Bull. When my grandfather died, she married Adolph Wise Spirits. The Wise Spirits are a very well-known family around here. So that's how that fits into my family.

I see that your children have the name McLaughlin. Can you explain how that happened?

Major James McLaughlin, the white Indian agent, was married to a Santee woman, a Dakota, and all of the children were enrolled members here on Standing Rock. I was married to Terrence McLaughlin. His father was Pat McLaughlin whose father was Henry McLaughlin whose father was Harry McLaughlin whose father was Major James McLaughlin. So my children are descendants of Major James McLaughlin.

Are they proud of that? James McLaughlin was a pretty controversial agent.

Major James McLaughlin had many Indian friends who admired him, but he also had many who disliked him. He was instrumental in the death of Sitting Bull. He did everything against Sitting Bull, so it depends on what side of the fence you sit on.

Like the McLaughlins, the Coudottes and the Black Hawks are mixed-bloods. Does that have anything to do with their sense of belonging on the reservation, or their possible involvement with the Spicer murders?

9. Healing

The white ancestor of the Coudottes was a French fur trader who came in from Quebec. He married a Chippewa woman, and his children came down to Pembina, North Dakota. One son went to Turtle Mountain and married up there on the Chippewa reservation. The other son came down here in the 1870s and married a Blackfeet woman, a Lakota. All the Coudottes on Standing Rock come from those two. So Alec came from a Lakota woman and a mixed-blood.

As for whether mixed-bloods feel like they belong at Standing Rock, the answer is "Yes and no." When you're within the mainstream part of a society, you have all of these people who are from within that society. The full-blood Lakota and Dakota and Nakota people all know each other. They all know who is related to who. And then you have the group that have moved in here now, the non–Indians with the military, agencies, the schools, and the government.

Then you have this group right in the middle, the mixed-bloods. They don't belong on one side, and they don't belong on the other, and that's where you find Black Hawk and Coudotte. They were mixed-bloods. They would have been looked on as suspicious by the full-blood people because in the past it was often the mixed-bloods who betrayed the people. Not all the time, but at times, and not everybody, just certain ones. But the minute people find out you have mixed-blood, they kind of ostracize you a little bit.

If you are a mixed-blood, you have your family, and the family will always take care of you, but to the group as a whole, you are an outsider. To the non–Indians, you are a mixed-blood. You do have some of their blood, but they see you as being an outsider. In times of change or transition or crisis, mixed-bloods have to decide where they stand. If you are a mixed-blood, do you stand with the hostiles, the traditional people? Do you stand with the people who are trying to assimilate and just live in peace? Do you stand with the non–Indian people? And we also have still another group of people, what we sometimes call the Texas cattle-drive people. These are the wranglers and cowboys who come up here with the big cattle drives. They hang out at the bars and the saloons. This other element that is here at the same time—the rabble rousing, bronco-busting people—can be an attractive culture for young people, especially mixed-bloods, to get involved in.

So, to answer your question, yes, it was difficult for mixed-bloods like Frank Black Hawk and Alec Coudotte. They belonged at Standing Rock, but didn't belong, too. They went over to Winona, maybe looking for a place they could belong, but found only whiskey, not respect or true friends. Interestingly, for a while the saloon keepers could legally sell liquor to mixed-bloods but not to full-bloods. Sometimes the mixed-bloods would buy whiskey and resell it to full-bloods.

The animosity between natives and non-natives was very high at that time. Oh, wait, it is still like that today.

Is it? How do you mean?

The animosity between natives and non-natives is huge. The non-natives around here have all kinds of illusions, myths, about who we are. The stereotypes have not changed. We still encounter a lot of hate and racism today. You can go across that river, and those people over there don't know us. They don't know anything about us, nor do they want to know anything about us. And so they have all these preconceived ideas about us.

We know that many people in the dominant culture across the river and across the nation have certain notions about us. They think that all Indians are alcoholics, but no one comes to see if it is true or asks us about it. They think we don't bathe, but in fact we are really obsessive about bathing. They think that Indians don't pay taxes, but in fact we pay all the taxes. They think Indians get things free, but in fact we don't get anything free.

Does it work both ways? Do Indians have preconceived notions about people on the other side of the Missouri?

Yes, the racism goes both ways. We have our issues with non–Indians. But we as native people are very bicultural today because we have been raised in American schools. We know from the start that we have to be bicultural to survive. We have to live in both worlds. The white people only live in theirs. Their survival does not depend on learning about us and our ways, our history, our religion. So as a result they don't.

You mention your religion. Do you want to say anything about your native religion or about the effect of Christianity on the Indian people?

[*Laughs.*] Are you trying to get me in trouble? Christianity was devastating to our culture. The churches saw us as savages to be converted from what we were to something they thought we should be.

But things are changing. In 1978 the United States passed the Freedom of Religion Act. It allowed us limited freedom of religion so we could actually pray out in the open without going to jail. Up to then, our native ceremonies, our traditional spiritual ways, had gone underground. Now we do them out in the open. So now our Sun Dances are huge, and attendance in Christian churches is down. The young people are coming slowly back to their own tradition and culture. And we have a large group of non–Indians who are coming for our spirituality today. We don't missionize them. They come to us.

Are they welcome?

In some cases, but not all. I go to closed ceremonies where no non–Indians are allowed. We have a proclamation from the Keeper of the Pipe which says that non–Indians cannot run our ceremonies.

Philip Ireland and Paul Holy Track went to a Catholic school. What does that suggest to you?

It's hard to say. There have been some reports or rumors of abuse — sexual abuse of Indian children — over the years, but I have no idea what happened, if anything, with those two.

I will tell you about myself personally. When I was born I was baptized Catholic, and then my aunts got mad and re-baptized me Episcopal. Then my grandma re-baptized me Mormon, and then Born Again — all by the time I was seven years old. In the hunger times we tended to go to the church that fed us.

When I was old enough, for the first and second grades, I was sent to St. Francis Mission, which was a Catholic school. And then when I was older, the Episcopal church took me to Massachusetts but when they got me to Massachusetts, they discovered that I was baptized in both churches. So I went to Catholic church and Catholic confirmation. And then I went to Episcopal church and Episcopal confirmation. One Sunday I went to a Catholic church, the next Sunday day I went to an Episcopal church. As a result, I grew up with the idea that the Christian doctrine is pretty much the same in all of the churches, and they all meant the same thing to me.

I never got too much into affiliation with Catholic, Episcopal, Lutheran, Baptist, or Mormon. Those are all the same thing to me because I belong to all of them, and yet I belong to none of them. You find a lot of the people here belong to a lot of the churches. When the government instituted the Indian missionary act in 1834 they sent the churches out to Christianize the Indian people. Standing Rock got Catholic, Episcopal, Congregational, and Baptist. Those were the four churches that were given money to come here to missionize us. You'll find that some of the people here belong to all four churches.

Here, whether they're Catholic, Episcopal, Mormon, Baptist, or Congregational really doesn't matter. The concept of one god and praying to one god is our concept, so the idea never changed. But now many Indians here are re-identifying with our native traditions.

Do the Christian churches still consider themselves to be missionaries and try to convert Indians to their religion?

Oh, my, yes. We get inundated in the summertime, especially. Part of my job is to speak to each one of these groups. They bring about 200 people every year, each church. So one week I did the Episcopals, I did the Catholics, I did the Baptists, and I did the Congregationals. All in the same week.

And what do you talk to them about?

I talk about history, the history of Standing Rock. That's what they want to know.

Do they go around individually to peoples' homes?

They go around to homes. They do little projects, fix up a house or a roof or something. They bring in all these kids from Virginia and Pennsylvania and every place to missionize us. They've been doing this for years. I just got off the phone with a man this morning. He asked, "Can you give me any ideas in how we can actually succeed in missionizing your people?" I cannot.

If they ask me my personal opinion, I tell them, "If you want to talk about Jesus, then see him through our eyes. He was native. Jesus had a vision quest for his people, fasted for his people, and sacrificed for his people. Native spiritual people did that, too."

I do help out at all the churches. We believe in our traditional ways. But we also respect other people's ways. We think that being accepting of everybody's way is the only way to be.

Is there anything else you'd like to say, especially about the Spicer murders and the lynchings?

You're asking about something that, as memories come back, is very painful to me. You are talking about an event for which there has been no healing. Traditionally, we have ceremonies and processes that we go through for healing. It might seem that when Indians kill innocent whites, then whites kill innocent Indians, and that balances things out and it's all healed up. But it never works that way. The wounds are not healed. The pain and anguish are still there. We see the lynchings not as justice or justified retaliation, but as vigilante lawlessness, similar to the racially motivated lynchings in the South.

We see the lynchings as a hate group killing us again. So that's how I see this whole thing — maybe not correctly because a bad thing happened, but because it was a vigilante hate group coming and hanging our people. They did not care what really happened. They were not seeking the truth. They did not care about the Spicer family. They cared about hate. That's what I see. And what I see is that there has been no healing.

Can there still be healing?

Of course. There can always be healing. We have ceremonies for that. We call it the Wiping of the Tears, where we invite the families of these people we have harmed, and we wipe their tears in ceremony. But it involves people on that side of the river, and that probably is not going to happen. We still have a lot of unresolved issues. For example, there is still a lot of violence against our people. Even today, to be a young girl on the reservation is to be very vulnerable. Ninety percent of all our young girls are raped by off-reservation men. And it seems that a non–Indian cannot be prosecuted here because the Supreme Court says so. So we cannot prosecute a non–Indian.

I am tempted to wonder why, in light of allegations like these, Indians have not done more violence against whites.

We were trying to survive. You have committed massacres. You have starved us. You have taken our land, our weapons, our buffalo. You have denied us our religion. You have poisoned us. You did medical experiments on us until 1989, when we went to the United States Supreme Court and said, "Stop experimenting on our people!" You did forced abortions on our women. You did forced sterilizations until 1982.

The crimes of Americans against our people have not stopped, they are continuing. America did not wake up and say, "Well, we've bothered the Indians enough. We'll leave you nice Indian people alone now."

We now prepare for the next battle, the battle over oil. The white oil companies want to come in here and dig or drill for oil. That is an extremely divisive issue.

About half the people welcome the drilling. After all, our people are impoverished. An average person on the reservation today lives on about $15,000 per year. How many people can live on $15,000 in America today? For the small percentage of people who have jobs here, most work for the tribe. Most of those have bachelor's and master's degrees. The majority of our people don't have that education. So, sure, these people want to bring on the oil companies and the jobs they will bring with them.

But the other half know that the oil companies will destroy the beautiful land we live on, will mess up the water, will bring more and more non-Indians onto the reservation, will alter this place that we love, alter it beyond recognition, will destroy this last little piece of America that we can still call our own.

I fear that oil will destroy us from the inside out. In this case it will not be the whites destroying us, it will be us destroying ourselves.

When you said a healing ceremony would involve people from the other side of the river, you mean they would have to come here and consent to be part of a ceremony? Do you think that could happen?

Anything can happen. Anything could happen. We would love it if they came over. I know that there are relatives of the Spicers over there. I think if the families sat down and talked with each other today, we might find common ground. We would not say, "Oh, we're innocent. We didn't do anything wrong." The Indian people would not say that. We would say, "Yes, we understand the pain you feel. We feel a similar pain."

I wonder if we might find common ground there, in those shared feelings of pain. And I wonder if we could agree about some things, like that vigilante groups and the hate groups cannot, by their very nature, bring about justice. All they bring about is more hate.

You know, I was really surprised that you agreed to talk to Anne and me about these painful subjects. Why *did* you agree to talk with us?

I tell stories all the time. Telling a story is a first step to healing. And then once you start healing, then life gets better for you. Maybe that is why I agreed to talk with you today. I am hoping that in this book you are writing about the Spicer murders and the lynchings you will maybe help the healing process. What happened more than a century ago affects my family still today. A long time ago when I decided to go to my people's ceremonies and follow our traditional ways, my only prayer was to heal my family. This is part of that healing. We have to heal as a nation and a people in order for us to go into the future. All of these events help us heal, to resolve all these unresolved issues. That's what it's all about.

Why did I agree to talk? Because I am hoping that we can someday heal the wounds on both sides of the Missouri. Because there are stories to be told on both sides of the river, and stories to be listened to. Telling stories and listening to stories can bring about healing. If the stories come from the heart, then the healing can begin. Isn't that what writing books is about, healing?

10

Epilogue

The documents in this book tell a story. The story is not a murder mystery about who murdered who. We know beyond any reasonable doubt that at least two Indian men from Standing Rock crossed the frozen Missouri River near Winona, North Dakota, and murdered a white family on February 17, 1897. We know beyond any reasonable doubt that at least thirty white men rode into Williamsport and murdered three Indians on November 14, 1897.

The story is not about whether either set of murders was justified. We know that both were dead wrong.

Rather, the story is about what made nine murders happen, about what caused good people to do really bad things. It is a story about the persistent racism and the demands for revenge that made those nine murders possible. It is a story about the attitudes of two groups of people who refused to understand each other, two groups of people who each thought they were the only ones who knew how to use the land, who thought they were the only ones who had a right to use it.

It is a story about a river that separated two peoples. One group crossed the river only to buy whiskey. The other group crossed the river only to make arrests. It is a story that no one can be very proud of. I hope it also proves to be a story about healing.

Is it so difficult to understand that in February 1897 Paul Holy Track and Philip Ireland needed to cross the Missouri River to became for one afternoon the conquerors of their white conquerors? Is it so difficult to understand that not long after, sober and safe, they wanted the world to know what they had done — by putting on display the treasures they had stolen and then confessing to the murders they had committed, knowing full well that to confess to murdering a white family was to invite death?

And, of course, death accepted the invitation.

Is it so difficult to understand why the white settlers who brought that death did not think of themselves as thieves of Indian lands? They had gotten their land by following the right legal procedures and were working hard to

10. Epilogue 233

A small ferry was used to bring people, mail, and supplies from Fort Yates and other locations across the Missouri River to Winona. To judge from the tilt of this one, it was probably bringing in mail or perhaps whiskey (State Historical Society of North Dakota 1952-5226).

scratch out a living on it. They did not think of themselves as vengeful murderers. They had tried to let the legal system punish the men who had murdered, without any provocation they could comprehend, a white family that had inflicted no intentional harm on Indians. When the legal system failed to provide anything they recognized as justice, the white settlers took the only course they saw open to them, riding off under cover of darkness to the Williamsport jail, demanding the keys to the cells, and dragging three prisoners to a beef windlass.

My goal in assembling these many documents is not to rake up painful memories, though they will undoubtedly do that. My goal is certainly not to renew the racial distrust that gave rise to the murders or to encourage any further retaliation for past actions. My goal is not, as Louise Erdrich's was in *The Plague of Doves*, to redo the story line in such a way that Holy Track and the other Indians are the innocent victims of the hasty and unreasonable anger of white settlers.

My goal, rather, is to offer to the good people living on both sides of the Missouri River avenues to understanding the people on the other side of the river.

Non-Indians reading through these documents can surely approach an understanding of the frustration that the Indians of Standing Rock felt in 1897. Non-Indians can understand that those Indians knew that they had been supplanted by white settlers who looked down on them as lazy, backward, brutish fiends. Non-Indians can understand that those Indians knew that their white neighbors were waiting, not very patiently, for them to die off. They can understand that these Indians had been cheated out of their land and livelihood by a United States government that had given them little in return but military massacres and abandoned promises. They can understand that these Indians despaired of any sort of productive future as they watched, in sickness and in poverty, as more and more white families took up homesteads on land they themselves had once used. Surely white people can approach an understanding of why a couple of angry young Indians, emboldened by whiskey illegally sold to them by white saloon-keepers, would murder a white farm family that had not personally harmed them.

Indians reading through these documents can surely approach an understanding of why the white settlers, working hard to make a living on homesteads offered to them by the United States government, would feel personally threatened when a neighboring family of six was brutally murdered by Indians. The white settlers had their own list of broken promises to contend with. The United States government had, after all, promised to protect them from the Indians. Not only had it failed in February to protect an innocent farm family from a brutal attack, but it had overturned in November the conviction of a suspect who had been declared guilty by a duly constituted jury. Surely Indians can approach an understanding of why a group of angry settlers, in the dead of night, emboldened by the absolute conviction that they were doing the right and just thing, would break into a county jail and drag to a beef gallows two confessed murderers and a man who had been sentenced by jury and judge to be hanged.

In understanding can be found the seeds of forgiveness, and in forgiveness can be found the seeds of healing. I hope that the good people on both sides of the Missouri River will come to understand that the river that has for so long separated them can also bring them together. It is a body of water that can cleanse, that can purify, that can irrigate, that can unite them by means of recreation, sports, boats, and bridges.

It is too much to hope that by growing to understand each other the Indians on the west bank and the non-Indians on the east bank of the Missouri River can by their own example model enlightened behavior for other groups that have refused to try very hard to understand each other — Republicans and Democrats leap to mind, as do Jews and Arabs, and management and unions. But it is not too much to hope that we can all come to understand the obvious: that feuding is both feudal and futile, and that those strange people on the other side of boundary rivers are just as decent as we are.

Key Dates and People

It may help readers to consult this list of key dates in 1897 and key people involved in the events that year in Emmons County, North Dakota.

Wednesday, February 17. Spicer family is murdered just north of Winona.

Tuesday, June 1. Opening date of the trial of Alec Coudotte. The trial ends in a conviction on Saturday, June 12. Coudotte is sentenced on Wednesday, July 14.

Monday, November 8. North Dakota Supreme Court in Bismarck announces that it has overturned the conviction of Alec Coudotte and calls for a new trial.

Sunday, November 14. Alec Coudotte, Paul Holy Track, and Philip Ireland are lynched in Williamsport in the early morning hours.

The Victims

Thomas and **Mary Spicer,** their daughter **Lillie Spicer Rouse** (wife of William Rouse, sometimes spelled Rowse), their twin grandsons **Alfred** and **Alvin Rouse,** and **Ellen Waldron**, mother of Mary Spicer. The six people, usually referred to collectively as "the Spicer family," were murdered in their home north of Winona, in Emmons County, North Dakota, February 17, 1897.

The Accused

Frank Black Hawk. Part African American, part Dakota Indian. He allegedly helped plan the murder of the Spicers but was probably not involved in the actual event. He was also known as Frank Pierre.

Alec Coudotte. Part French, part Lakota Indian accused of involvement in the Spicer murders. He was tried, pled not guilty, found guilty by the jury, and sentenced by the judge to be hanged. The state supreme court reversed the decision and called for a new trial. Lynched November 14, 1897.

George Defender. Dakota Indian. Tried for murder, but a hung jury failed to convict him. Died of tuberculosis a year after the lynching of Alec Coudotte, Paul Holy Track, and Philip Ireland.

Paul Holy Track. Young Dakota Indian whose father, Wandbi Wanapeya (Eagle That Scares, sometimes mistranslated as Scares the Eagle or Rushing Eagle), transferred to Fort Peck, Montana. His mother remained at Standing Rock and remarried Siyaka. Paul is listed on one tribal list as Oye Waken (Holy Tracks). When he started school he was assigned the name Paul, and Tracks became singular. Paul Holy Track confessed to the Spicer murders in at least four separate and conflicting ways. Lynched on November 14, 1897.

Philip Ireland. Young Dakota Indian, also known as Philip Turning Bear, a name usually mistranslated as Standing Bear. He took his lead from Paul Holy Track. Lynched on November 14, 1897.

The Law

Henry A. Armstrong. State's attorney for Emmons County. He led the investigation of the Spicer murders and prosecuted the trials of Alec Coudotte and George Defender.

J. M. Bartholomew. A justice in the North Dakota Supreme Court. Wrote the judgment overturning the conviction of Alec Coudotte.

Guy C. H. Corliss. Chief justice of the state supreme court that reviewed and overturned the conviction of Alex Coudotte.

John W. Cramsie. U.S. government agent to the Standing Rock Indians from 1895 to 1898. He was headquartered at Fort Yates, just across the Missouri from Winona.

William M. Derr. The Emmons County coroner who cut down the bodies of the three lynched Indians.

Charles H. Edick. Justice of the peace in Emmons County who authorized the arrest of Alec Coudotte and Frank Black Hawk.

Thomas Kelly. Deputy sheriff who guarded the three Indians in the Williamsport jail the night a mob entered the jail, took his keys, released the three prisoners, and lynched them.

W. B. Livermore. Deputy sheriff of Emmons County.

George W. Lynn. Appointed defense attorney for Alec Coudotte. He actually served as assistant to R. N. Stevens, a more experienced trial lawyer.

James McLaughlin. Indian agent to the Standing Rock Indians from 1881 to 1895, when he was replaced by John W. Cramsie. He was married to a Santee Sioux woman. His mixed-blood sons **Harry McLaughlin** and

Charles McLaughlin translated at the trials of Alec Coudotte and George Defender.

Thomas J. Reedy. Chief of Indian police at Standing Rock.

O. E. Sauter. Presiding judge at the trial of George Defender.

Peter Shier. Sheriff of Emmons County.

R. N. Stevens. Defense attorney assigned to defend Alec Coudotte and George Defender.

Aaron C. Wells. Boss farmer on the Standing Rock reservation. His main job was to teach the Indians how to farm the land, but he also served as a detective. He was a part–Mohawk mixed-blood.

Walter H. Winchester. Presiding judge at the trial of Alec Coudotte.

Others

Frederick "Red" Caldwell. Winona saloon owner arrested for illegally selling liquor to Indians, particularly Alec Coudotte and Frank Black Hawk.

Scar Faced Charley. Bartender in Winona who worked for Red Caldwell and regularly sold liquor to Indians. His real name was James Jacobs.

Sitting Bull. Hunkpapa Lakota medicine man and military leader who led the Indian defeat of George Armstrong Custer's army at the Little Bighorn in 1876. Killed at Standing Rock in 1890 by tribal policemen sent by agent James McLaughlin.

Dr. Ralph H. Ross. Doctor at Standing Rock who said that he had seen Alec Coudotte at his mother's house on the reservation the afternoon of February 17, 1897.

D. R. Streeter. Editor of the *Bismarck Daily Tribune*, occupied a room above the jail the night of the lynchings.

George "Win" Tracy. One of the lynching party that forced its way into the Williamsport jail and seized Alec Coudotte, Paul Holy Track, and Philip Ireland.

R. M. Tuttle. Editor of the *Mandan Pioneer* and court stenographer for the trial of Alec Coudotte. Published articles deeply critical of agent John W. Cramsie.

Questions for Discussion

Besides being interesting in its own right, this book would be useful as a supplemental text, particularly in American studies and Native American studies classes. Stimulating discussions can be had on a wide range of topics, such as the varieties of racism in America, the extent to which citizens have the right to bypass a legal system that seems not to guarantee justice, Indian access to whiskey during a time when their access to whiskey was forbidden, and the psychology of "criminals" like Paul Holy Track.

The book would also be a stimulating choice for discussion groups, perhaps in conjunction with National Book Award winner Louise Erdrich's *The Plague of Doves*. The list below provides a start, though many more questions will occur to readers as they read through the various chapters.

General

1. Is it possible to reconstruct from the various conflicting testimonies given in Alex Coudotte's trial the actual sequence of events on that bloody February Wednesday?
2. Who done it, and what precisely is the "it"?
3. There is plenty of blame to go around for the troubling events in Emmons County, North Dakota, in 1897. Who or what is *most* to blame?

Paul Holy Track

1. What other options did Paul Holy Track have than the one he chose? After all, many Indians shared his frustration but did not take an axe to their white neighbors.
2. Is it a sign of strength, weakness, cleverness, or something else that Paul Holy Track "confessed" in three or four different ways?

3. In what sense, if any, is Paul Holy Track a heroic figure?
4. Why did Paul Holy Track openly wear jewelry he had stolen from the Spicer house?
5. Paul Holy Track says he committed the murders because he needed money. Is it so simple? How would you complete this sentence: Paul Holy Track attacked the Spicers because _____?

Alec Coudotte

1. Was Alec Coudotte guilty? If so, of what was he guilty? Did he murder Thomas Spicer? Was he even at the Spicer farm on February 17, 1897?
2. Why did Alec Coudotte stab himself? Was it a sign of guilt or innocence? Strength or weakness?
3. What do you make of Dr. Ross's efforts to provide Alec Coudotte with an alibi?

Racism

1. What are some of the terms that white people use to describe Indians — "fiends," "bucks," and so on? Why do they use such terms, since they know that Indians are really not devils or animals. Or do they?
2. Racist attitudes lurk everywhere in the Spicer murders and in what follows. What is racism, and in how many ways does it show itself?
3. "For all its high-sounding liberalism, the North Dakota supreme court statement written by Justice Bartholomew is deeply racist and could be said to call for the lynching that followed." Would you rather defend or refute that statement?
4. Why did mixed-bloods seem to have such a difficult time?
5. Do you detect evidence of racism in the statements of the modern Indians?

Alcohol

1. To what extent was whiskey the key ingredient in the Spicer murders?
2. Does their use of alcohol provided by white saloon-keepers in any way ameliorate the guilt of the killers?
3. Do you think Red Caldwell should have been tried for murder?

Lynching

1. Is lynching ever justified? Can you think of any historical figures who should have been lynched by concerned citizens? Osama bin Laden? Adolf Hitler? John Wilkes Booth? Lee Harvey Oswald?
2. Were the citizens of Emmons County justified in lynching Alec Coudotte, Paul Holy Track, and Philip Ireland?
3. Should the thirty-plus mob members have been arrested and tried for murder?

Lawyers, Agents, and Journalists

1. Do the events of 1897 speak well for the legal profession?
2. Does the newspaper coverage of the events of 1897 speak well for journalists?
3. Would you vote for Henry A. Armstrong for public office?
4. Would you appoint John W. Cramsie as an Indian agent?

Heroes and Villains

1. Who (or what) do you think is the most culpable villain in the 1897 murder/lynching? Defend your answer.
2. Who (or what) do you think is the most honorable hero in the 1897 murder/lynching? Defend your answer.
3. Did any good come out of the terrible events of 1897?

If It Had Been You

1. If you had been Thomas Spicer, Mary Spicer, or Lillie Rouse, how might you have avoided the violent deaths that they suffered on February 17, 1897?
2. If you had been Paul Holy Track or Philip Ireland, how do you think you would have responded to the frustrations of being a young Standing Rock Indian in 1897? Would you be proud of yourself for taking the path that they took?

Fact into fiction

1. If you were writing a novel based on the events of 1897, how would you approach your subject? For example, which character would you focus on, who would be your narrator, and what would be the theme of your novel?

2. What obligation, if any, do writers of fiction have to be true to the facts that inspired their novels? For one analysis of some of the changes Erdrich made in transforming the factual events into her fictional novel, see my "'Imagined places and characters': Louise Erdrich's Recasing of *The Plague of Doves*" in my website PeterGBeidler.com.
3. How would your novel have differed from Louise Erdrich's *The Plague of Doves*?

Index

Agaard, Louis 45, 105, 151
Allard, LaDonna Brave Bull 192; interview 217–32
Allen, Edward S. 59, 180, 182–83
Armstrong, Henry A. 3, 81–82, 84, 92–93, 106, 117, 119–23, 129, 131–37, 150, 167–69, 170, 189–90, 236, 241; recollections 197–209; testimony in Coudotte trial 122–23

Bad Horse 86, 128, 133
Bales, Oliver 216
Bangs, Tracy M. 48–50
Bartholomew, Judge J.M. 154, 182–84, 236, 240
Baxter 168
Bear Face 224
Bear Shield 67
Beck, Paul N. 12
Beede, Aaron M. 194–95
Big Foot (Spotted Elk) 29
Big Horn Association 23–25
Bingenheimer, George H. 150
Black Hawk, Frank (Frank Pierre) 1–4, 7, 45, 50, 55–59, 63–77, 80–89, 94–99, 100, 106–8, 114, 119, 129–34, 151–52, 157, 172–73, 179–80, 186–87, 189–92, 194, 203, 205–7, 211, 213, 216, 226–27, 235; testimony in Coudotte trial 135–37
Black Hawk, Peter 226
Black Hills 25
Blue Boy, John 61, 67, 72, 99, 110
Blue Shield, Peter 105, 133
boarding schools for Indian children 20–22
Bouillier, Charles 170
Bowers 188
Braddock 168
Brave Bull, Sarah 236
Briggs, Governor 173, 180, 192–93
Bruguire, Frank 211–12

Buffalo Bill 22
Burke, Steve 82
Burke, William 116, 132
Bussey 171

Cabe, Baptiste 131–32, 136
Caldwell, Frederick P. ("Red") 3, 48–52, 55, 70, 77, 80–81, 86–88, 95–96, 103, 130–31, 134–37, 212, 237, 240
Caldwell, Ruby ("Mrs." Caldwell) 48–49, 80–81, 92, 137–38
Carignan, J. M. ("Jack") 211–12
Casey, Dennis 168
Catch the Bear 28
Charging Eagle, Joseph 124–26, 138–40
Chase 131
Cheyenne River reservation 29
Chilcot, Spencer 122
Clark, Joe 214
Cochrane, Dr. 120
Cooper, James Fenimore 84–85
Corliss, Judge Guy C.H. 181–85, 236
Corrigan 112
Coudotte, Alec 1–5, 7, 45, 49–50, 55–59, 63–77, 80–88, 155, 167–71, 176–87, 194, 200, 203–4, 206–7, 211, 213, 227, 235, 240; state supreme court decision reversing conviction 155–61; testimony 128–35; trial proceedings 89–153
Coudotte, Marciana (Mrs. Alec Coudotte) 127–28, 138
Coudotte, William 123–24, 127–29, 131
Cramsie, John W. 37, 48–54, 60–61, 80–84, 144–51, 169, 184, 190–91, 195–96, 202, 236, 241; testimony in Coudotte trial 115–17
Crawler, Mary 226
Crazy Horse 10
Custer, George Armstrong 1, 12, 47, 226

Dakota-Lakota-Nakota bands of Sioux tribe 7, 223–24
Dawes Act of 1882 (General Allotment Act) 51
Defender, George 2–4, 7, 49, 56, 81–88, 89, 94–98, 100, 104–6, 109, 111, 114, 124–25, 129, 132, 134, 138, 150–53, 172–73, 179–80, 187–91, 194, 200, 204–7, 211, 213, 216, 225, 236
Defender, George, Jr. 224
Defender, Mrs. George 124–26, 139
Derr, William M. 166, 169, 172, 236
Dorman, Isaac 226
Drew, Frank 16
Duncan, Alexander 43

Eastwood, John 38
Edick, Charles H. 58, 82, 236
Edick, John 59, 153
Eppinger's store 188
Erdrich, Louise 4, 233, 242

Farrel 171
Featherston, Lee 188
Fire Cloud 11
Fiske, Frank Bennet 200–13
Flynn, Jack 136, 173, 202, 211–13
Flynn, Paddy 211–12
Fool Bear, Archie D. 16–19, 168–69
Fort Dodge 10
Fort Laramie Treaty of 1868 23
Fort Rice 46
Fort Ridgely 13
Fort Yates 1, 26
Frederickson, Gus 206
Fuller, Joe 136
funeral of Spicer family 42–44

Gardner, Abbie 10–12
Gardner, Rowland 10
Ghost Dance 27–31
Grey Eagle 123, 128–29
Grey Hand Woman 222

Hagedorn, Herman 25
Hampden Institute 226
Hansbrough, Senator 186–87
Hanson, Jean Marilyn Tracy 214
Hart, Jerry 85
Henry Lott 10
High Eagle, Placidus 116, 129, 142–43
Holtz, Paul 131
Holy Track, Paul (Scare the Eagle) 2–4, 7, 32, 49, 56, 61–88, 89, 91, 105–12, 114, 117, 128–29, 131–34, 137, 140–42, 145, 150–51, 153, 155–56, 161, 163, 168–71, 176–82, 187, 193–94, 200–1, 203–4,

206–8, 211, 213, 217–21, 228, 232, 236; testimony in Coudotte trial 94–103, 127
Homestead Act of 1862 20
Hunkpatina Indians 15

Inkpaduta 9–12, 15
Ireland, Agatha 22
Ireland, Philip (Standing Bear) 2–3, 7, 16, 32, 49, 56, 61–88, 89, 97–98, 102, 110–11, 114, 128–29, 131–34, 137, 140–42, 151, 153, 155–56, 161, 163, 168–71, 176–82, 187, 193–94, 203–4, 206–7, 211, 213, 218–21, 224, 228, 232, 236, 239–40; testimony in Coudotte trial 103–9, 200
Iron Face 224

Jaszkowiak 168
Jefferson, Thomas 50

Keiffer, Jess 215–16
Keiffer, Tom 215
Kelly, Thomas 3, 60, 153, 166–68, 170, 178, 207, 215–16, 236
Kent 164, 175
Knudsen, Pete 215–16
Kurtz, S.E. 170

Lake Oahe 209
The Last of the Mohicans 84–85
LeBrock 35, 40
Lincoln, Abraham 14, 17, 20, 226
Little Bear 224
Little Bighorn battle 1, 12, 17, 22, 27, 47, 226
Little Crow 10, 13–16
Livermore, W.B. 56, 85, 92, 113, 152, 180, 236
Lochren family 4
Lynn, George W. 59, 89, 103, 142, 236
Lyons 133

Mackey, Sam 129–30
Martin, Moses 122–23, 129
Martin, Thomas 124–26
McConville, Frank 214–15
McCormack, James 167–68
McCrory, Jack A. 36, 85, 120, 136, 210–11, 214
McDonald 168
McGinnes 168
McIntyre, Charles 207
McLaughlin, Charles 237
McLaughlin, Harry 92–94, 112–15, 119, 154, 205, 226, 236
McLaughlin, Henry 226
McLaughlin, James 11, 25–28, 114, 115, 154, 184, 205, 226, 236

Index

McLaughlin, Pat 226
McLaughlin, Terrence 226
McSorely, John 213
Miles, Nelson A. 28
Miller, General 180–81
Minnesota massacre of 1862 12–15
Moccasin, Mary 16–17, 223–24
Modern Woodmen of the World 166–67, 171, 178
Moves Robe Woman 226
Muench, Dr. 113
My Friend the Indian 25–26

Naaden, Christ 215
Normand 164, 175

Oehler, C.M. 13
Old White Woman, Charlie ("Joseph") 139

Packineau, Joe 152
Packineau, Mary 21–22
Parker 141
Pepper 135–36
Pine Ridge reservation 29
The Plague of Doves 4, 233, 242
Pope, Alexander 47
Pope, John 14
Procunier, Harry 171, 173

Rain in the Face 224
Red Cloud 29
Red Thunder 224
Reed, George 42, 151
Reedy, Thomas J. 56, 61, 63, 72, 81, 100, 106–7, 112, 116–17, 129, 131, 136, 237
rewards 43, 56, 192–93
Rice, James K. 47
Roach, Senator 186–87
Roosevelt, Theodore 25
Root, Joseph Cullen 166
Ross, Dr. Ralph H. 90, 128, 132–33, 181–83, 237, 240; testimony in Coudotte trial 113, 117–122
Rouse, Alfred 2, 32, 39–41, 43, 65, 71–74, 85–88, 94, 156, 165, 167, 192, 198, 201, 211, 235
Rouse, Alvin 2, 32, 39–41, 43, 65, 71–74, 85–88, 94, 156, 165, 167, 192, 198, 201, 211, 235
Rouse, Lillie Spicer 2, 33–43, 65, 71–77, 85–88, 94, 97, 156, 165, 192, 198, 201, 211, 213, 235
Rouse, William 35, 79, 215–16, 235
Rush, Mike 168, 172, 179, 207, 216

Safton, Tom 215–16
Sand Creek massacre 10
Santee Indians 9, 13–15, 26
Sauter, Judge O.E. 150–52, 164, 190, 206, 237
Scar Faced Charley (James Jacobs) 48–49, 80–81, 135–36, 237
Schofield, John McAllister 28, 30
Schultz, Duane 13–14
Schwandt, John 13
Sharp, Aaron 33
Shaved Head 224
Sheridan, Philip Henry 23, 69
Shier, Peter 55–56, 59–62, 79, 82–84, 119, 129, 133, 136, 152, 171, 173, 178, 180, 192–93, 203, 207, 213, 215, 237
Short, Tom 211, 213
Sibley, Henry 12, 14, 16, 18
Sintominiduta 10
Sioux uprising of 1862 12
Sitting Bull 10–12, 22–32, 223–24, 226, 237
Sitting Bull College 28
Siyaka (Rushing Eagle) 76–77, 219
Slater, Andrew 127, 130–31, 135–37
Sleasing, Tom 215
Slippery Dick 211
Smee, H.M. 46–48
Smell the Bear, Leo 124–26, 139
Smith, Frank 60
Smith, Thomas P. 185–87
Smyth, F.D. 170
Spicer, Ella 35
Spicer, John ("Jack") 33–34, 202
Spicer, Maggie 35, 37
Spicer, Mary 1–3, 33–41, 63–65, 68–69, 78, 88, 94, 97–98, 104–7, 164, 192, 198, 200–1, 211
Spicer, Thomas 1–3, 33–41, 63–65, 68–69, 78, 86–87, 92–95, 98, 102–4, 109, 156, 164, 192, 197–98, 200–2, 211, 213, 235
Spirit Lake 10, 15, 26
Spirit Lake massacre of 1857 9–12
Standing Rock Sioux reservation 1, 11, 19–20
Standing Soldier 116, 202, 208
Stevens, R.N. 90, 100, 118, 122, 128, 134–35, 141–43, 150–51, 154, 173, 182, 190, 206–7, 211–12, 216, 237
Stiles, J.A. 36
Stowell, John 154
Streeter, D.R. 167, 169–70, 237
Streeter, Frank 168
Sully, Alfred 15–18
Swidenski 164, 175

Taylor, Sheriff 79, 85, 172, 181, 190–91
Tracy, George "Win" 191, 214–16, 237
Treaty of 1851 9–10, 13

Tuttle, R.M. 89, 93–94, 144–52, 191, 237
Twin, Joseph 111
Two Hearts 62

Waldron, Ellen 2, 34, 63–65, 78, 86, 94, 99, 105, 107–8, 156, 164–65, 192, 201, 235
Waldron, Jack 34
Wallace, Frank 216
Welch, Charles "Billy" 79, 82, 101, 132, 157
Wells, Aaron C. 61–63, 65, 81–84, 91, 100, 106–7, 111–13, 119, 132–33, 203, 211, 215, 237
White Bull, Charles 126–27, 131–32
Whitestone Hill massacre of 1863 15–19, 222

Whitside, Samuel M. 29–30
Wilson, Horatio M. 35, 109–10
Wilson, Mary Louise Defender 21–22
Winchester, Judge Walter H. ("the court") 89, 140–43, 161, 164, 190, 206, 215, 237
Winter 131
Wiping of the Tears ceremony 18, 230
Wise Spirits, Adolph 226
Wounded Knee massacre 17, 19, 29–32, 222–23
Wovoka 27

Yanktonai Indians 15
Yates, George 1
Yeater, Bill 168, 216
Yellow Lodge, Patrick 74, 111, 133